KOVELS' AMERICAN ANTIQUES
1750 TO 1900

KOVELS' AMERICAN ANTIQUES
1750 TO 1900

by Ralph and Terry Kovel

RANDOM HOUSE
REFERENCE
New York

Kovels' American Antiques

by Ralph and Terry Kovel

Copyright © 2004 by Ralph and Terry Kovel

This book is available for special discounts for bulk purchases for sales promotions or premiums. Special editions, including personalized covers, excerpts of existing books, and corporate imprints, can be created in large quantities for special needs. For more information, write to Special Markets/Premium Sales, 1745 Broadway, MD 6-2, New York, NY, 10019 or e-mail specialmarkets@randomhouse.com.

Please address inquiries about electronic licensing of reference products for use on a network, in software or on CD-ROM to the Subsidiary Rights Department, Random House Reference, fax 212-572-6003.

Visit the Random House Web site: www.randomhouse.com

Cover and interior design by Geraldine Sarmiento

Photos on front cover:
1. Wedgwood sardine box (Skinner, Inc.)
2. Pewter teapot (Museum of Fine Arts, Boston)
3. Glass vase (James D. Julia, Inc.)
4. Furniture detail (Peter Harholdt/Corbis)

Photos on back cover, left to right
1. Toy (Theriault's)
2. Tray (Conestoga Auction Company)
3. Jewelry (Ralph and Terry Kovel)
4. Tobacco box (Ralph and Terry Kovel)

Library of Congress Cataloging-in-Publication Data is available.

First Edition

0 9 8 7 6 5 4 3 2 1

ISBN: 0-609-80892-3

Dedicated to

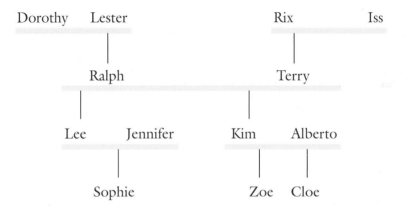

Dorothy — Lester   Rix — Iss

Ralph   Terry

Lee — Jennifer   Kim — Alberto

Sophie   Zoe Cloe

The past is always with you.

Try to understand it.

TABLE OF CONTENTS

Introduction

The year 2000 was the beginning of a new century. The words "made in the last century" now refer to the 1900s, not the 1800s. Our best-selling book *Kovels' Know Your Antiques*, written in 1967, was out of date. A revision wasn't enough—a whole new book with a new look was needed.

Kovels' American Antiques, 1750 to 1900, focuses on the antiques made or used in America before 1900. European and Asian wares imported and used in American homes are included. What may have been considered merely a nineteenth-century collectible when *Kovels' Know Your Antiques* was written may now be included in this book as an antique. The 1960s book was written using a typewriter with carbon paper; the new book has been keyed into a computer. The old book included only black and white illustrations. This book includes more than 400 color pictures of antiques and 340 drawings of marks. We deliberately chose to picture antiques that were used by the average family as well as outstanding pieces now found in museum collections. Most of the research for the old book was done in libraries, through interviews with experts, or with the help of the files of information we had gathered while writing our newspaper column. This time we have added the capabilities of the Internet and the information we have gathered while researching our 90 books, 50 years of newspaper columns, and 30 years of articles for *Kovels on Antiques and Collectibles*, our subscription-only newsletter.

It is surprising how much has changed in 35 years. Excavations and other research have proved that what were thought to be facts in the 1960s are sometimes wrong. Many pieces of pottery attributed to the Bennington factories are now questioned. *Whittle* marks on glass are not caused by the rough surface of a wooden mold but by the way hot glass cools in a cold metal mold. Some artists and factories that were almost unknown in the '60s are now popular, and some wares, like majolica, that were out of style and thought to be in poor taste are now in demand. In the 1960s few museums displayed Victorian furniture and decorative arts; even fewer cared about the art nouveau movement. Several subjects in this book—like advertising and store collectibles, toys, tools, and Victorian silver plate—were considered too commercial, and not worthy of study by serious history and art students. But times have changed. Today the life and artifacts of the common man and woman are just as relevant as the furnishings of the rich and famous. People care about researching the history of their family possessions.

Some things, however, have not changed. Marks remain important as a quick guide to the identification of ceramics or metals, so we include many marks with the name of the maker and the dates that the marks were used. For many types of antiques, we have included lists of the most important designers and factories with dates, locations, and marks. The collector's vocabulary can be tricky, so we explain the most confusing terms; for instance, *metal* is the correct name for molten glass being blown and shaped into a bottle. There are also stories of discoveries, tips on care, bits of interesting history, and warnings of fakes and fantasy items.

At the back of the book is an appendix that lists jewelry and metalwork designers and manufacturers. A short bibliography suggests sources for further information about material in each chapter.

This is a book written for the novice, the collector, and the history buff. It is not written for museum curators or art experts with advanced degrees. It covers eighteenth- and nineteenth-century furniture, glass, pottery and porcelain, silver, and other decorative arts of greatest interest to the twenty-first-century collector. And what about those treasures from the last century? We are already working on the Kovels' book about American collectibles and decorative arts made between 1900 and 2000!

Ralph and Terry Kovel
June 2004

Acknowledgments

The photographs in this book have come from many sources, including collectors, auctions, museums, and companies. Each picture used is credited, and the addresses of the sources are on pages 369 to 371. A number of the photos were taken by Benjamin Margalit, who has done photography for our books for many years. We appreciate the efforts of the many people who went out of their way to provide pictures, like Anne Trodella of Skinner Inc., who put in extra hours and found the "unfindable" for several chapters. Ruth Hancock, an archivist at the Syracuse China Archives at Libbey Inc., located the Onondaga cracker jar and had a photograph of it taken for this book.

Our vision of this book required some special attention by editors and artists at Random House Information Group. They were able to create an even better book than we could have imagined. Fabrizio La Rocca, creative director, put extra effort into creating a stylish design, but also kept in mind that the information was as important as the illustrations. The art department's skill and talent made the tables of marks and names attractive and easy to use. Dorothy Harris, our editor for many books, made sure everything went well and did what a good editor does for authors. David Naggar, president of Random House Information Group; Sheryl Stebbins, vice president and publisher of Random House Reference; and John Whitman, senior production editor, kept an eye on the work and made sure everything was on time and up to

Random House's high standards. Others who contributed are: Nina Frieman, Tigist Getachew, Lindsey Glass, Lisa Montebello, Geraldine Sarmiento, and Linda Schmidt.

The Kovel staff helped in many ways—finding sources, doing research, and checking facts. But without Heidi Makela, editor, researcher, and organizer; and Karen Kneisley, photo editor and computer maven, this book would have suffered and taken years longer. Marcia Goldberg, editor and punctuation-grammar expert, and Liz Lillis, Linda Coulter, and Julie Seaman, list-makers extraordinaire, also had special roles in the writing of *Kovels' American Antiques*. Grace DeFrancisco, Doris Gerbitz, Gay Hunter, Katie Karrick, Kim Kovel, Tina McBean, Nancy Saada, June Smith, and Cherrie Smrekar are others who helped. We also consulted experts who gave us suggestions and advice about their specialties that led to clarification of old information or discovery of little-known facts.

The 21st century and new technologies made it possible at last to write a book with exceptional color illustrations. The computer methods of transmitting pictures made extra clarity possible. New research methods have added to the information to be found in books and manuscripts.

We thank all of these talented people. They worked hard to create a book with only the Kovel name on the cover. They know that we know the truth—we share credit for *Kovels' American Antiques* with all of them.

Chapter 1

Pottery and Porcelain

POTTERY, PORCELAIN, BONE CHINA, ironstone, majolica, stoneware, and dozens of other kinds of dishes have been made through the centuries. But each of these types of ceramic is different, with its own characteristics, strengths, and flaws.

Pottery is opaque. You can't see through it. Porcelain is translucent. When a porcelain dish is held in front of a strong light, it is possible to see the light through the dish. If a piece of pottery is held in one hand and a piece of porcelain in the other, the porcelain will be colder to the touch. If a dish is broken, a porcelain dish will chip with small shell-like breaks (conchoidal fractures), while pottery cracks on a line. Pottery is softer and easier to break, and it stains more easily because it is more porous. Porcelain is thinner, lighter, more durable, and usually more expensive.

The way to identify an antique dish is to use the most obvious clues first. Turn the dish over. There may be a mark on the bottom. The most commonly found mark is the English design registry mark. This is the most useful mark for dating any piece of English

In the nineteenth century ceramic collecting was a popular hobby as shown in this hand-painted plate. The verse reads "China's the passion of his soul: A cup, a plate, a dish, a bowl, Can kindle wishes in his breast, Influence with joy, or break his rest."

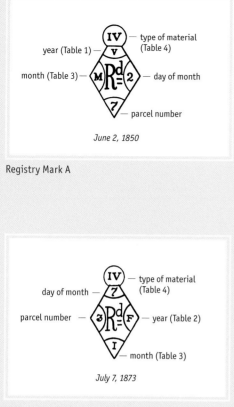

year (Table 1) — type of material (Table 4)

month (Table 3) — day of month

parcel number

June 2, 1850

Registry Mark A

day of month — type of material (Table 4)

parcel number — year (Table 2)

month (Table 3)

July 7, 1873

Registry Mark B

Rd Nº 821265.

Registry Mark C

pottery and porcelain. Registry marks were used for other decorative art designs as well, including furniture and items made from wood, glass, metal, paper, or fabrics. The mark tells the earliest possible date of the design.

From 1842 to 1883, diamond-shaped registry marks were used. Each mark contained the abbreviation *Rd* (for registered) in the center and coded information about the patent date and manufacturer. If there is a letter at the top inside the diamond, the dish was designed between 1842 and 1867. This type of registry mark is illustrated here as Mark A. If a number from 1 to 31 appears inside the top of the diamond, the piece was designed between 1868 and 1883. This type of registry mark is illustrated here as Mark B. The year was indicated by a letter (for Mark A, see Table 1; for Mark B, see Table 2). The month was also indicated by a letter (see Table 3). The type of material or class was indicated by a Roman numeral in a circle at the top of the diamond (see Table 4). The parcel number relates to the factory, retailer, or wholesaler.

In 1884 the diamond-shaped mark was replaced by the letters *Rd No* and a number indicating the year the piece was registered. This new mark is illustrated as Mark C. If the number is from 1 to 351,600, the piece was registered between 1884 and 1900. Larger numbers indicate a piece made after 1900. For example, 751,160 was the first number

English Registry Marks

Table 1 ❧ Mark A

Year the Design Was Registered: 1842–1867

A - 1845	J - 1854	S - 1849
B - 1858	K - 1857	T - 1867
C - 1844	L - 1856	U - 1848
D - 1852	M - 1859	V - 1850
E - 1855	N - 1864	W - 1865
F - 1847	O - 1862	X - 1842
G - 1863	P - 1851	Y - 1853
H - 1843	Q - 1866	Z - 1860
I - 1846	R - 1861	

Table 2 ❧ Mark B

Year the Design Was Registered: 1868–1883

A - 1871	I - 1872	U - 1874
C - 1870	J - 1880	V - 1876
D - 1878	K - 1883	W - March 1-6, 1878
E - 1881	L - 1882	X - 1868
F - 1873	P - 1877	Y - 1879
H - 1869	S - 1875	

Table 3 ❧ Mark A or B

Month of the Year the Design Was Registered

A - December	H - April
B - October	I - July
C or O - January	K - November (and December 1860)
D - September	M - June
E - May	R - August (and September 1–19, 1857)
G - February	W - March

Table 4 ❧ Mark A or B

Type of Material or Class

I	Metal
II	Wood
III	Glass
IV	Ceramics
V	Paper hangings
VI	Carpets
VII	Printed shawls
VIII	Other shawls
IX	Yarn
X	Printed fabrics
XI	Furniture
XIIi	Other fabrics
XIIii	Damasks
XIII	Lace

Table 5 ❧ Mark C

Year the Design Was Registered: 1884–2000

1884	1
1885	20,000
1886	40,800
1887	64,700
1888	91,800
1889	117,800
1890	142,300
1891	164,000
1892	186,400
1893	206,100
1894	225,000
1895	248,200
1896	268,800
1897	291,400
1898	311,677
1899	332,200
1900	351,600
1930	751,160
1950	860,854
2000	2,089,200

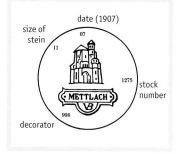

size of stein

date (1907)

07

11

1275 stock number

METTLACH

998

decorator

Mettlach castle mark

issued in 1930, and 860,854 was the first number issued in 1950. Beginning in 2000, pieces were registered as 2,089,200 and above.

Information on English patents is available online at www.patent.gov.uk. Information on registry marks before 1964 may be available from the Public Record Office, Rushkin Avenue, Kew, Richmond, Surrey, England. For information on registry marks in and after 1964, contact Designs Registry, Patent Office, Chancery Lane, London WC2A 1LR, England. Or you can e-mail the English Public Records Office at enquiries@pro.gov.uk.

If the name of a country is on the bottom of a dish, the dish was probably made after 1891, when the United States government passed a law requiring that the name of the country of origin (where the dish was made) appear in writing on each piece of pottery or porcelain imported into the United States. But some countries, particularly England, put the country name on pieces years earlier. So if a country other than England is printed on the dish, it was probably made after 1891; but if England is in the mark, the dish may have been made as early as 1850. The words *Made in . . .* were usually used after 1915. There are exceptions to all these rules: Some pieces made in the twentieth and twenty-first centuries may have been marked only with a paper label. These labels are easily removed and may be lost.

If no country name appears, examine the mark. Initials or short names usually appear on older pieces. Fancy trademarks were used beginning in the last half of the nineteenth century through the early twentieth century. The word *trademark* was used on English wares after 1855. Most marks that include the letters *Ltd.* (abbreviation for *limited*) were made after 1880. *Limited* is an English term with a meaning similar to the American word *incorporated*.

There may be some small impressed numbers on the bottom of your dish. Several factories marked dishes using a date-number system. If your dish was made by Wedgwood (see page 33) or Rookwood (see page 65), or if you have a Mettlach stein (see above and page 54), the numbering system used on it is easy to understand. Some other small impressed marks on dishes are just factory model numbers, models, painters, or patterns, however, and provide no help in dating the dish.

If your dish has only a pattern or factory name on the bottom and no country name, it is still relatively easy to judge the age of the dish. Many books are devoted to pottery and porcelain marks. If you know nothing about the plate, use a book such as *Kovels' New Dictionary of Marks*, which pictures thousands of marks according to their shape. If you are sure that the dish is English, German, or French, look in any of the special marks books listed at the end of this book. Almost every English mark can be traced to its source. Books on French, German, Russian, or Scandinavian pieces are available in the United States, but some are not translated into English.

THE SHAPE TELLS THE TALE

Plates

If there is no mark on a dish, it is still possible to determine the age of the dish. Earlier wares are heavier than later ones of the same type. The change in weight was due to improved manufacturing methods that used less clay. Early plates often have no rim on the bottom. Nineteenth-century wares have a foot rim. The foot rim is often unglazed on plates made before 1850 and on most Asian plates. Twentieth-century dishes usually have a foot rim, but some very modern shapes omit it.

Some early plates show three small marks on the face of the plate where the spur rubbed. The spur is a three-prong piece that separated plates during firing. Although spurs were not used extensively after 1825, the spur or stilt mark can still be found on some inexpensive pieces of later pottery. Sometimes an old plate will be slightly uneven. Old dishes should show some signs of wear, even if it is only a scratch in the glaze from years of use.

Cups

Teacup shapes have changed through the years. The earliest European tea sets were copies of Chinese sets. The Chinese drank

Opposite page, top left: Early round shape, 1710–1780. Meissen teapot.

Top right: Inverted pear-shape, 1730–1760. Sèvres teapot.

Middle left: Cylindrical body shape, 1740–1810. Unmarked blue-and-white salt-glazed teapot.

Middle right: Rounder and fatter shape, after 1810. Unmarked black basalt teapot with relief decoration.

Bottom left: Fanciful Victorian shape, after 1850. Worcester double-body teapot.
(Photos: William Bunch Auctions)

lukewarm tea, so they held the body of the cup and no handle was needed. Eighteenth-century tea sets made in Europe and America included teacups without handles. Only coffee cups and chocolate cups had handles. Cups without handles are usually older than those with handles. By the nineteenth century, most cups had handles. The oversize coffee cups that many believe are a new idea were made as early as 1820. The large cup held as much as two regular-size coffee cups.

Teapots

The teapot shape in silver, pewter, pottery, or porcelain also went through a series of changes. Early teapots were much smaller than later ones. Tea was an expensive beverage during the eighteenth century, so tea was served in small cups, and only a small teapot—one that would hold just one or two of today's cups—was necessary.

The teapot gradually changed in size and shape. The round pot was in fashion from about 1710 to 1780. The pear-shape teapot was also in use from about 1730 to 1760. From 1740 to 1810 the teapot body was cylindrical. After 1810 the pot became rounder and fatter, and by 1840 some pots also had a flared base. The teapots made in the last half of the nineteenth century were adaptations of earlier types or strange, fanciful shapes.

In addition to considering the size and shape of a teapot, there are several other ways to judge a teapot's age. Look inside the pot at the holes that lead to the spout. Eighteenth-century pots have fewer holes than later pots—sometimes as few as three—and the holes are often jagged and uneven. The lid on an eighteenth-century pot was usually held in place by a deep rim.

A piece of pottery or porcelain can reveal not only its age, but also the country where it was made. Because the Chinese were able to make a teapot and lid and then glaze and fire the piece with the lid in place, there is no shiny glaze where the lid rests. The English and other Westerners were not as skilled as the Chinese. They had to glaze the lid and pot separately, so on a European or American teapot, the top and the rim at the teapot's opening are covered with glaze.

A pattern of peonies and leaves decorates this brown transfer Wedgwood plate. Another version of the design was made by adding green, gold, and rose to parts of the transfer design. Manufacturers often added color to enhance a design.

DECORATIONS CAN DATE DISHES

The type of decoration on a dish can also give a general hint about its age.

Blue or black transfer designs: End of eighteenth century

Green, pink, or brown transfer designs: c. 1830 (See Staffordshire on page 30.)

Flow blue—a dark, blurry decoration: 1830–early 1900s

Golden sponged edging with blue: Late nineteenth century

Hand-painted plates: 1870–1900

Plain gold bands on white dishes: c.1876

Portrait plates: 1880s

First Christmas plate in Denmark: 1895

Decal designs: Late nineteenth and early twentieth centuries

LEARN THE PROPER NAMES

Belleek

The glaze on belleek closely resembles a piece of polished mother-of-pearl. It is creamy yellow. Occasionally, pieces are decorated with gold or very pale colors.

The open basketwork designs are, perhaps, the most famous. Dishes were made to resemble shells or flowers. A few pieces were made of belleek with a Parian figure incorporated into the design so the texture of the two types of ceramic added to the beauty of finished pieces. (For more on Parian, see page 19.)

Belleek Pottery Limited in County Fermanagh, Ireland, has made Belleek pottery since 1863. The firm, which is still working, gained the legal right to use the name *Belleek* as part of its trademark in 1929. Since then, no other firms may use the word *Belleek* with a capital *B* as part of their mark or advertising.

Belleek made in Ireland is almost always marked, although a few unmarked pieces have been identified. The mark is an Irish wolfhound, a harp, a round tower, and a shamrock with the name *Belleek* imprinted on it. This mark can be green, brown, black, red, or blue. The words *Belleek-Fermanagh* were also used.

Factories in the United States produced belleek, but the designs are easily distinguished from the Irish products. Ott and

Brewer of Trenton, New Jersey, hired William Bromley to make belleek ware from about 1882. Its *BELLEEK* mark is sometimes within a crescent.

The Knowles, Taylor and Knowles Company made a true belleek that was marked *Belleek* and another porcelain similar to Irish Belleek marked *Lotus Ware*. This velvety glazed bone china was made from 1890 to 1900 and is marked *KTK* or with a special mark that includes the words *Lotus Ware*.

Willets Manufacturing Company and the Ceramic Art Pottery, both of Trenton, New Jersey, made belleek. Walter Scott Lenox, a founder of Ceramic Art Company in 1899, learned about belleek at the Ott and Brewer and Willets factories. He became sole owner of the Ceramic Art Pottery in 1896 and added the word *Lenox* to the CAC mark. The company became Lenox, Inc. in 1906. It made a ware similar to belleek, but more translucent and warmer in color.

Biscuit or Bisque Ware

Bisque, or biscuit, porcelain has been made for many years. Any piece of unglazed porcelain is bisque. It gained popularity during the Victorian era, when bisque figurines were mass-produced by the millions.

Belleek Pottery Company mark (1863–1891)

Ott & Brewer belleek mark (c.1883–1894)

Knowles, Taylor and Knowles belleek mark (1889+)

Knowles, Taylor and Knowles Lotus Ware mark (1891–c.1898)

Willets Manufacturing Company mark (1879–1912+)

Ceramic Art Company mark (1889–1906)

During the Victorian period, many people claimed the best bisque was made in Austria. Today collectors know that excellent bisque was made before the late nineteenth century by factories in England, France, and other countries.

Bone China

Almost every type of animal bone can be burned and the ashes used in the manufacture of bone china. Bone ash is added to clay to make a porcelain body. The Spode Museum in England has a punch bowl that was made from bones left after a banquet. When the guests at the party finished eating, the bones remaining on their plates were collected, burned to ashes, and added to clay to make a new ceramic bone china that was shaped into a punch bowl. Bone china was developed about 1800 and is still made today.

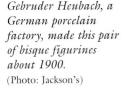

Gebruder Heubach, a German porcelain factory, made this pair of bisque figurines about 1900.
(Photo: Jackson's)

Delft

Delft is a special type of faience, a tin-glazed pottery that has been popular for centuries. Early delft was made in Holland and England during the seventeenth century, and it is still being made. It was usually decorated with blue on a white surface; but some delft, called polychrome, was decorated with green, yellow, and other colors. Most delftware was *useful ware*—the dishes needed for everyday living. Delft figures were made from about 1750 to 1800 and are very rare. They were copied from the designs of the Meissen potters of Germany.

With some study, it is possible to differentiate old delft from new. Delft crumbles and chips easily, so old delft dishes and tiles should show some signs of wear. The blue decorations on old delft are slightly darker, and old wares are much thicker and heavier than new ones. New pieces have much whiter bodies and much clearer designs than older pieces. Take a look at the mark. If the word *Holland* appears, the piece was made after 1891. If the word *delft* appears, the pottery is probably a twentieth-century piece. But the easiest way to judge whether your delft is old or new is to compare

Opposite page: Geometric patterns, a landscape scene, and heraldic devices decorate this nineteenth-century Dutch delft ewer.

it with a new, fresh-from-the-gift-shop piece of delft. Pieces marked *Blue Delft* were made in the twentieth or twenty-first century, probably in Asia or Germany.

Majolica

The general term *majolica* means any pottery with an opaque tin enamel glaze that conceals the color of the clay body. This would include delft, faience, and the more familiar majolica of England, Spain, Germany, Italy, and the United States. Although majolica was made during the fourteenth century, the average collector is interested in the type made since the mid-nineteenth century.

Majolica serving pieces were often made with three-dimensional handles and decorations. A can of sardines fit perfectly into this sardine box.
(Photo: James Julia)

During the sixteenth century, the famous and eccentric Bernard Palissy made his unusual majolica wares in France. He used natural designs, but the most famous of his wares were plaques covered with three-dimensional fish, snails, lizards, and snakes. The inspiration for later wares, they have been copied in every century and in almost every country. Many copies were made in Spain and England in the nineteenth century.

The Whieldon factory of England, which was the forerunner of the famous Wedgwood factory, made a type of majolica about 1740 that was inspired by the works of Palissy. (For more on Wedgwood, see page 33.) Majolica was popular until the early nineteenth century, then fell out of favor for about fifty years. About 1850 the majolica craze hit Europe and North America again, and the ware was made in quantity by English, Dutch, Italian, French, Spanish, and American factories. Victorian-era majolica ware is the type usually found today.

Victorian majolica is thick and heavy, and it has brightly colored glazes that make it easy to recognize. But the quickest way to learn more about a piece is to look for a mark (unfortunately, much of it was not marked). The piece is English if one of these names is impressed on the bottom: Adams & Co.; Brown-Westhead, Moore & Company; William Brownfield & Company; W. T. Copeland & Sons; Joseph Holdcroft; George Jones; Minton; Royal Worcester; or Wedgwood.

Griffen, Smith and Hill majolica mark (c.1878–1889)

The words *Etruscan Majolica* or the letters *GSH* appear on the most famous of the American majolica, the work of Griffen, Smith and Hill of Phoenixville, Pennsylvania. The firm, which worked during the 1880s, made Etruscan ware with a variety of designs from nature, including cauliflower, bamboo, shell, and seaweed patterns. The company used a marking system that can help today's collector. Each dish was marked with a number-letter combination. The letters, from *A* to *O*, indicated the shape of the piece, and the numbers the style of decoration.

ETRUSCAN MAJOLICA

Griffen, Smith and Hill majolica mark (c.1880)

Other American majolica makers were Edwin Bennett Pottery, Chesapeake Pottery, Faience Manufacturing Company, Hampshire Pottery, Morley & Company, New Milford Majolica Company, and Wannopee Pottery Company. Important European makers include Haviland, Sarraguemines, Utzschneider & Company, and Villeroy & Boch.

Ironstone

Ironstone china was first made by Miles Mason, an English potter, who began making ceramics about 1780. Mason sold Chinese export ware in England and was unable to get replacements for broken dishes. Rather than disappoint his customers, he decided to make a ware that could be used with the Chinese export dishes. Charles James Mason, the son of Miles, patented ironstone china in 1813. All large pieces were marked. The marks were blue underglaze with the name *Mason* appearing on most of them.

Mason's ironstone ware was made from slag left from processing iron. It was combined with flint, Cornwall stone and clay, and blue oxide of cobalt. Some experts believe the name *ironstone* came from the slag, but others think it derived from the fact that the ware was as hard as iron. The name *ironstone* was used by Mason. Other firms that copied the popular tableware called their products by names such as *white granite, Parisian granite, stone china, granite ware, opaque porcelain, semi-china,* and, later, *semi-porcelain.*

Ironstone was used as the base for some flow blue and historic blue plates. Mason and other English firms made ironstone decorated to resemble porcelain patterns that were popular in England, Europe, America, and Asia. It is not difficult to distinguish ironstone from porcelain. Ironstone is heavy and thick and not translucent. The same firms also later made simple, undecorated white wares. Ironstone went out of fashion in the early 1900s but made a comeback in popularity in the 1950s. It is still being made.

Dating Ironstone
Use the type of decoration—or lack of it—and the color of the ironstone design to date a piece if a maker's mark is missing. Ironstone patterns were copies of porcelain patterns of the period until about 1830. Pieces were decorated with only blue or had Asian-inspired multicolored patterns. Blue, pink, purple, green, black, and sepia transfers were used from about 1830 to 1845. Purple, black, and light blue were used until about 1850, when flow blue became popular. Light-colored transfer prints of pink, green, light blue, or puce were favored until about 1860.

About 1855 a type of *Gaudy ironstone* was popular. It was decorated with orange and blue Imari (Japanese-inspired) designs. Many pieces were marked with a maker's name. Do not confuse Gaudy ironstone with Gaudy Dutch or Gaudy Welsh (see page 41), which were wares made for the American market.

Gaudy ironstone, with bright colors, luster, or gold included in the decoration, was in vogue from 1855 to 1865. Luster-decorated ironstone, with tea-leaf or Chelsea grape-type decorations, was made mainly between 1870 and 1880. Plain white ironstone with raised decorations was most popular from about 1875 until 1900.

The shape of a white plate helps to date it. Round plates had plain rims until 1820, when slight indentations appeared in the rim. There was very little raised decoration. Makers began using scalloped rims between 1830 and 1840; and by 1840 to 1860, geometric, octagonal, and other shapes were introduced. Round plates came back into favor between 1860 and 1880, but the plates were flatter than earlier ones and often had a raised design as the border. From the 1880s on, mass production led to classic round, oval, and square shapes.

Ironstone wares are still being made in many of the early shapes; fortunately, most of these new wares are not attempts to fool the collector and are plainly stamped with a modern maker's mark.

A blue-and-white transfer design of an oriental scene was applied to this Mason's ironstone china plate. Then it was decorated over the glaze with green, red, and yellow enamel.

White Ironstone Patterns

During the peak of its popularity in the mid-nineteenth century, plain white ironstone evolved through a series of trim and handles that were molded as part of the piece. Wheat pattern ironstone was made by several English firms between 1855 and 1865. Other patterns pictured grain and botanical designs, such as corn and oats, grapes, grape leaves and vines, ivy (late patterns have buds), morning glory, lily of the valley, and other flowers, as well as geometric shapes with border designs. About 1875, fancy embossed overall designs were discontinued, and plain white ironstone became popular.

Tea-leaf Ironstone

The tea-leaf pattern, which pictured a luster tea leaf on a white ironstone dish, was made by more than three dozen English factories after about 1850. The brown tea-leaf pattern became quite popular during the 1870s. The idea of a tea leaf painted at the bottom of a cup may have been suggested by the superstition that it was lucky if a whole tea leaf unfolded in your cup. Many variations in the shape and number of tea leaves were used on dishes. Tea-leaf dishes are still being made.

American Ironstone

Many firms made ironstone ware in the United States. Potters in Trenton, New Jersey, were making ironstone by the 1850s. John Wyllie, working in East Liverpool, Ohio, by 1874, is said to have been the first potter to manufacture ironstone west of the Allegheny Mountains.

American ironstone manufacturers believed their product would sell better if the label hinted that the piece was of English origin. Many manufacturers adopted the seals of the United States or Great Britain for their factory marks. The lion and the unicorn holding a shield were used in many ways. Some marks used two lions or two unicorns to hold a shield, making a new American mark. The English-style marks were used until 1891, when the word *England* was required by law to appear on dishes imported from that country.

Luster

Luster glaze has been used on porcelain for centuries. Sixteenth-century Spain produced some of the finest early luster decorations. About ninety-four out of every one hundred early luster-glazed pottery dishes broke during the firing. The glaze shrinkage was difficult to handle, which accounts for the rarity and high cost of early luster.

The fifteenth and sixteenth centuries saw blue, reddish-gold, copper, or green luster decorations, while seventeenth-century luster included bright red, copper, and golden yellow. Metallic gold, silver, copper, and pink lusters were made during the late eighteenth and nineteenth centuries. A pearly luster was used during the nineteenth and early twentieth centuries.

Luster glaze was made from a mixture of platinum, copper, or gold salts. The gold made pink, purple, or copper-color luster.

Most English luster was made in the Staffordshire district. It was most popular between 1775 and 1830. It has remained popular and is still being made.

Old luster ware is heavier than new ware. The potting rim at the base of new ware is smoother and shallower. Some experts can recognize a new piece from the color, because new luster is brighter.

Many luster pieces of the eighteenth and nineteenth centuries were almost entirely covered with metallic glaze. The silver-coated pieces were made in shapes that resemble solid silver or silver-plated pitchers or tea sets. Copper luster pitchers were very popular.

Opposite page: Tea-leaf pattern dishes were named for the copper luster design showing the leaves of a tea plant. This 7½-inch-high English pitcher was made by Anthony Shaw.

Some solid luster pieces were decorated with bands of colored flowers or figures about 1830. By 1850 plain luster pieces imitating metal were discontinued. The cheaper process of electroplating metal had been discovered, and the plated metal was inexpensive and unbreakable.

Early luster pieces had the same glaze on the inside as on the outside. Most nineteenth-century pieces had luster on the outside but were white on the inside.

Many English factories made copper, silver, pink, and gold luster during the Victorian era. Some late nineteenth-century pieces, especially copper luster pitchers, can still be found.

Pink luster is a special decorative pink glaze that appears metallic and glossy. The Leeds, Newcastle, and Sunderland pottery factories in England made wares with pink luster decoration. The most famous wares were made in or near Sunderland. The name Sunderland, however, is often incorrectly given to any pink luster piece.

Two general types of pink lusterware were made. Some had luster lines or leaves painted into the design for added glimmer, but the most spectacular pieces were made with wide bands of bubble pink luster. Large bowls, pitchers, and picture frames were made this way. Black transfer patterns with added hand-painted color pictures of sailors, ships, bridges, drinking scenes, sporting events, and so on, were used on pink luster made during the mid-nineteenth century. Some pieces were made with verses and political slogans which help to date the lusterware.

Pink bubble luster is always eye-catching. This Sunderland jug is decorated with three vignettes—The Rich Widow, Cast Iron Bridge Near Sunderland, and a four-line verse.
(Photo: James Julia)

The famous Chelsea-grape pattern is typical of patterns made with small luster designs. A small bunch of grapes was made in a raised design on a white plate. The grapes were colored lavender, blue, or purple luster. Most

Chelsea-grape ware is unmarked and was probably made by the Coalport factory in England before 1840. It was *never* made by the Chelsea factory in England. The pattern was also called Aynsley or Grandmother. Chelsea Sprig is similar but has a sprig of flowers instead of a bunch of grapes. Chelsea Thistle has a raised thistle pattern.

In 1860 a luster with the appearance of iridescent mother-of-pearl was developed. Though it was attractive, the iridescence washed off after a few years. This luster became popular again about 1900 to 1915 and was used by Japanese and German factories.

Parian Ware

Parian ware is an unglazed biscuit porcelain resembling Parian marble. It was first made by the English Spode factory in the 1840s. Many other English and American firms manufactured Parian ware after that date. Usually Parian ware is white, but some pieces are partially colored. It was often used to make statues and figurines that looked like marble carvings.

NAMES YOU NEED TO KNOW

ABC or Alphabet Plates

Most *ABC plates* were made between 1780 and 1860. The dishes were teaching aids for young children who were learning to read. The outside border had the letters of the alphabet with pictures of a hero, a famous landmark, a character from Aesop's fables, or a storybook character decorating the center of the plate. The plates were made of glass, tin, pottery, pewter, or silver plate. Most of them were made in England. Some unusual examples include the alphabet in Braille or in sign language for the deaf.

An organ-grinder and children are pictured in the center of this ABC plate. The letters of the alphabet are embossed around the border.

Bone Dishes

During the late Victorian era, diners placed their discarded fish bones in small plates called *bone dishes.* Hotels often gave the dishes to diners as souvenirs. Most bone dishes were crescent shaped, but

some were shaped like a fish. Bone dishes were used during the late 1890s and early 1900s.

Butter Pats

Small dishes that held a single pat of butter were another Victorian tableware. These dishes were called *butter pats* or *butter chips*. They were used only during the late nineteenth and early twentieth centuries.

Where to put the bones from a fish dinner? The Victorians had an attractive solution. Each place setting included a bone dish like this crescent-shaped example.

Coffee Cans

The term *coffee can* or *coffee cann* is English and refers to what Americans call a *mug*. It was a popular china form in the eighteenth century. Most English potters made coffee cans as well as cups and saucers and sold them as parts of dinner sets. A straight-sided can was 2½ inches high and 2½ inches in diameter. Any other size, even one with a half-inch difference, is a collector's rarity.

Fairings

Souvenirs have always been sold at fairs. Small trinket boxes and figurines called *fairings* were popular during the nineteenth century. Hundreds of designs were made between 1855 and 1870, when the boxes were in great demand for pins, matches, and other small objects. The figurines were often sentimental gifts for a mother or girlfriend or were slightly off-color jokes. The work was crude, but the designs were amusing and the pieces colorful. Most of the fairings were made in Germany or in the Staffordshire district of England.

A fairing is a small souvenir originally sold at a country fair. Many were humorous or even risqué. This German fairing is part of a set about courting and marriage. The husband holds a baby while the wife watches. It is titled Three o'clock in the morning.

Fish and Game Plates

A *game plate* is any type of plate decorated with pictures of birds or wild game. Most fish and game plates came in sets of twelve plus a serving platter. Most of the game plates were made in Germany, Bavaria, and France during the 1880s. Decorations were either hand painted or decals.

Hot-water Dishes

The *hot-water dish* looks like a covered soup bowl with a lower section that can be filled with water. Hot water was poured inside to keep the upper plate warm and the food hot. The hot-water dish was popular after 1830.

Lithophanes

A *lithophane* is a transparent panel of biscuit porcelain. The design was made by varying the thickness of the panel. When a lithophane is held to the light, the thick parts appear dark and the thinner ones light.

The process for making lithophanes was developed in 1827 by Baron Paul de Bourgoing of Paris. They were made in Berlin and Meissen, Germany, and in Holland, France, Denmark, and England.

Lithophanes were popular between 1834 and 1860. They were hung in windows, mounted

A lithophane had to be displayed in front of a light. This KPM colored lithophane with an acid-etched, ruby overlay glass frame was made to hang in a window. It is 14½ by 16 inches.

in lampshades, placed on candlestands, and even used at the bottom of children's milk glasses or adults' beer mugs. Most lithophanes were white, but colored ones also were made. In the late nineteenth century, beer steins were made with lithophanes in the bottoms. In the early 1900s, the Japanese made tea sets with lithophanes at the bottoms of the cups. If you hold the empty cup or stein to the light, you will see a picture. The lithophane became popular again in the 1960s, and new lithophanes are still being made.

Moriaga

A style of relief decoration called *Moriaga* (also spelled *Moriye*, *Moriya*, or *Moriage*) was used on Japanese and other pottery from about 1870 to 1900. This raised overglaze decoration looks like squeezed toothpaste has been applied to the piece. The word *moriaga* means squeezed.

Moss Rose China

The moss rose was a very popular flower during the early nineteenth century. Gardeners prized the fuzzy flower, and because of its popularity it was often pictured on china and glassware. The earliest *Moss Rose china* was made about 1808. The fad was over by the late 1890s, and the pattern was discontinued.

Because the moss rose is being grown again and sold in many parts of the United States and Canada, old dishes picturing the flower have become popular with collectors.

The moss rose is an old-fashioned plant variety that is difficult to find today. The buds have a fuzzy covering that suggested the rose's name. The flower was very popular in Victorian times and inspired the dish pattern.

Mustache Cups

Many men wore flowing mustaches after the Mexican War ended in 1848. Proper care of a mustache included curlers, oil, dye, brushes, combs, and even nets that held it curled at night. After all his efforts to take care of his mustache, no man wanted to dip it in hot coffee and spoil his appearance. To keep his mustache dry and clean, a man would use a *mustache cup,* which was a large coffee cup with a porcelain ledge near the rim. The curled mustache could rest on the ledge, safe from peril.

The first factory to make a mustache cup was Harvey Adams and Company of Longton, Staffordshire, England, about 1850.

Mustache cups of silver, tin, pottery, or porcelain were made by many famous factories. In Queen Victoria's day, mustache cups inscribed *To Pop, Forget Me Not, Love the Giver, Birthday Greetings, Present,* or *Remember Me* were given as gifts.

Left-handed mustache cups were made, but old ones are a rarity. Modern fakes are known.

Mustaches and mustache cups went out of fashion in the early 1900s, but large, flowing mustaches came back in style in the 1970s and a few new mustache cups were made.

Pâte-sur-pâte

Pâte-sur-pâte is a special type of decoration. The French name means *paste on paste*. Thin layers of liquid porcelain clay were applied to an unfired clay piece. The thin clay, or slip, formed a raised decoration. The piece was then glazed and fired.

Pâte-sur-pâte was developed by Marc Louis Solon, who was trying to copy an early Chinese vase. His mistakes and efforts led to the development of a new decorative technique. Solon worked at the Sèvres factory in France until 1870, when he moved to the Minton firm in England.

Pâte-sur-pâte ware is beautiful and expensive. It required many time-consuming applications of the slip. The ware was in great demand. Solon trained Birks, Hollins, Mellor, Morgan, Rhead, Rice, Sanders, and Toft, and all of these men made and signed work for Minton.

As the demand continued, other European potteries began making pâte-sur-pâte. Artists at several factories, such as Sèvres and Worcester, signed the ware. It was also made in the United States from about 1910 to 1914 at the University City Pottery in St. Louis, Missouri.

Pâte-sur-pâte is a type of decoration that used slip to create a raised design. This pâte-sur-pâte example by Meissen pictures the archangel Michael.

Most firms no longer made pâte-sur-pâte by 1890. It was still in demand, but it was slow and expensive to manufacture and therefore not a profitable ware.

Pot Lids

Pot lids are china tops that were used on commercial soap, cosmetics, and mustache-wax boxes. The lids have become popular with collectors and are often framed and hung as a group.

F. and R. Pratt Company made pot lids in Fenton, England, during the late 1840s. The first pot lid with a colored transfer print was made in 1846 and was called *Polar Bears*. Hundreds of different lids were made during the next forty years. Pratt also made dishes and small porcelain objects. Other pot lids were made with black and white printed decorations, often just the name of the product.

Puzzle Jugs

Several types of *puzzle jugs* were made by the practical jokers of their times. One jug, the simplest of the puzzles, had a frog on the bottom. When the unwary tippler drank his grog, the frog appeared—a startling, lifelike visitor. Many hard drinkers must have had a real fright from this jug. Another type of jug had holes under the handle at the neck of the jug. It was the original dribble glass, spilling the contents of the jug all over the drinker. If you knew it was a puzzle jug, you could safely drink from it by covering all but one of the holes with your fingers. Then you drank through that hole.

Puzzle jugs can be dribble jugs. There are holes around the neck and in the center of this piece. To drink, suck on one of the two knobs on the neck. They act like straws. On the side of this jug is a poem, "From Mother Earth I took my Birth, I'm made a Joke for Man, And now am here fill'd with good Beer, Come tate it if you can."

One type of puzzle jug was copied from an earlier oriental design for a wine pot. The Cadogan pot, named after the Earl of Cadogan, was made at Nottingham, England. This pot had no lid. It was shaped like a peach, with trailing vinelike designs twined about it. There was a hole in the bottom of the pot, but no other opening except at the end of the spout. If you filled the pot from the bottom and turned it over, no water would spill, though water would pour from the spout.

Stirrup cups are not true puzzles but are often collected with puzzle jugs. They were made to hold alcoholic beverages at a hunt or other special event. The cup was shaped like the head of an animal, such as a fox or a dog, and could not be put down until it was empty because the bottom wasn't flat. Stirrup cups were popular in the eighteenth and nineteenth centuries.

Saltglaze

Legend has it that a farm girl was pickling pork in a saltwater brine when the brine boiled over onto a hot earthenware pot. When the pot cooled, it had a bright, hard glaze. It's a nice story, but we doubt that it really is the origin of saltglaze, which was made by throwing salt into the kiln while pottery was being fired. This late seventeenth-century method has been refined for today's manufacturing methods.

Shaving Mugs

Shaving mugs were most popular between 1860 and 1900. Many men went to the local barbershop each day for a shave. A shaving mug was kept for each patron in a mug case at the barbershop. Occupational shaving mugs were decorated with the owner's name and fire engines, milk wagons, or other easily identifiable trade items or with a picture of the owner's house. The coal-scuttle shaving mug was given its name because of its peculiar shape. The small pocket that protruded in front held a shaving brush. The first of these mugs was made as a soap package. The mugs were made in Germany, the United States, and Japan.

Tiles

Decorative tiles have been made for centuries. Most popular with collectors are tin-glaze earthenware tiles, such as faience, delftware, and majolica. Tile making was brought to England from the Netherlands in the late sixteenth century. By the eighteenth century, Liverpool, London, and Bristol were the centers of tile making in England. Most designs copied Dutch delftware. Delftware production in England ceased by the end of the eighteenth century, but tile production there slowly revived with the development of dust-pressed encaustic tiles. In the last quarter of the nineteenth century, tile making reached a new peak and featured a variety of decorating techniques, including transfer printing, hand painting,

HINTS ON CARE OF POTTERY AND PORCELAIN

Wash antique dishes in the same manner as you would any fine modern china. A dishwasher can handle anything that is not crazed or does not have gold decorations. Dishes with any damage or gold must be washed by hand.

Tiles that were this rectangular shape and size were used as the top of a fireplace surround. This 6-by-18-inch green tile showing mother and children was made by the American Encaustic Tile Company of Zanesville, Ohio.

sgraffito, and pâte-sur-pâte. Major tile makers included Minton, Maw, Copeland, Boote, and Wedgwood.

All tile used in the United States was imported from Europe until the middle of the nineteenth century, when American potteries began to manufacture tile. Tiles with raised relief decorations were not made in the United States until after the Centennial Exposition in 1876. Art tile production flourished in the United States from 1870 to 1930. Chelsea Keramic Art Works, J. & J.G. Low Art Tile Works, the Star Encaustic Tile Company, and the American Encaustic Tiling Company were among the best known American tile makers.

Toby Jugs

The *Toby jug* was named for Toby Philpot, a notorious drinker mentioned in a British song written in 1761. The jug was shaped to resemble a seated person. Toby jugs were very popular from 1776 to 1825, but many later versions have been made. A jug shaped like a person's head and shoulders is *not* a Toby jug. ᦉ

A Toby jug is shaped like the full figure of a man or woman. This portly man was made in the Staffordshire district of England.
(Photo: James Julia)

Chapter 2

British Pottery and Porcelain

𝒸ℴ FASHIONS IN CLOTHING, furniture, and pottery and porcelain change. Spatterware, majolica, ironstone, and moss rose pattern have gone in and out of fashion, but by the 1980s collectors and museums began to realize the artistry of some of the pieces. Included here are some of the factories and artists of most interest to museum curators and collectors today.

The Doulton pottery in Lambeth made this 9¼-inch-high stoneware stein, signed Hannah B. Barlow, in 1895. (Photo: Dargate)

Doulton and Royal Doulton

After completing a seven-year apprenticeship at the Fulham Pottery in 1812, John Doulton moved to a small pottery in Lambeth, South London. He became a partner three years later, and in 1820 the firm became Doulton and Watts. Doulton and his three sons formed Doulton and Company in 1854. It began making fine bone china under the name Doulton and Co. in Burslem, England, in 1882. Doulton made tableware, vases, and ornamental pieces using talented artists and new techniques, including raised gold outlining and on-glaze enamel painting. Decorative figures were introduced in 1893. Doulton also made earthenware pottery, like flowerpots, kitchenware, and spittoons.

Doulton
1879–1902
Impressed
England added
after 1891

Royal Doulton
First Royal
Doulton mark
Printed or
impressed
1902–1922,
1927–1932
Made in England
added after
1930

Minton
1860s
Printed

Minton
1863–1872
Printed

Minton
c.1873+
Printed *England*
added in 1891
Made in England
added
c.1902–1911

The Leeds factory made this creamware plate with a blue feather edge. Green was also used as a border color on pieces.

In 1902 King Edward VII honored Doulton by granting it the right to use the word *Royal* to describe its wares, and the name *Royal Doulton* appeared in its marks. The factory is still working and still making the figurines, character jugs, and animal figures so popular with collectors today.

Leeds

Leeds was a popular English factory during the eighteenth and early nineteenth centuries. The factory, which operated from 1760 to 1878, was best known for its cream-colored earthenware. *Leeds ware* has a distinctive appearance and several characteristics that are easy to recognize. The handles on pitchers and mugs were usually made of twisted, entwined strips of clay. The rims of plates were often beaded. The creamware body was tinted green or blue at the rim. Leeds also made many other types of pottery. Best of all for positive identification, if everything else checks, it is nice to find the word *Leeds* impressed on the bottom—a rarity but a possibility.

Minton

Thomas Minton, after working for other potters, started his own firm in Stoke-on-Trent in 1793. The family business made a wide variety of tablewares and decorative pieces. By 1846 it was making Parian ware, and later it made majolica, tiles, bone china, and art pottery.

From 1873 to about 1912, the name on the mark was usually *Mintons*; then it again became *Minton*. A special code of symbols was stamped or impressed on wares starting in 1842. Each year was represented by a different picture. The firm became part of the Royal Doulton Tableware group in 1968, but the wares continue to be marked *Minton*.

James Macintyre and Company (Moorcroft)

William Moorcroft worked from 1898 as a designer for James Macintyre and Company of Burslem, England. In 1913 he set up his own firm, making many of the wares he had developed at Macintyre. His designs often include stylized flowers and distinctive glaze colors. He worked with flambé glazes (flame colored) and won many awards for his work.

Potter to H.M. The Queen was added to the marks after 1928 when he was given a Royal Warrant by King George V.

Poole Pottery

Poole Pottery was founded by Jesse Carter in 1873 in Poole, England. The company specialized in architectural ceramics like tiles and decorative trim used in buildings, but soon began to make other pottery. In 1908 the firm was incorporated as Carter and Company, Ltd. In 1921 a subsidiary company, Carter, Stabler and Adams, was formed to develop art pottery. This firm's name was changed to Poole Pottery Ltd. in 1962.

Spode

Spode pottery, porcelain, and bone china were made at a factory founded by Josiah Spode about 1770 in Stoke-on-Trent. The firm

James Macintyre (Moorcroft) 1898–c.1904 Printed brown; painted signature

James Macintyre (Moorcroft) 1898–1935 Printed brown; painted initials

Poole Pottery/Carter and Company 1873–1921 Incised or printed

Copeland and Garrett c.1833 Printed

W.T. Copeland and Sons c.1885 Printed

This plate was made soon after Spode began adding mined feldspar to its porcelain in 1821. It is marked Spode, feldspar porcelain. The plate, in the Etruscan shape, is decorated with blue and overglaze gold designs.

was named Copeland and Garrett from 1833 to 1847, then W.T. Copeland or W.T. Copeland and Sons until 1976, when it merged with Royal Worcester to become Royal Worcester Spode Ltd. Most collectors include all the wares under the more familiar name of Spode.

The word *Spode* appears on pieces made by the companies, and some pieces have pattern numbers. The low numbers are on the earlier pieces, but more than 5,000 pattern numbers were used by 1833.

Staffordshire

Staffordshire is a district in England where hundreds of pottery factories have made many types of wares since the mid-eighteenth century. Flow blue and historical blue transfer-printed dishes, as well as figurines for the mantel, were made in the district.

The potteries of the Staffordshire district made almost every kind of saleable ceramics, not just figurines or transfer design plates. This 1770s black-glazed teapot has a solid silver rim, spout, finial, and trim. It is 11½ inches high. (Photo: Skinner)

When collectors refer to *Staffordshire* wares, they can mean a transfer-decorated ware, or a ware similar to the antique pieces made by the Wood family, or any ceramic wares made in the Staffordshire district—no matter how new.

Ralph Wood (1715–1772) and possibly his brother Aaron (1717–1785) made rustic pottery figures. Ralph made the famous Staffordshire groups, showing everyday life or famous events. The pottery made by Ralph and his cousin Enoch Wood (1759–1840) are among the most famous early Staffordshire wares. Enoch Wood set up his own works around 1784. About 1790, his pottery changed its name to Wood and Caldwell, and in 1818 to Enoch Wood and Sons. The factory closed in 1846.

The Wood potteries also made other sorts of Staffordshire wares, including transfer-printed earthenware, black basalt, jasperware, and Toby jugs. Other Staffordshire makers produced small figures of the same general type as the Wood figures. Neale and Company of Hanley, John Walton of

Burslem, and Ralph Salt of Hanley all made figures that were sometimes marked.

Victorian Staffordshire figures are easier to find and less expensive than those dating from the early nineteenth century. These figurines are not only examples of the potter's art, but also symbols of a specific historical time. The first Victorian Staffordshire portrait figures were representations of Queen Victoria and Prince Albert. The couple was married in February 1840, so any figure depicting their lives can easily be dated. Their children were represented in later figures. Many American collectors mistakenly believe that Staffordshire figures are limited to large figurines of dogs or other animals, or of royalty and other important historical people or places. But through the years, figurines of political figures, murderers, murderers' homes, actors, sports heroes, and other famous people were made.

Victorian figures are different from earlier Staffordshire figures in many ways: The clay is whiter, the parts are molded and not handmade, and more gold was used in the decorations. The figures made after 1850 do not try to imitate the earlier porcelain figures, and were designed to be made from pottery.

Other factories in England, Scotland, and Wales made Staffordshire portrait figures between 1840 and 1900. Many Staffordshire figures are being reproduced today. The old glazes are not as perfect as modern glazes. The finish on the early figures tends to craze in a fine network of lines, and the bottoms are different. Old bases are often solid; new ones show that the figure is hollow. A comparison of an old and a new piece will also show a difference in the colors used as decoration.

Many collectors search for animals made by Staffordshire potters. The Staffordshire spaniel is a flat-faced dog called a King Charles spaniel or a comforter dog. These dogs, as well as poodles, sporting dogs, domestic animals, and zoo animals, were made in quantity.

Printed Staffordshire

To a large group of antiques collectors, the word *Staffordshire* means "printed dishes that are usually blue and white." If you go to your library to get a book about Staffordshire ware, it is likely that most of the books on that subject will discuss these printed plates, some of the books will discuss the Victorian portrait figures, and only a few books will cover the early English wares made in eighteenth-century Staffordshire.

Most of the historic blue Staffordshire plates were made in England from about 1818 to 1848, but copies have been and still are being made. Each English maker had his own characteristic border design. The views were transfer-pattern pictures of actual events or cities applied to a white china. The blue patterns were the earliest. Blue transfer designs were used at the end of the eighteenth century and during the nineteenth century. Black was also one of the early colors used. Pink, green, red, purple, lavender, and brown transfer designs were popular from the 1820s to the 1840s. The combination of several colors began about 1840. American historical views on china bring higher prices than European scenes, although the same factories made the wares at the same time. Historical china was made from about 1800 to the 1860s. Plates picturing similar scenes have been made ever since, but collectors are interested in the early ones. *Romantic Staffordshire*, with attractive scenic views, was made from the 1820s to the 1860s. Many of the designs have been reproduced. The quality of the pottery, transfers, and design have varied widely.

This is a Staffordshire warming plate. It looks like any other plate, but it has an added bottom piece that held hot water. The warm plate kept food from getting cold, a problem in the nineteenth century when the kitchen was outside.

Flow-blue Staffordshire

Flow-blue china was made in England, the Netherlands, and the United States from about 1830 to the 1920s. The designs—often oriental motifs, floral patterns, romanticized landscapes, or historical scenes—were transfer printed on the plates, and the cobalt coloring that was used to create the design on the plate flowed beyond the lines of the pattern. The smeared effect was colorful and hid most defects in the pottery. Almost all flow blue was printed on white ironstone china. (See the section on "Ironstone" on pages 13–14.) Ironstone was cheaper than porcelain and did not chip, stain, or craze as easily.

Historical china is often of the flow-blue type. Collectors differ in their judgments of the best type of flow blue. Some like the very dark, heavily smeared blue pieces, while others prefer the lighter blue with more legible designs. Historical designs are judged by rarity of design and the amount of blue.

Wedgwood

Wedgwood pottery is one of the most famous and important English pottery factories. Josiah Wedgwood came from a family of potters, but his brother did not want him in the family business, possibly because he was physically disabled. Josiah went into partnership with several other men after 1752 and invented many types of pottery and glazes. He became the head of his own firm in 1759 and continued with his experimentation and work. Wedgwood's early work in partnership with Thomas Whieldon resulted in several types of earthenware: agateware, white stoneware, and marbleized wares. He discovered a green glaze that made it possible to make earthenware pieces resembling cauliflowers, pineapples, and other natural fruits. The cauliflower ware was made from about 1750 to 1770 and was copied by European majolica makers during the last half of the nineteenth century. Cauliflower ware was also made in the United States. (See the section "Majolica" on pages 12–13.)

By 1765, Josiah Wedgwood developed a cream-colored pottery that was used by Queen Charlotte, wife of King George III. *Queensware* quickly became a popular style.

The Wedgwood factory made many kinds of stoneware, such as black basalt, *rosso antico* (redware), and caneware. In later years, it made lusterware, majolica, bone china, and, from 1811 to 1816, porcelain.

STAFFORDSHIRE BORDERS

These are sample border designs used on Staffordshire china.

The most famous of the Wedgwood products is jasperware. It is a nonporous pottery made in light blue, dark blue, lavender, green, yellow, black, or some other color. The decorations are of a raised material that is usually white. Some pieces are made from a solid-colored clay with applied raised designs of a contrasting colored clay. Other pieces are made entirely of one color clay with a color dip to create the contrast in design. The most famous piece of jasperware is the Portland vase, which is a copy of an early Roman cameo glass vase. Jasperware was so popular that it was copied by many factories, especially by German firms during the late nineteenth century.

Wedgwood is almost always clearly marked. The quality of Wedgwood products is so obvious that it takes only a short time to recognize copies. Use the marks as a quick reference. Be wary if there is no mark. One word of warning: The word *Wedgewood* (with a second letter *e*) is found on china that was *not* made by the famous factory of Josiah Wedgwood. William Smith and Company of Stockton-on-Tees, England, made a cream-colored ware marked *Wedgewood* from 1826 to 1848. The mark was a deliberate attempt to mislead the public and to misrepresent the china as that of the more famous factory. The English courts agreed that there was an infringement of rights and forced the company to stop using the mark.

Wedgwood merged with Waterford Crystal in 1986 to form Waterford Wedgwood PLC.

Worcester and Royal Worcester
Worcester porcelains have been made in Worcester, England, at several locations since the middle of the eighteenth century. Almost

Wedgwood's Queensware was popular as soon as it was introduced in 1765. This covered sardine box with a realistic fish handle is decorated with hand-painted flowers and butterflies.
(Photo: Skinner)

Wedgwood Date-Letter System

The Wedgwood date marking system was introduced in 1860 and used three capital letters, with the first representing the month, the second the potter, and the third the year the piece was made.

MBT

Marks Indicating Months

January	J	July	V (1860–1863)
February	F		L (1864–1907)
March	M (1860–1863)	August	W
	R (1864–1907)	September	S
April	A	October	O
May	Y (1860–1863)	November	N
	M (1864–1907)	December	D
June	T		

Marks Indicating Years: 1860–1929

The mark indicating the years from 1860 through 1929 ran in cycles with letters from A to Z. The first cycle began with O for 1860 and continued to Z for 1871. The second cycle began with A for 1872, and so on. After 1907 instead of a letter indicating the month, a number was used to indicate the cycle. For example, the letter code *3BS* means 1916.

Cycle 1	Cycle 2		Cycle 3		Cycle 4
O - 1860	A - 1872	N - 1885	A - 1898	N - 1911	A - 1924
P - 1861	B - 1873	O - 1886	B - 1899	O - 1912	B - 1925
Q - 1862	C - 1874	P - 1887	C - 1900	P - 1913	C - 1926
R - 1863	D - 1875	Q - 1888	D - 1901	Q - 1914	D - 1927
S - 1864	E - 1876	R - 1889	E - 1902	R - 1915	E - 1928
T - 1865	F - 1877	S - 1890	F - 1903	S - 1916	F - 1929
U - 1866	G - 1878	T - 1891	G - 1904	T - 1917	
V - 1867	H - 1879	U - 1892	H - 1905	U - 1918	
W - 1868	I - 1880	V - 1893	I - 1906	V - 1919	
X - 1869	J - 1881	W - 1894	J - 1907	W - 1920	
Y - 1870	K - 1882	X - 1895	K - 1908	X - 1921	
Z - 1871	L - 1883	Y - 1896	L - 1909	Y - 1922	
	M - 1884	Z - 1897	M - 1910	Z - 1923	

In 1930 the company discontinued this confusing system. A new system was devised that represented months with the numbers 1 to 12, the potter by letter, and the year by the last two digits. Thus the mark "6 P 50" means June 1950.

The English registry marks were also used. (See pages 2–4.)

(See pages 2–4.)

JOSIAH WEDGWOOD MARKS

Wedgwood

1769–present

WEDGWOOD

1780–1795

OTHER "WEDGWOOD" FIRMS

Other firms run by relatives of Josiah Wedgwood have used the name in their marks, although they did not produce the famous Wedgwood porcelain. Wedgwood & Co. was established in Tunstall, Staffordshire, in 1860. The name was changed to Enoch Wedgwood Tunstall Ltd. in 1965 to avoid confusion with Josiah Wedgwood and Sons Ltd. In 1979 Josiah Wedgwood and Sons Ltd. purchased the Tunstall firm.

The Worcester factory made this demitasse cup and saucer in the late nineteenth century. Notice the asymmetrical designs done in the Japanese manner.

Royal Worcester standard mark 1862–1875 The numeral *73* below the mark indicates the year 1873.

Royal Worcester standard mark 1876–1891 Letter underneath changed every year.

Royal Worcester standard mark 1891–1963

Chamberlain and Company c.1840–1845

Opposite page: The impressed mark Bretby *is on the bottom of this English art pottery vase. The two-tone blue vase is 9½ inches high.*

every type of porcelain, from simple blue and white to elaborate multicolor pieces, was produced. Majolica was made during the nineteenth century. The Worcester Porcelain Company, established by Dr. John Wall, William Davis, and thirteen other partners in 1751, is the best known. Porcelains can be identified by the name of the owners of the factory at the time the porcelain was made. Each period had its own marks. The Dr. Wall period was from 1752 to 1783; the Flight period, 1783–1792; the Flight and Barr period, 1792–1807; the Barr, Flight, and Barr period, 1807–1813; and the Flight, Barr, and Barr period, 1813–1840. Robert Chamberlain, a decorator at the factory, started his own studio in 1786. His mark, which sometimes included the name of the city of Worcester, appears on pieces as early as 1790. Chamberlain's firm merged with the Worcester Porcelain Company in 1840. W. H. Kerr and R. W. Binns purchased the company in 1852, and the years until 1862 were called the Kerr and Binns period. The company's name was changed to the Worcester Royal Porcelain Company, Ltd., in 1862. Collectors refer to the porcelains made after 1862 as Royal Worcester. In 1976 the firm merged with W. T. Copeland and Sons to become Royal Worcester Spode Ltd.

Thomas Grainger and John Wood founded another important china factory in Worcester in 1801. It was first called Grainger Wood and Company. When Grainger died in 1839, his son George continued the business. It was called George Grainger & Company and was bought in 1889 by Worcester Royal Porcelain Company.

British Art Pottery

Art pottery was first made in Great Britain about 1865. Art critic and writer John Ruskin and poet and artist William Morris argued that it was time for craftsmen to create individual pieces rather than

British Art Potteries

Pottery and Location	Dates of Operation	Mark
Aller Vale Pottery Newton Abbot, Devon	1887–1901	ALLER VALE
Ault, William Swadlincote	1887–1923	
Bailey, C.J.C. & Co. Fulham, London	1864–1889	
Barons Pottery Rolle Quay, Barnstaple	1899–1939	BARON. BARNSTAPLE
Barum	See *Brannam, C. H.*	
Belleview (Bellevue) Pottery	See *Rye Pottery*	
Bingham, Edward (Hedingham Art Pottery) Castle Hedingham	1864–1901	
Bishops Waltham Hampshire	1866–1868	BISHOPS WALTHAM
Bramfield ware	See *Pearson, James, Ltd.*	
Brannam, C. H. Barnstaple	1879–1979	C. H. BRANNAM BARUM
Bretby Art Pottery Woodville, Derbyshire	1883–1933	BRETBY
Burmantofts Pottery Leeds	1882–1904	B &F
Cadborough Pottery Rye, Sussex	1840–1871	RYE POTTERY
Carter & Co. Poole, Dorset In 1921 Carter, Stabler & Adams was established and added as a subsidiary. Both firms were referred to as the Poole Potteries.	1873–present The name was changed to Poole Pottery Ltd. in 1962.	

Pottery and Location	Dates of Operation	Mark
Commondale Pottery Stokesley, Yorkshire	1872–1884	COMMONDALE POTTERY
Crane, Walter (designer) London	1865–1915	
De Morgan, William Chelsea, Merton Abbey, Fulham	1869–1907	W. D e MORGAN
Della Robbia Pottery Birkenhead, Cheshire	1893–1906	D R
Doulton & Watts **Doulton & Co.** Lambeth and Burslem	1815–1854 1854–1956 "Royal Doulton" mark used after 1902–present	DOULTON & WATTS LAMBETH POTTERY LONDON
Dresser, Christopher (designer) Yorkshire, Swadlincote, London (others)	c.1870–1890s	Chr.Dresser
Elton's Sunflower Pottery **(Sir Edmund Elton)** Clevedon, Somerset	1879–1930	Elton
Grovelands Potteries (S. & E. Collier) Reading	1850s–1910	TRADE MARK
Hedingham Art Pottery	See *Bingham, Edward*	
Kensington Fine Art Pottery Hanley	1892–1899	K. F. A.
Lauder & Smith Barnstaple, Devon, Pottington	1876–1914	Lauder Barum
Linthorpe Pottery Middlesbrough, Yorkshire	1879–1889	LINTHORPE
Macintyre & Co. Burslem	1890s–1913	FLORIAN WARE
Martin Brothers London, Southall, Fulham	1873–1923	RW Martin & Brothers London & Southall

Pottery and Location	Dates of Operation	Mark
Maw & Co. Shropshire	1851–1888	MAW & CO.
Minton's Art Pottery Kensington Gore, London	1871–1875	
Pearson, James, Ltd. (Bramfield ware) London	1884–1939	Items not marked.
Pilkington Tile & Pottery Co. Manchester	1893–1938	P
Poole Pottery	See *Carter & Co.*	
Ruskin Pottery West Smethwick, Worcestershire	1898–1935	
Rye Pottery Cadborough Pottery, Belleview (Bellevue) Pottery Rye, Sussex	1840–1871 1869–1939; reopened in 1947 as Rye Pottery	
Salopian Art Pottery Co. Shropshire	1882–1912	SALOPIAN
Spode Copeland & Garrett W.T. Copeland or W.T. Copeland & Sons Royal Worcester Spode Ltd. (merged with Royal Worcester) Stoke-on-Trent	c.1770–present 1833–1847 1847–1976 1976–present	
Stiff, James & Son Lambeth	1840–1913	J. STIFF & SONS
Torquay Terra-Cotta Co. Hele Cross	1875–1909	
Wardle and Co. Ltd. Hanley	1871–1935	
Watcombe Pottery Co. Staffordshire, Torquay, Devon	1867–1901	
Wedgwood, Josiah & Sons Ltd. Burslem, Etruria, Barlaston	1759–present	WEDGWOOD

become part of the standardized world of the Industrial Revolution. They encouraged artists and craftsmen to produce pottery in the manner of the Arts and Crafts movement.

Most of the British art potteries were small shops with just a few workers. The style created by these artists influenced the larger potteries, and some, like Doulton and Company, began making similar wares in a special art department.

This English art pottery bowl is so light in weight it surprises those who lift it. The light and dark blue crystalline glaze is on a very thin clay base. It was made by the Ruskin pottery in 1921.

English Wares for the American and Canadian Markets

Gaudy Dutch, Gaudy Welsh, and Others

Gaudy Dutch pottery was made in England and exported to the United States after the War of 1812. It has been said that Staffordshire potters made the pottery only for the German settlements of Pennsylvania, but that is probably not true as it was sold in quantity in Pennsylvania, Ohio, New Jersey, and Maryland.

Gaudy Dutch is a white earthenware with bold Japanese Imari-style decorations in rusty red, blue, green, yellow, and black. Today's collectors have named each pattern of Gaudy Dutch pottery: Butterfly, Carnation, Dahlia, Double Rose, Dove, Grape, Leaf, Oyster, Primrose, Single Rose, Strawflower, Sunflower, Urn, War Bonnet, Zinnia, and No Name are modern names and were not used when the ware was first sold.

A few pieces were marked with factory names, such as Riley (1802–1827), E. Woods and Sons, Burslem (before 1814), and Rogers (1815–1842).

Gaudy Dutch dishes were made in only sixteen patterns, all using the same colors of rusty red, blue, green, yellow, and black. This is a piece in the Carnation pattern.

Gaudy Welsh is a similar but later pottery that was also copied from Imari patterns. It was made in England after 1820, but the china is heavier and the coloring cruder than the Gaudy Dutch. Gaudy Welsh had many patterns. Its most popular ones include Tulip, Oyster, Sunflower, Wagon Wheel, and Grape Leaf. Some of the wares had impressed borders, but most of them had dark blue scalloped borders with large flowers or leaves in blue, red, green, or gold.

Gaudy Dutch and Gaudy Welsh wares are easy to identify. Almost no copies of these wares have been made that could confuse even the inexperienced collector.

Gaudy Ironstone is the collector's name for ironstone wares with bright patterns similar to Gaudy Dutch. It was made in England in the early 1850s for the American market.

Mocha Ware

Mocha ware was a utilitarian pottery made in England from the late eighteenth century through the twentieth century. Some was also made in America. It was most popular before 1875. Mugs, bowls, and jugs are the most common forms.

Rowland & Marsellus c.1893–1900 United States importer's mark

Mocha refers to the distinctive slip-glazed decorations used on the ware rather than to the color of the clay body. Mocha ware was made of various types of earthenware: creamware, pearlware, yellowware, or white ware. Decorations included patterns called banded, checks, circle, cat's eyes, cable, geometric, and fan. Glaze colors are blue, brown, green, gray, buff, orange, black, and white.

Mocha ware was discovered by collectors in 1945, when an article on banded creamware was published in *Antiques* magazine. Since that time the interest and prices have risen.

Mocha ware was usually unmarked. Early pieces were decorated with a variety of distinctive patterns like this double zigzag earthworm.

Mocha ware was exported to the United States and Canada in quantity from 1800 to about 1850, then in lesser amounts. It was rarely marked. A few pieces with the name Adams or Leeds have been found. The older the mocha, the lighter the color. The almost-yellow-colored kitchen bowls of the 1880s to 1920s were the last of the ware. The name *mocha ware* is sometimes used incorrectly for kitchen pieces from the 1930s and later.

Rowland and Marsellus Company
Rowland and Marsellus Company is a mark that appears on Staffordshire wares dating from the late nineteenth and early twentieth centuries. The company was a New York importer that sold English wares in the United States from 1893 to about 1937. The products they imported were made by British Anchor Pottery, S. Hancock and Sons, and others. Many American views were pictured on the plates. Often a retail store name appeared with the Rowland and Marsellus mark. One special type of plate is called a *rolled edge* by collectors. It has a central design showing a building or scene, and several other related scenes in cartouches on the rolled-over edge of the plate. More than 400 different scenes of American cities and towns are known. The company also made a few matching cups and saucers.

Spatterware and Spongeware
Spatterware made in Staffordshire was most popular from about 1800 to 1850. The spatter may cover the entire dish, or it may be just around the border. Many pieces have a hand-painted design in the center. Favorite motifs are flowers, birds, or houses. Large quantities of spatterware were exported to the United States, where it was especially popular with Germans who had settled in Pennsylvania.

Spongeware is a less expensive earthenware that has designs or borders created with sponges or crumpled cloth. Natural sponges were cut to create a pattern that could be repeated. Flowers, stars, circles, arcs, and chain-links can be found, both as borders and as part of a cen-

The borders, grass, and leaves of this cup and saucer are spatter, and the center is a painted red schoolhouse. The finished plate is very childlike and very collectible. (Photo: Pook & Pook)

Is it spatterware or spongeware? It's easy to tell. Spatterware dishes are decorated with what looks like paint spattered from a brush.

Spongeware looks as if the paint was dabbed on with a sponge. Through the years, authors and collectors have jumbled the names until almost all of these types of decoration are lumped under the name *spatterware,* even if the dishes appear to be spongeware. To be correct, avoid the terms *design spatter, stick spatter,* and *cut sponge,* all of which are inaccurate names for types of spatterware and spongeware.

tral design that is hand painted. Easiest to identify are the white crockery pieces decorated with blue sponged decoration in a random overall pattern. Spongeware was first made in Scotland about 1835. The technique soon spread to the rest of Britain and to Holland, Russia, and America. This type of decoration was used on pottery until about 1930. Reproductions are being made today.

Portneuf or Canadian Spongeware

A special type of spongeware called *Portneuf* was made for the Canadian market. It was originally believed that the crude earthenware was made in Portneuf, Quebec, but studies have proved that it was probably made in Scotland for sale in Canada. Portneuf is very similar to the spongeware that was made for sale in Pennsylvania and New England. It is a thick pottery and was decorated with elk, deer, robins, wildflowers, ferns, leaves, or stylized designs, and it often had sponged decorations. The ware was usually decorated in green, blue, or other muted tones.

Right: *Portneuf is the name for this type of Canadian spongeware. The borders and the flowers have been sponged on this pitcher.* (Photo: Waddington's)

Chapter 3

EUROPEAN POTTERY AND PORCELAIN

IN THE 1940s most of a museum collection of works by Taxile Doat, a pottery artist who worked both in France and in St. Louis at the University City Pottery, was deaccessioned through a sale at a department store. Today museums search for his works. Opinions of what is good or bad art change with time. Some factories like Haviland or Mettlach have been recognized as makers of important ceramics for many years. Some, like Massier and Gouda, were not fully appreciated until the 1970s.

AUSTRIA

Teplitz

Teplitz refers to a town in Central Europe in what is now Austria. Several companies in the Turn-Teplitz area manufactured art pottery during the late nineteenth and early twentieth centuries. The Amphora Porzellanfabrik (Amphora Porcelain Works) was run by Riessner, Stellmacher, and Kessel. The firm used a variety of marks with the word *Amphora* or the initials *RS&K*. Another company making pottery was the Alexandra Porcelain

Amphora pottery vases often have applied three-dimensional figures, leaves, and flowers climbing up the sides. This 21½-inch-high vase has putti, blackberries, and leaves.
(Photo: Jackson's)

Works. The firm, started by Ernst Wahliss, sold the RS&K wares until 1910, when it started making its own faience.

DENMARK

Bing & Grondahl
Bing & Grondahl was established in Copenhagen, Denmark, in 1853 by Frederick Vilhelm Grondahl, who had worked at the Royal Copenhagen Porcelain manufactory, and M. H. and J. H. Bing, owners of a stationery department store. At first, overglaze and biscuit porcelains were made. Underglaze blue decoration was started in 1886. The annual Christmas plate series was introduced in 1895. Dinnerware, stoneware, and figurines are still made today.

Royal Copenhagen
A factory to produce hard paste porcelains was established in Copenhagen, Denmark, in 1775. The firm was supported by the king, and when he assumed ownership of it in 1779, the company was named the Royal Copenhagen Porcelain Manufactory. Although the firm became privately owned in 1868, the name was not changed.

Early wares included inexpensive blue decorated porcelain and more elaborate types, including the famous Flora Danica service with raised flowers introduced in 1790. Tablewares such as the Blue Fluted dinner service, made since 1775, and Blue Flowers, Julian Marie, and Saxon Flower, all made since about 1800, are still in production.

Flora Danica is one of the oldest dinnerware patterns still being made. Flowers and leaves are hand modeled and applied to the pieces. Piercing, beading, and gold trim are added. The flowers are botanically correct.
(Photo: Skinner)

The wares decorated with a blue underglaze developed by Arnold Krog about 1884 have remained popular. The figurines with pale blue and gray glazes have been in production since the nineteenth century. Christmas plates were first made in 1908.

FRANCE

Haviland

Haviland china was the "company" dish set of your grandmother's or great-grandmother's day. Dishes made by Haviland were popular because of their beauty, quality, and low price. Many complete sets of Haviland can still be found, and many are still in use. Four generations of the Haviland family made tablewares.

David and Daniel Haviland founded D.G. and D. Haviland Co. in New York City in 1838. They imported tableware from France. David moved to France in 1841, and six years later he opened a porcelain-decorating shop in Limoges, France, where many other factories made porcelain. At first, the French Haviland firm decorated plain porcelain produced by other Limoges firms, but it soon built its own kilns. By 1876 Haviland made all the white ware it decorated.

A third brother, Robert, joined the New York firm in 1852, and the company became Haviland Brothers and Company. This firm closed in 1863, and the Limoges factory became Haviland and Company. The Limoges factory was owned by David Haviland and his two sons, Charles Edward and Théodore. Charles Edward and his son Georges became sole owners of the company in 1892, and it remained in business until 1931. Théodore opened his own workshop, Théodore Haviland Company, in 1893. Théodore's son William took over the firm when his father died and also operated a business in the United States from 1936 to 1957. By the twentieth century, some Haviland china was made in France but decorated in the United States. Other Haviland family members who made tableware included Charles Field Haviland, his grandson Robert, and Jean Haviland, son of Charles Edward.

The name Haviland appeared in many marks on porcelain made at other factories run by several branches of the family. As a result,

Amphora
Porcelain Works
1892–1918

Amphora
Porcelain Works
1892–1905

DANISH MARKS

Bing &
Grondahl
1853

B. & G.

Bing &
Grondahl
1898+

Royal
Copenhagen
1775–1820,
1850–1870
Blue

Royal
Copenhagen
c.1892
Blue

Haviland Family Tree and Various Haviland Marks to 1900

William

Edmund

Daniel Griffin

David

(1814–1879)
Founded **D.G. & D. Haviland**, a New York City importing company, with his older brother, Daniel G., in 1837–38. In 1841 he moved to Limoges, France, where he founded a porcelain decorating firm (a subsidiary of the New York company) in 1847. He opened his own china factory in Limoges in 1853; after **Haviland Bros. & Co.** closed during the Civil War, the Limoges firm became **Haviland & Co.**, and David's sons joined in ownership.

Richard

Charles Edward

(1839–1921)
Managed **Haviland & Co.** in France and maintained control of the company until he and his brother, Théodore, decided to split up and close the firm on Dec. 31, 1891. Reopened **Haviland & Co.** with his son Georges the very next day, Jan. 1, 1892. It remained in business until 1931.

Théodore

(1842–1919)
In charge of promotion and distribution of **Haviland & Co.** porcelain in the United States from the 1860s until his father's death in 1879, when he returned to France to manage manufacturing at the company until 1891. Opened his own workshop, **Théodore Haviland Co.**, in 1893.

THÉODORE HAVILAND COMPANY MARKS

c.1892	1892+	1893+
1893+	1894+	1895+

William David

Took over operation of the **Théodore Haviland Co.** in 1919.

Guy

Assisted William David in running **Théodore Haviland Co.** from 1920 to 1940.

Georges

Took over control of **Haviland & Co.** when his father died in 1921.

Jean

Founded **Johann Haviland Company** in Bavaria in 1907. It was bought out in 1924 and by 1934 was part of Rosenthal.

Frank

Operated own decorating studio (1910–1925).

Robert Barclay

(1803–1885)
Traveled to France in the late 1830s to investigate supply sources for fine china. Joined brothers Daniel and David at the New York importing firm, which by 1852 was renamed **Haviland Bros. & Co.** After dissolution of that firm in 1863, created a new company with his sons and two other partners, Mr. Churchman and Mr. England.

Frederick

Charles Field

(1832–1896)
Apprenticed with his uncle David in Limoges in the early 1850s. Founded a company with his uncle Richard in 1859 and began decorating porcelain from Casseaux Works. Acquired his first porcelain manufacturing company about 1868 and took over his father-in-law's white ware factory, Alluaud, in 1876. Retired in 1881.

Charles Field
Haviland
Mark
1870–1882

André

Robert

(1898–?)

HAVILAND BROTHERS & COMPANY, HAVILAND & COMPANY MARKS

*Various Haviland companies continued to work into the twentieth century and used various marks, some of which can be confused with early Haviland marks. Haviland china is still being made in the twenty-first century.

there is understandable confusion about the marks used by the Haviland family.

Today old and new Haviland china is still popular. Many sets of Haviland are passed from generation to generation but may be missing a few pieces. There are matching services that can find the missing pieces. Dealers can help identify the patterns.

Limoges

Fine quality hard paste porcelain has been produced in Limoges, France, since the late 1700s. In America Haviland china is the best known of the Limoges factories, but fine porcelain was made by many Limoges firms, including Coiffe, Delinieres & Company, William Guerin and Company, A. Lanternier, Jean Pouyat, and Martial Redon & Company. Collectors are most interested in the porcelain produced in Limoges from the mid-1800s until about 1930.

Quimper

Tin-glazed, hand-painted pottery has been made in Quimper (pronounced *kam pair*), a town in the French province of Brittany, since the late seventeenth century. Three firms worked in Quimper, and the names and marks have changed because of marriages and mergers. The earliest firm, founded in 1685 by Jean Baptiste Bousquet, was known as HB Quimper. Another firm, founded in 1772 by François Eloury, was known as Porquier. The third firm, founded by Guillaume Dumaine in 1778, was known as HR or Henriot Quimper. All three firms made similar wares decorated with designs of Breton peasants and sea and flower motifs. The Eloury (Porquier) and Dumaine (Henriot) firms merged in 1913. Bousquet (HB) merged with the others in 1968. The company, purchased in 1984 by an American holding company, is now called Société Nouvelle des Faienceries de Quimper HB and is still in operation.

Sarreguemines

Utzschneider and Company, a porcelain factory, made ceramics in Sarreguemines, France, starting

Opposite page: The Haviland company made many types of tablewares. This tureen, made to hold oyster stew, has an oyster-shaped finial. It is the work of Albert Dammouse, who also worked at the Sèvres factory. It was made between 1876 and 1889. (Photo: Gene Harris)

The word Limoges is on this covered container. It has a hole in the bottom so a condensed milk can or jam jar could be put inside. This is for jelly because it is hand painted with currants.

Left: This 4-inch-high mustard jar is decorated with a colored transfer of French peasants at a fair. It is marked Obernai, the pattern name, and Faienceries Sarreguemines. The pattern has been made for 100 years.

Garnitures were popular fireplace mantel decorations in the nineteenth century. This three-piece Sèvres garniture is decorated with romantic scenes, raised gilt scrolls, and gilt bronze trim. It is marked Chateau de Longpre, France, with the interlaced L's mark. (Photo: Jackson's)

in 1770. Transfer-printed wares, often picturing French peasants, and majolica were made in the nineteenth century. Some pieces were marked *Faienceries Sarreguemines.*

Sèvres

Porcelain has been made in Sèvres, France, since 1769, when the Manufacture Royale de Porcelaine de France was established. Soft paste porcelain had been made in nearby Vincennes, France, since 1743, but that factory merged with the new one in Sèvres. Eighteenth- and early-nineteenth-century Sèvres porcelains were known for their jeweled decorations and for enamel decorations in colors like royal blue, turquoise, rose, and gold.

In the nineteenth century, the factory made a variety of ceramics, including majolica, soft paste porcelain, stoneware, and pieces with pâte-sur-pâte decoration. Tablewares, figurines, utilitarian items, and decorative pieces were made in many styles. Early pieces were marked with interlaced *L*'s and a center letter, but this is one of the most frequently forged marks in ceramics. Sèvres porcelains continued to be made in the twentieth century.

GERMANY

Meissen the Town, Meissen the Porcelain Factory

The term *Meissen* is frequently misused. Meissen is a town in Germany where a porcelain factory was built about 1710. Over the years, country borders were redrawn by numerous wars, so although the Meissen factory never moved from its original location, its address changed to Saxony, then Prussia, and finally Germany.

This 6-inch figurine of Neptune, god of the sea, is an early nineteenth-century Meissen porcelain. It is marked with blue crossed swords.

The word *Meissen* should mean any ware, regardless of whether it is a porcelain or stoneware, that was made at the original Meissen factory from 1710 to the present time. The English refer to Meissen as *Dresden*, and the French use the word *Saxe*. Until the mid-nineteenth century the term *Dresden china* was used to refer to genuine Meissen porcelain. After that time, the same term was applied to a large number of other porcelains that only resembled the work of the famous factory. Most of it is from factories in or near the city of Dresden, which is 15 miles from Meissen. French, Italian, English, and other factories copied Meissen china. These pieces are Meissen-type or Dresden-type. These terms are interchangeable. Dresden porcelain sold today is *not* made by the famous original Meissen factory.

True Meissen china may be unmarked or may have one of several marks, such as the famous crossed lines or crossed swords, imitation Chinese letters, the *KPM* mark, the letters *AR* or *KHC*, or some other letter combination. The crossed-swords mark was first used by the Meissen factory in the 1720s, and variations of the mark have been used ever since. The factory's name changed over the years, but the marks used did not always match the concurrent factory names. The mark *KPM* stands for Königliche Porzellan Manufaktur, or Royal Porcelain Manufactory. The *KPF* mark is for Königliche Porzellan Fabrik, or Royal Porcelain Factory. The *MPM*

Quimper
Bousquet
Mid–19th
century

Quimper
Eloury
c.1860

Quimper
Dumaine
c.1886–1926

Sarreguemines
Utzschneider
and Company
Before 1890

Sèvres
interlaced
L's mark

MARKS WITH CROSSED SWORDS, "KPM," OR "MEISSEN"

The crossed-swords mark of the Meissen factory has been copied by many firms in Germany and other parts of the world. The initials *KPM* can be confusing because other German companies used the same letters in their marks. Krister Porzellan Manufaktur, Kister Porzellan Manufaktur, and Kranischfelder Porzellan Manufaktur used KPM marks in the late nineteenth and early twentieth centuries. The word *Meissen* as all or part of a mark was used by another factory in Meissen, Germany, that was founded in 1864 by Carl Teichert, and by other factories. The name even appears as a pattern name on twentieth-century dishes that were not made in Germany.

Meissen
1725+

K.P.M.
KPM
1832–
present

ONION MEISSEN

The blue-and-white onion Meissen was first made around 1739. The design is Chinese in origin, and it pictures peaches and pomegranates, mistakenly referred to as onions. The fruit on the border pointed only toward the center of the plate before 1800, while later patterns used fruit that alternately pointed in and out. Twentieth- and twenty-first-century pieces have the fruit pointing either way. The design has been simplified, and fewer of the "onions" or pomegranates are shown in the plate border. A pink version of the onion pattern and a Red Bud onion pattern date from the mid-nineteenth century. The Red Bud onion pattern had added gold and red overglaze decoration. Onion Meissen was made by many German, French, English, Japanese, and United States factories. It is still being produced.

mark represents the Meissener Porzellan Manufaktur, or the Meissen Porcelain Manufactory, and was first used about 1722. All three marks were used on the porcelain made at the Meissen factory beginning about 1722. In addition, all these marks were used during the nineteenth and twentieth centuries, sometimes by other factories. If these letters appear either alone or with some symbol, verify the mark in a book about porcelain marks.

Old Meissen by the original factory may be differentiated from new Meissen by the same factory by careful study. Many of the eighteenth-century figures were reproduced by Meissen during the nineteenth, twentieth, and twenty-first centuries. Old Meissen was carefully decorated. It is heavier than new Meissen. The colors used in the decorating can help determine the age of the piece. Maroon and yellowish chrome green were never used during the eighteenth century. Almost all the eighteenth-century figures had brown eyes. Blue or brown eyes appeared during the nineteenth, twentieth, and twenty-first centuries. The porcelain used for early Meissen has a slightly green color, while later porcelains were dead white.

Mettlach Steins

The stoneware steins of Germany have been popular with collectors for years. The most famous steins came from the pottery factory of Villeroy & Boch, located in the town of Mettlach, Germany. The company, which is still operating, was founded in 1836 by Jean François Boch and Nicholas Villeroy. The factory was in an old abbey that had been restored, and it is pictured as part of the company's castle mark. The firm made stoneware starting in 1842.

Several types of improvements were developed at the factory. The company had a process for making inlaid stoneware, mosaic ware, or chromolith ware in which colored clay was inlaid into a body clay to form designs. The method was expensive at first, but it was gradually improved and the price reduced.

The steins were made during the nineteenth century. The ware was popular in America and won awards at the world's fairs in 1876, 1893, and 1904.

Mettlach steins and plaques can be recognized by the workmanship. Steins have lids of solid pewter or pewter inset with a piece of matching stoneware. Most steins were numbered, lettered, and marked with the Mettlach castle mark after 1874.

RS Prussia

The Schlegelmilch name is common in the Thuringia region of central Germany. In the late nineteenth and early twentieth centuries, several members of two unrelated Schlegelmilch families operated porcelain factories in the Saxony province. Porcelain production became a major export industry.

Leonhard Schlegelmilch founded the Erdmann Schlegelmilch factory, named for his father, in 1861. Located in Suhl, Thuringia, it operated until 1937. Leonhard's son Carl ran a branch of the Erdmann Schlegelmilch factory in Mäbendorf from 1882 until 1918. Oscar Schlegelmilch, another son of Leonhard, opened a plant in Langewiesen, Thuringia, in 1892. It is still in production.

Reinhold Schlegelmilch, who was not related to the Erdmann Schlegelmilch family, opened a porcelain factory in Suhl in 1869 and a second one in Tillowitz, Silesia (now Poland), in 1894. The factories were consolidated in Tillowitz during World War I, taken over by the Polish government in 1945, and are still in operation.

Each of these factories had its own set of marks that used its initials or name with the words *Germany, Prussia, Thuringia,*

The Mettlach castle mark (1907) has the name *Mettlach* in the center and, around the edge, numbers that indicate the date, size of stein, decoration number, and stock number. (See page 4.)

∾∾

Many RS Prussia porcelain plates had embossed rims and scalloped edges that were decorated with a raised pattern or left uncolored when decoration was added to the plate's center. This cobalt blue bowl is made from the Carnation mold.

(Photo: Woody)

R. S. PRUSSIA

 Erdmann Schlegelmilch 1880s–1890s

 Reinhold Schlegelmilch Late 1880s– 1917

 Carl Schlegelmilch 1882–1919

 Oscar Schlegelmilch 1890s

GOUDA

 Zenith Pottery Factory 1891+

 Regina Art Pottery 1898–1910

*Gouda is the collectors'
term for the pottery
made by many factories
in Gouda, Holland.
This ewer is marked
Zuid Holland.*
(Photo: Smith & Jones)

Tillowitz, Silesia, or *Suhl.* Collectors generically refer to Schlegelmilch porcelain as RS Prussia.

HOLLAND

Gouda

Gouda pottery has been made in Gouda, Holland, since the 1700s. Collectors group all pottery marked *Gouda* into one class, although many factories made these wares.

Pieter Van der Want founded the Plateelbakkerij/Zenith in 1749. *Plateelbakkerij* is the old Dutch word for *Delftware pottery.* Several other companies were founded by descendants. The Zenith pottery remained in the family until 1898, when one descendant, Gerrit Van der Want, formed the Regina factory. Another family member, Otto Adrianus Van der Want, kept the Zenith pottery. His son expanded the factory with another plant.

The potteries of Gouda and nearby cities made blue and white delftwares, and after 1890, distinctive, colorful pieces with art nouveau designs.

Other European Pottery and Porcelain Factories and Makers

Pottery and Location	Dates of Operation	Mark
Arte Della Ceramica Florence, Italy	1896–1906	
Boch Frères La Louvière, Belgium	1841–present	
Dalpayrat, Pierre-Adrien Bourg-la-Reine, France	1876–1888	
Deck, Theodore France	1859–1891	
Delaherche, Auguste France	1894–c.1940	
Doat, Taxile Sèvres, France United States	1877–1905 1909–1911	
Gallé, Emile Nancy, France	1874–1935	
Gustavsberg Gustavsberg, Sweden	1827–present	
Haga Pottery Holland	1904–1907	
Longwy Pottery France	1798–present	
Rörstrand Stockholm, Sweden	1726–present	
Rozenburg The Hague, Holland	1883–1916	
Zsolnay Manufactory Pécs, Hungary	1853–present	

Chapter 4

AMERICAN PORCELAIN AND POTTERY

POTTERY WAS MADE IN THE UNITED STATES by the middle of the seventeenth century, but the first recorded attempt to make porcelain was by Andrew Duche in Georgia about 1738. Other potters tried with little success until the late 1760s. In 1770 Bonnin and Morris (also called the American China Manufactory), a Philadelphia firm that operated only until 1772, actually made and sold porcelain, and pieces can be seen in museums today. Other successful attempts were made by Dr. Henry Mead of New York City between about 1813 and 1824, and the Jersey Porcelain and Earthenware Company of Jersey City, New Jersey, between 1825 and 1828. Early American porcelains are so very rare that the average collector will never find one.

In 1826 William Ellis Tucker made some experimental porcelain in Philadelphia. The factory operated by Tucker made a clear white porcelain that was decorated with colors and gold in the French manner. The firm worked from 1825 to 1838 and made wares that were as fine as any made in Europe. Thomas Hulme became a partner in 1828, and the firm was called Tucker and Hulme until the end of 1829. It became Tucker and Hemphill in 1831 when Judge Joseph Hemphill joined the company, which

Faience Manufacturing Company of Greenpoint, New York, made this earthenware potpourri keeper about 1885. The 19-inch-high piece is decorated with piercing, raised flowers, painting, and gilding in the elaborate style of the day. (Photo: Charlton Hall)

Smith, Fife and
Company mark

Syracuse mark
(1893–1898)

*Opposite page:
Onondaga Pottery
Company made this
biscuit jar in the
Marmora shape. The
jar, made in 1886, is
in the collection of the
Syracuse China/Libbey
Inc. Archives.* (Photo:
Hal Silverman Studio)

*This Ceramic Art
Company vase was
hand painted by
Sigmund
Werkner. He
created a portrait
of the Empress
Josephine
surrounded by
flowers, ribbons,
and gilding. It is
marked with the
CAC/Lenox stamp
and the artist's
signature.* (Photo: David
Rago)

*Ott & Brewer made
some pieces in unusual
shapes. This
11-inch-high covered
jar is decorated with
daisies and clouds and
is marked with a red
crown.*

continued to work until 1837. Tucker porcelain was rarely marked and was so similar to the French porcelain of the same period that even some museums have had cases of mistaken identity.

Smith, Fife and Company was established in Philadelphia about 1830 and made a porcelain that was almost identical to the Tucker porcelain. A few pieces of Smith, Fife and Company porcelain marked in red still exist, but the factory was in business for only a few years.

William Boch and Brothers was founded about 1844. The firm made porcelain door hardware and tableware. Thomas C. Smith bought it in 1861 and renamed it the Union Porcelain Works. The firm continued operations until 1890.

Charles Cartlidge of Greenpoint, New York, opened a porcelain factory in 1848. His firm closed in 1856.

Knowles, Taylor and Knowles of East Liverpool, Ohio (1870–1929) made belleek and also Lotus Ware, a porcelain that resembled belleek (See pages 8–9.)

The Onondaga Pottery Company was established in Syracuse, New York, in 1871, and it purchased the Empire Pottery Company that year. At first Onondaga made white graniteware. The company began to make Imperial Geddo porcelain in 1888. Although it started to make china marked Syracuse in 1893, it wasn't until 1966 that the name of the company was officially changed to Syracuse China Corporation. The company made fine porcelain and semiporcelain dinnerware and toilet sets for home and commercial use. The company was purchased by Libbey, Inc., in 1995.

Other important nineteenth-century porcelain makers were United States Pottery of Bennington, Vermont (1849–1858); Kurlbaum & Schwartz of Philadelphia (1853–1859); American Porcelain Manufacturing Company of Gloucester, New Jersey (1854–1857); and Greenwood Pottery (1869–c.1933), Ott and Brewer (1871–1893), and Ceramic Art Company (1889–1906; became Lenox, Inc. in 1906), all of Trenton, New Jersey.

WELL-KNOWN AMERICAN POTTERY MAKERS

Susan Frackelton made unusual art pottery in Milwaukee, Wisconsin, after 1883. This gourd-shaped salt-glaze stoneware vase is decorated with abutilon blossoms and leaves. It is 6¾ inches high.

Bennington

The pottery made in Bennington, Vermont, is some of the most famous American ceramics. Two factories whose products are now referred to as Bennington pottery were in the town, and neither company was named Bennington. The Norton pottery, established by Captain John Norton in 1793, produced utilitarian earthenware and stoneware. The pottery was known for its decorations, which featured flowers, birds, and animals. Before production ceased in 1894, the firm's name changed many times, but it always included the word *Norton*. Christopher Webber Fenton, who worked briefly with Julius Norton, founded the United States Pottery Company in 1847. The firm made yellowware with Rockingham and flint enamel glazes, agate and granite wares, porcelain, and parian. It closed in 1858. Pottery production in Bennington had ended by the close of the nineteenth century.

For many collectors, Bennington pottery remains a mystery. In the 1990s, excavations and studies proved that many pieces formerly thought to be Bennington were not. Some pieces are pictured and identified as Bennington in early books. Some information in the books is now known to be incorrect. Most Bennington ware is unmarked. It is almost impossible to say that a piece is Bennington if it has no mark. For example, the United States Pottery made hound-handled pitchers, but so did many other potteries. The United States Pottery didn't mark much of its work, and it is impossible to identify an unmarked hound-handle pitcher as Bennington ware. Only exact duplicates of marked pieces should be considered Bennington.

American Art Pottery

America's art pottery movement began at the 1876 Centennial Exhibition in Philadelphia. Many artists who eventually worked for art potteries were inspired by work displayed at the exhibition. Mary Louise McLaughlin, an amateur potter from Cincinnati, saw the French Haviland pottery. Hugh Robertson was inspired by *sang de boeuf*-glazed (red) pieces in the Chinese exhibit. Susan Frackelton of Milwaukee,

Wisconsin, won a medal for a piece at the Centennial. William Long, a druggist from Steubenville, Ohio, who started Lonhuda Pottery in 1892, became interested in making pottery because of displays in Philadelphia. The unfamiliar designs seen in the Chinese and Japanese exhibits led to the creation of exotic decorations by American potters.

The term *art pottery* now refers to the works, including commercial florist lines, of the many companies that made art pottery from 1870 to about 1930. Sometimes it includes the work of studio potters from the 1920s through the 1940s.

Art pottery was hand-thrown and hand-decorated. It was made to be a thing of beauty, not just a utilitarian vessel. Later pieces, also considered part of the art pottery movement, were made with underglaze slip decoration, matte glaze, or high-gloss glaze, and with carved, molded, or applied decoration. Many of the art potteries started as one-man or one-woman operations and then grew to become large successful financial ventures with hundreds of employees.

Chelsea Pottery/Dedham Pottery

In 1866 Hugh C., George W., and Alexander Robertson started the Chelsea Pottery in Chelsea, Massachusetts. The firm was renamed Chelsea Keramic Art Works in 1875 and was reorganized in 1891 as the Chelsea Pottery U.S. The firm made many kinds of pottery, including red bisque and gray earthenware, and many colored glazes with a hard, brilliant finish. In 1895 the pottery moved to East Dedham, Massachusetts, and was renamed Dedham Pottery. The pottery was famous for its soft gray glazed crackleware that was fired, glazed, freehand decorated with blue, then glazed again. Border designs such as Rabbit, Iris, Turkey, Elephant, or other animals and plants were hand painted on full sets of crackleware dishes. Dedham Pottery closed in 1943.

The monogram for Chelsea Keramic Art Works or the name *Chelsea Keramic Art Works, Robertson & Sons* was used from 1875 to 1889. A cloverleaf with the initials *CPUS* was used from 1891 to 1895, and a rabbit after 1893.

Dedham Pottery mark (1895–1932)

Dedham Pottery mark (1896–1943)

This small cream pitcher made by Chelsea Keramic Art Works is 3¾ inches high. It has applied flowers and leaves as decorations.

Fulper Pottery

The Fulper Pottery, established in 1860 by Abraham Fulper in Flemington, New Jersey, produced only utilitarian items at first. It began making its artware line, Vasekraft, in 1909. The line used classical and oriental shapes and several kinds of glazes. In 1920 Fulper introduced the first solid-colored glazed dinnerware produced in the United States. It moved all operations to Trenton, New Jersey, in 1929 and continued to make a limited amount of artware at this plant until 1935. The artware was marked *Vasekraft*, and other pieces had the word *Fulper* in the mark. J. Martin Stangl bought the firm in 1930, and production shifted to dinnerware marked with the *Stangl* name. However, the company's name was not officially changed to Stangl Pottery until 1955.

Grueby Faience Company

The Grueby Faience Company was founded in Boston in 1894 by William Henry Grueby. It made architectural tiles and art pottery. Most of the pottery had a matte green glaze. Grueby Pottery Company, created as the art pottery division of the firm in 1898, was incorporated in 1907 and closed in 1911. Grueby Faience went bankrupt in 1909, and  a new company, the Grueby Faience and Tile Company, was started to make tiles only. This company continued until 1920. The Grueby Faience and Grueby Pottery marks were both used, although after 1905 all artware was marked Grueby Pottery.

Newcomb Pottery

Sophie Newcomb College in New Orleans, Louisiana, started a pottery and classes in 1895. Distinguished potters such as Paul Cox and Joseph Meyer taught and worked there. For a short time George Ohr was an employee. The pottery sold the students' work.

Between 1900 and 1910, most wares were blue-green with incised decoration emphasized with black. From about 1910 to 1930, low molded relief designs and matte glaze were used. Designs reflected the landscape of the South. Commercial production by students was limited after 1931, and by 1939 the pottery was used only for teaching purposes. Pieces were marked with *NC* and the designer's initials. Some pieces had a paper label that said *Newcomb Pottery*.

George E. Ohr

George Ohr, the "Mad Potter of Biloxi," Mississippi, operated his own art pottery from about 1883 to 1909. Ohr's unique pottery style was reflected in his free-form pieces, which were formed from twisted, folded, and crimped clay. He also made inkwells or whimsies in the shape of realistic hats, animals, and houses. Pots were decorated with snakes and lizards made from folded clay. Glazes were usually flowed on, and flaws were common.

Rookwood Pottery

The Rookwood Pottery Company was started by Maria Longworth Nichols in 1880 in Cincinnati, Ohio. It made commercial tableware and art pottery. At first pieces were marked Rookwood. The earliest pieces of Rookwood, made before 1886, were signed with the year. The monogram R P with the R reversed was introduced in 1886. Each year after that, a flame was added to the mark. By 1900 there were 14 flames, and after that a Roman numeral was added that indicated the year. For example, XV was used in 1915. Other letters impressed into the bottom of a Rookwood vase denote the size of the piece or the color of the clay. Many artists signed their

Weller
Pottery mark
(1895–1918)

Fulper Pottery
mark
(1922–1928)

Grueby Faience
Company mark
(1897–1911)

GRUEBY

Rookwood
Pottery mark
(1902)

George E. Ohr
mark (1899–
1906)

GEO. E. OHR
BILOXI, MISS.

Roseville
Pottery
Company mark
(c.1905)

Each piece of George Ohr pottery is unique, hand thrown and trimmed, and often crumpled, crimped, or pleated. A snake with a folded body winds around the top of the 6-inch crimped blue vase.

works with either names or initials. The company closed briefly in 1941, but reopened later that year under new ownership. After changing owners several times, the plant was moved to Mississippi in 1960 and closed in 1967.

Roseville Pottery

Roseville Pottery was started by George F. Young in Roseville, Ohio, in 1892. The company made utilitarian stoneware jars and flowerpots. The company added another factory in Zanesville in 1898 and started making art pottery in 1900. Roseville's first line of handmade art pottery was an underglaze, slip-decorated, dark brown ware called Rozane. A light background Rozane and other lines followed but were still called Rozane. Many lines featured molded raised designs of realistic flowers. By 1920 the handmade artware was replaced by commercial pottery. Production ended in 1954. Early Roseville pieces were marked with a capital *R* and a small *v*. The artware was marked *Rozane*. Later marks included the word *Roseville*.

Weller Pottery

The Weller Pottery was started by Samuel A. Weller in 1872 in Fultonham, Ohio, and moved to Zanesville, Ohio, in 1882. Artware was introduced in 1893. Hundreds of lines of pottery were produced, including Louwelsa, Eocean, Dickens Ware, and Sicardo. By 1915 Weller Pottery was the largest art pottery in the world. Weller's prestige lines of pottery were discontinued at the end of World War I, and commercial lines were substituted. The pottery closed in 1948. Most Weller pottery is marked with the name of the company.

Nineteenth-Century Art Potteries

Pottery and Location	Date	Mark
American Art Clay Works Edgerton, Wisconsin (Renamed Edgerton Art Clay Works in 1895)	1892–1895	Samson Bros. & Co. American Art Clay Works Est'd 1892 Edgerton, Wis.
Avon Pottery Cincinnati, Ohio	1886–1888	AVON
Edwin Bennett Baltimore, Maryland	1845–1936	E. Bennett 1896. Pottery Co
John Bennett New York, New York	1877–1883	Bennett. 101 Lex. Ave N.Y. 1888
Brush Guild New York, New York	c.1897–1908	[mark]
Chelsea Keramic Art Works Chelsea, Massachusetts	1875–1889	C K A W
Chelsea Pottery Chelsea, Massachusetts	1866–1875	Items not marked.
Chelsea Pottery U.S. Chelsea, Massachusetts (Renamed Dedham Pottery in 1895)	1891–1895	[clover mark]
Chesapeake Pottery Baltimore, Maryland (Renamed Haynes, Bennett and Company in 1890)	1880–1890	[oval mark 276]
Cincinnati Art Pottery Company Cincinnati, Ohio (Do not confuse with Pottery Club of Cincinnati.)	1879–1891	C.A.P. Co.
Dallas Pottery Cincinnati, Ohio	1865–1882	DALLAS
Dedham Pottery East Dedham, Massachusetts (Formerly Chelsea Pottery U.S.)	1895–1943	DEDHAM POTTERY
Edgerton Art Clay Works Edgerton, Wisconsin (Formerly American Art Clay Works. Became Norse Pottery in 1903)	1895–1899 1902–1903	Samson Bros. & Co. American Art Clay Works Est'd 1892 Edgerton, Wis.
Edgerton Pottery Edgerton, Wisconsin (Formed by shareholders of bankrupt Pauline Pottery)	1894–1902	Rock Pottery. Edgerton Wis.
Faience Manufacturing Company Brooklyn, New York	1880–1892	[monogram mark]

Nineteenth-Century Art Potteries

Pottery and Location	Date	Mark
Frackelton China Decorating Works Milwaukee, Wisconsin (Susan Stuart Goodrich Frackelton)	1883–1902	
Fulper Pottery Flemington, New Jersey Trenton, New Jersey	1860–1929 1929–1955	
Graham Pottery Brooklyn, New York	1880–1900	
Grueby Faience/Grueby Pottery Boston, Massachusetts	1894–1911	
Hampshire Pottery Keene, New Hampshire	1871–1923	
D. F. Haynes and Son Baltimore, Maryland (Formerly Haynes, Bennett and Company)	1896–1924	
Haynes, Bennett and Company Baltimore, Maryland (Formerly Chesapeake Pottery. Renamed D.F. Haynes and Son in 1896)	1890–1896	
Knowles, Taylor and Knowles East Liverpool, Ohio	1870–1929	
Lonhuda Pottery Steubenville, Ohio	1892–1895	
J. W. McCoy Pottery Roseville & Zanesville, Ohio (Became Brush-McCoy Pottery in 1911)	1899–1911	LOY-NEL-ART McCOY
Middle Lane Pottery Long Island, New York	1894–1946	
Moravian Pottery and Tile Works Doylestown, Pennsylvania	c.1898–present	
Matt Morgan Art Pottery Cincinnati, Ohio	1883–1884	
Newcomb Pottery New Orleans, Louisiana	1895–1939	
Odell & Booth Brothers Tarrytown, New York	1880–1885	O&BB
George E. Ohr Biloxi, Mississippi	1883–1909	GEO. E. OHR BILOXI, MISS.

Pottery and Location	Date	Mark
Owens Pottery Company Zanesville, Ohio (Founded by John B. Owens)	1891–1907	
Pauline Pottery Chicago, Illinois Edgerton, Wisconsin (Reopened in 1894 as Edgerton Pottery)	1883–1888 1888–1893	
Peters and Reed Pottery Zanesville, Ohio	1897–1921	Items not marked.
Pottery Club of Cincinnati Cincinnati, Ohio (Do not confuse with Cincinnati Art Pottery Company)	1879–1890	Pieces signed by artists.
A. Radford Pottery Virginia, Ohio, West Virginia	1890–1893, 1903, 1904–1912	RADFORD JASPER
Red Wing Red Wing, Minnesota	1878–1967	
Roblin Pottery San Francisco, California	1898–1906	
Rookwood Pottery Cincinnati, Ohio	1880–1967	
Roseville Pottery Roseville and Zanesville, Ohio	1892–1954	ROSEVILLE POTTERY
Stockton Terra Cotta/Stockton Art Pottery Stockton, California	1891–1902	
Teco-Gates Terra Cotta, Illinois	1887–1930	
Volkmar Pottery New York and New Jersey	1879–1911	
W. J. Walley West Sterling, Massachusetts	1898–1919	W J W
Wannopee Pottery New Milford, Connecticut	1892–1903	
Weller Pottery Zanesville, Ohio	1872–1948	WELLER
T. J. Wheatley & Company Cincinnati, Ohio (Founded by Thomas Jerome Wheatley)	1880–1884	

Chapter 5

Asian Pottery and Porcelain

WHEN YOU FIND A PIECE of Asian porcelain or pottery, you must always remember that the writing in the mark does not always indicate the maker or age; instead you may have a later exact copy. Chinese and Japanese ceramics represent a difference in artistic practice between the modern Western ceramicist and the Asian ceramicist regarding imitation. If an Asian artist considered a design, glaze, or shape beautiful, he or she often copied it, line for line, even to the mark. This was an accepted practice and not a type of faking.

Japanese, Chinese, and Koreans borrowed freely from each other's designs. Europeans copied the Asian work, and Asian artists made pieces to suit the European taste. So a piece with European designs may have been produced in Asia, and a dish with Asian-style decoration may have been made in Europe.

CHINESE EXPORT PORCELAIN OR CHINA TRADE PORCELAIN

Chinese potters made restrained, well-designed pottery or porcelain for use in their own country. When the first few pieces were brought back to Europe by Marco Polo in the late thirteenth century, Chinese porcelain was considered a rarity worth more than

Opposite Page: Rose palette porcelains made in China and known to collectors today as Famille Rose became popular for export by the 1750s. This 17½-inch-tall vase has panels picturing figures, birds, and butterflies. It was made in the late nineteenth century. (Photo: Brunk)

gold. Europeans were not able to make porcelain until the eighteenth century when the secret was discovered at Meissen, Germany.

During the eighteenth century, when trading with the Orient became more common, the ships of England and Holland brought back dishes that we now call Chinese export porcelain or China trade porcelain. The wares in demand by Europeans were very different from those made in Asia for Asians. The porcelain was not as fine in quality, and the design was often distinctly European. Dishes with family coats of arms, figures dressed in European clothes, American flags, ships, biblical and mythological scenes, and local mottoes and symbols were ordered for the European and American markets.

Special Designs

Chinese export porcelain was made for many markets, and each country favored special designs. The English ordered dinnerware called armorial china, which had a family's coat of arms or crest emblazoned in the center of each plate. It was made to order in China and sent by ship to England. When a piece was broken, the replacement was often ordered from the English porcelain factories of Worcester, Spode, Wedgwood, and Leeds. The English firms copied the design onto the English porcelain. Chinese export porcelain had a grayish-colored body. The English firms made their ware to match the Chinese sets. Because the English porcelain was white, the English firms often tinted the glaze.

An unusual coat of arms featuring a chessboard and a dragon is in the center of this Chinese export porcelain charger. The 13-inch plate was made about 1800. (Photo: Waddington's)

Americans had no coats of arms, so similar heraldic-type symbols or eagles were pictured in the center of dishes. The border was frequently decorated with blue bands with gold stars or another motif inspired by the flag. Italians liked the black-and-white or Jesuit designs. Biblical scenes were painted on some of the plates. The Dutch ordered porcelains with decorations that resembled the designs on delft. The French liked pieces decorated with flowers and scrolls that resembled Sèvres patterns.

The term *China trade porcelain* or *Chinese export porcelain* means not only eighteenth-century Chinese porcelain, but also some of the later products from Asia. Canton ware, a blue-and-white china, was made at potteries near Canton or north of Canton, China. Much of the decorating was done by families living in the city of Canton. The earliest Canton ware was made about 1785. Dishes were decorated with blue pictures of a scene showing a teahouse, bridge, willow trees, and birds, a version of the blue willow pattern. True Canton ware never pictured a person on the bridge. The Canton ware made before 1890 is popular with collectors today.

European shapes were often copied in Canton. This typical blue and white decorated tureen was used to serve soup at the table. Notice the boar's head handles.
(Photo: James Julia)

Nanking china is a blue-and-white porcelain ware that was shipped from Nanking, China, during the eighteenth and early nineteenth centuries. It was decorated with Chinese subjects, usually landscapes or buildings, and often showed people standing on a bridge. Nanking china has a spear-and-post border and may have gold decoration.

Rose Palette Porcelains

Famille Rose (rose family) porcelain is a five-color Chinese porcelain that has rose as its predominant color. Three different patterns of Famille Rose are seen for sale today: Rose Medallion, Rose Mandarin, and Rose Canton. All of the patterns have four or more panels of decorations around a central medallion and a background design of tree peonies and leaves. The Rose Medallion pattern has a bird or peony in its central medallion, and the surrounding panels show birds and people. The Rose Mandarin pattern has panels with only people, no birds. The Rose Canton pattern has just flowers, no people or birds. All patterns are still being made today.

Early pieces were made during the reign of Emperor Yongzheng (1723–1735). Toward the second half of the reign of Emperor Qianlong (1736–1795), Famille Rose porcelain was made both for domestic use and for export to Europe and America. Sets of dishes in European shapes like soup tureens or urns were

DETERMINING THE AGE OF FAMILLE ROSE

The age of the Famille Rose porcelains can be best determined by color and glaze. A 1982 exhibit of Famille Rose at the China Trade Museum in Milton, Massachusetts, demonstrated that the early examples had a thick, opaque, muddy mauve pink glaze. By the 1730s, the glaze was opaque rose pink often mixed with white and applied in thick relief. By the end of the eighteenth century, the rose glaze was thin and almost translucent. Late eighteenth-century pieces are considered superior to later brilliantly colored and carelessly painted late nineteenth-century pieces. Twentieth-century pieces made in many countries are of uneven quality.

decorated in the rose patterns. Some even included English crests as part of the design. The Rose Medallion pattern was especially popular from about 1830 to 1930 and continues to be popular today. Rose palette porcelain that was made after 1891 is marked *Made in China* or *China*. Unfortunately sometimes the mark is on a removable paper label.

The popularity and value of Famille Rose porcelain has changed as information on its manufacture has become available. In the late nineteenth and early twentieth century, many collectors and museums thought these porcelains were made before the fifteenth century. They were considered fine quality porcelains. Then from 1900 to 1950 tastes changed, and more information on early Chinese ceramics became available. Many museums and collectors thought that all Famille Rose was poor quality late nineteenth-century export ware. It took until the late 1970s for the porcelain to be appreciated again. Now rose palette porcelains are popular, and the decorative qualities have been reappraised by experts. Once again Famille Rose, especially Rose Medallion, is considered important.

Willow Pattern

The willow pattern that pictures a bridge, three figures, birds, trees, and a Chinese landscape was first introduced to England in 1780 by Thomas Turner at the Caughley Pottery Works. The pattern was inspired by a similar Chinese design without figures on the bridge. Early English versions of the pattern show two or three figures, and some of the late nineteenth-century versions show no people. Early pieces were hand painted, but transfer designs were used on later ones. There is no pattern that has been copied as often as willow. English factories, as well as German, Japanese, American, and other factories, have made it and still are making it.

The legend connected with the willow pattern was invented long after the Chinese pattern first arrived in England. The English devised a tale to describe the willowware design: the two figures on the bridge are lovers who are fleeing from a cruel father who wants to stop their marriage. The gods take pity on the lovers and change them into birds so they can escape. While it is true that the willowware scene is Asian in origin, the legend of a romantic pair fleeing from a cruel father is not Chinese in concept. China was a land of arranged marriages and not one of romantic love. The Chinese version of the design did not picture the lovers, so the English story could not have described the original design.

There is, however, one Chinese legend that may be the true story of the willow pattern. At some time in Chinese history, a political group tried to overthrow the government. They circulated the dishes to remind the people of their aims. The three figures represented three Buddhas: past, present, and future. The doves were the souls of those slain in battle, and the pagoda was a symbol of shelter for escaping monks. There are no early Chinese examples of the design with the figures, but the legend claims they were all destroyed by the government.

The willow design has been and is still being made by many firms. It is virtually impossible to distinguish the old from the new without checking the marks on the bottom of a piece. Both pottery and porcelain dinnerware sets were made.

JAPANESE CERAMICS

Often the name of a type of Japanese ware represents both a geographic area and a pattern. The definitions used here are those you will find in common use, and they may differ from those accepted by scholarly sources.

The willow design was used on plates for hundreds of years in dozens of countries. This version shows the pagoda, the lovers as birds, and the three people on the bridge.

AN INTERESTING CHINESE EXPORT PATTERN

There is an interesting Chinese export pattern picturing the signers of the Declaration of Independence. The design, copied from a painting by John Trumbull, was created by Chinese artists and shows Asian, not Caucasian, men. The pattern was once thought to date from 1800, but now experts say it was made after 1840. Many think it was made for the Centennial of 1876.

Arita, a Town

Arita ware, a fine white porcelain, has been made by many potteries in the small town of Arita on Kyushu Island since 1616, when Korean potters came to Arita and made porcelain from the white clay found in the area. When civil war in China in the 1640s disrupted trade, Dutch traders turned to Japan for porcelain to sell in Europe. The Japanese export porcelain industry flourished until the 1740s. The Dutch no longer bought porcelain from Japan because the Chinese made a less expensive porcelain. Interest in Japanese porcelain returned in the 1850s following the opening of Japan to trade with the West.

Three types of porcelain were made in the Arita area: Arita ware, Imari, and Kakiemon.

Arita Ware

Early seventeenth-century Arita ware typically had underglaze blue designs that resembled Chinese Ming styles. By the 1640s, Arita potters also made a polychrome porcelain with designs of flowers, birds, and geometric patterns in bright colors, including red, yellow, green, black, and gold. In the eighteenth century, Japanese designs had become more popular than Chinese decorations. Arita is still home to many modern potteries.

Imari, a Port and a Pattern

Arita export porcelain was shipped from Imari, a nearby port. The Dutch traders asked for an overall brocade design that would be popular throughout Europe. The resulting ceramic was a porcelain with a blue underglaze and iron red and gold decoration. Yellow, brown, green, and turquoise were used on some pieces. The design became so popular it was copied by Chinese, English, and many European factories, and no matter where it is made, it is known as Imari or Imari—style today. The pattern is still being made. The Japanese Imari wares degenerated to less finished decoration and uneven colors by the middle of the nineteenth century. Pieces exported to the United States were marked after 1896.

Opposite page: Flowers and branches decorate this Arita footed planter. The 12-inch-high jardiniere was made in the late eighteenth or early nineteenth century.
(Photo: Brunk)

This Imari charger has the typical blue underglaze and iron red and gold brocade design surrounding a central medallion with a vase of flowers.
(Photo: Brunk)

Kakiemon, a Pattern

There is both Kakiemon porcelain and Kakiemon style, so any definition must explain the differences. The Sakaida family's kiln near Arita made a multicolor enamel-decorated porcelain ware with asymmetrical decorations. Red, blue, turquoise green, and yellow were favored, with some use of gold. Most designs were from nature—flowers, branches, animals, and birds. Sakaida Kozoemon, who developed the colored enamel technique, took the artistic name Kakiemon I. The Kakiemon kilns continue today, supervised by Kakiemon XIV.

The Kakiemon pattern was so popular it was copied by several English potteries. This 8¼-inch dish was made by the Worcester factory in England during the 1790s.

Kakiemon porcelains were popular with the European market, and the Dutch imported many pieces. By the eighteenth century, the popular Kakiemon porcelains were being copied in China and Europe. These pieces are known as "Kakiemon style."

Banko, a Rustic Pottery

Banko is a rustic Japanese ware first made by eighteenth-century potter Numanami Gozaemon and revived in the middle of the nineteenth century. Most familiar are small, reddish brown stoneware teapots with decorative, animal-shaped knobs, and pots of glazed gray clay. True marbleized wares were made from a blending of several colors of clay. These pieces often have the Banko mark, a small incised oval with Japanese characters. Other incised or raised decorations were added to the clay by pressing it into a mold or by using a stamp. The knobs of teapots and sugar bowls were trimmed with a touch of gold. The knobs were made to turn freely, a construction feature not seen in other pottery or porcelain.

Banko pottery is easy to recognize. The marbleized pattern made from colored clays, the raised decorations trimmed with gold, and the knob on the lid are not found on Asian pottery from other areas. This tea set has the incised oval mark.

Imari—See page 77.

Kakiemon—See above.

Kutani, a Province

The kilns in the village of Kutani first produced porcelain from about 1639 to the beginning of the 1700s. The porcelain made there at that time is called old Kutani (Ko Kutani). Blue green Kutani (Ao Kutani) is the most famous. The porcelain has a deep blue-green glaze with designs of birds, flowers, and landscapes. Some pieces were entirely covered with green and yellow glaze with no undecorated porcelain showing.

This nineteenth-century plate was made at the Kutani kilns. The diameter is 7¼ inches, the size of a salad or dessert plate.

Work at the kilns revived about 1824. This later Kutani used colorful overglaze enamel patterns in green, blue, purple, yellow, orange, black, and gold, and pictures of warriors, animals, and birds. A red and gold brocade design was used on some of these wares, which were called Red Kutani. Eggshell porcelains were also made. Many of these pieces were marked with the Japanese characters for *Kutani*. Most collectors today find only the porcelains from nineteenth-century Kutani kilns.

To confuse the collector even more, the word *Kutani* has been used to describe a number of other nineteenth-century porcelains, earthenwares, and stonewares. These may or may not be marked with the Japanese characters for Kutani.

Satsuma, a Province and a Pattern
In England, the word *Satsuma* means pottery or porcelain made in the Satsuma area. In the United States, the same word usually means a special type of crackle-glazed ware with an identifiable decoration of flowers or figures. Pottery was made in the Satsuma province from the beginning of the seventeenth century. Skilled Korean potters were brought to Japan to make the pottery. Early pieces were made from brown or reddish brown clay. Glazes were dark, and the decorations were simple. The ware was decorated with detailed drawings of flowers and trees. The first pieces had floral designs asymmetrically spaced in the Japanese manner, with much open space. No human figure appeared on the early pieces.

The crackle-glazed cream-colored ware Americans call Satsuma today was made for export to Europe from about 1865. Pieces had overall designs, *diapering* (repetitive, geometric designs that are connected with one another), or elaborate designs of birds, flowers, landscapes, mythical animals, or human figures. The designs

Warriors and royalty are pictured on the center section of this 20-inch-high Satsuma floor vase. Elaborate border designs use typical Satsuma patterns. The vase was made in about 1860.

SUMIDA GAWA

The word *gawa* means river in Japanese. Sumida pottery was made near the Sumida River and has sometimes been referred to as Sumida Gawa pottery. However, pottery marked *Sumidagawa* is a raku ware, a low-fired ware that is soft and porous. It was made near the Sumida River, but not by the same potters who made Sumida pottery.

Right: The bright orange color and the raised figure on this earthenware mug are typical of decorations on Sumida ware. An oval tablet on the side of the mug says "Ryosai." (Photo: Duomo)

became more and more elaborate. Decorations were crowded. Dragons, plants, animals, and people were added in raised designs. The Thousand Face pattern—an overall design of faces—appeared about 1880. As the century progressed, the faces became fewer and larger and the backgrounds became darker. Some pieces included designs of a group of men with halos. These figures are called the "immortals." By the end of the nineteenth century, the design became very dark and the "glowing immortals" had a sinister appearance.

A collector will find a variety of wares from the light cream crackle glaze to the dark glazed pieces with crude designs, all of which are called Satsuma. The design of Satsuma gradually changed over time, but the pottery's basic cream-colored clay and crackle glaze remain. Some pieces of Satsuma were hand painted in the United States by American women during World War I and the early 1920s, when they couldn't get undecorated dishes from Germany. Collectors refer to these pieces as "American Satsuma."

The word *Satsuma* also describes wares that were made in these patterns through the nineteenth and twentieth centuries by many artists and many factories and not just at the original Satsuma kilns.

Sumida, a River

Sumida is a Japanese pottery made from about 1870 to 1941 in the area of Tokyo near the Sumida River. Pieces are usually everyday objects, including vases, jardinieres, bowls, teapots, and decorative tiles. Most pieces have a heavy orange-red, blue, brown, black, green, purple, or off-white glaze with raised three-dimensional figures as decorations. The unglazed part is painted red, green, black, or orange. Sumida was sometimes mistakenly called *Poo Ware* after a similar pottery made by a Chinese potter named Poo You-she.

Chapter 6

GLASS

ALMOST EVERYONE OWNS a piece of old glass that has been in the family for years, and every piece seems to have a glamorous history associated with it. Most of the stories are fable, not fact. There were stories in our own family about six green glasses that had belonged to our grandfather. Each grandchild was given one of the priceless green glasses and told the wonderful story of its rarity. We finally looked up the priceless glasses and learned the green pressed glass with its gold decorations was a pattern called Delaware. It was made for the Atlantic and Pacific Tea Company about 1890 and *given away free* with the purchase of coffee. We still display Grandpa's green glasses in a special place and fondly recall the fantastic stories of the "rare" green glass. Our heirloom is just another piece of glass that has now become old enough to be considered an antique, but is too ordinary to be considered priceless.

Our family's "famous" Delaware pattern emerald green tumbler has worn gold trim. It is part of a set of six glasses and a water pitcher.

The study of glass requires time and effort. Colored glass was not popular until after the Civil War. Some colored glass was made

IMITATION IS THE SINCEREST FORM OF FLATTERY

A sad word of wisdom: Almost every known type of glassware—pressed, blown, colored, clear—has been reproduced or reissued since the nineteenth century. Many reissues were made from original molds, which makes identification more difficult but not impossible. Some reproductions even have fake marks.

Top right: This free-blown creamer with an added, applied handle and foot is in the Twelve Diamond pattern. It has a pontil scarred base. It was probably made at a Midwestern glass house. (Photo: American Bottle Auctions)

Right: This cruet, probably made in England, was made in a three-piece mold. It has a pressed glass stopper. The cruet holds eight ounces of liquid. It was made between 1860 and 1890.

earlier, and many eighteenth-century pieces were produced from aqua, amethyst, olive, or green glass; but glassmakers focused their efforts on making glass look like rock crystal—as clear as possible—until about 1860. After that time, many new types of colored glass were developed.

To identify glass, it helps to understand the basic methods of manufacture and a few of the technical terms. The basic materials that are used to make glass, such as sand and various alkalis, are measured and mixed together to form a *batch*. The batch is heated and the resulting molten glass is called *metal*. When the molten glass reaches the appropriate temperature, the glassworker gathers a blob of metal with a *blowpipe*. The blob, called a *gather*, is inflated by blowing through the blowpipe, then transferred to a *pontil* (also called a *punty rod*). After the item is shaped with paddles and tools, it is removed from the pontil. A rough spot, called a *pontil mark*, is often left on the bottom of the item where the pontil was attached.

There are many ways to shape glass. Ancient glass was shaped around a solid ceramic core or with a blowpipe. The earliest blown glass was *free-blown*, meaning that all of the shaping was done by hand. Decoration was added by shaping with tools or by engraving, and the finished item was a unique luxury item.

The next type of glassmaking was *pat-ternmolding*. German glassmakers used *dip-molds* to add a design to glass as early as 1400. American glassmakers were using the technique by the late 1700s. The glass was blown into a small cylindrical mold, which was sometimes hinged, with an interior pattern. When the glass was removed, heated again, and blown to the desired size, the impression of the mold remained on the glass. The finished piece had geometric swirls, ribs, or designs like diamonds or feathers. The swirls on the finished piece were smaller at the ends because the blowing process stretched the design at the center. Imagine a design drawn on a toy rubber balloon. When the balloon is inflated, the design distorts in much the same way as the swirls of blown-molded glass. Because the items still required shaping, pattern-molded glassmaking was still expensive.

The use of the *three-piece mold* between 1820 and 1880 increased the availability of glassware in the United States. Hot glass was blown into full-size molds with two to four hinged parts that shaped items from top to bottom. Very little offhand work was required to finish the piece. Three-piece mold-blown items can be recognized by the seams created by the edges of the mold parts.

The invention of the mechanical press in the mid-1820s meant glass could be made inexpensively. Instead of blowing hot glass into a shape, glassmakers pressed the glass into a mold with a weight. A *pressed glass* item takes on the design and shape of the mold. Many patented pressing processes were developed in the mid-nineteenth century. Pressed glass tableware is the easiest glassware to identify. Companies made dishes and accessories using their own designs, and many patterns are named in advertisements and catalogs.

VERY EARLY AMERICAN GLASS, 1760–1830

Glassmaking was one of the earliest industries in Colonial America, but imported glassware from England and Ireland competed with East Coast glasshouses, resulting in the failure of many early American glasshouses. Midwestern glasshouses had less competition, but production was limited until the invention of the mechanical glass press.

If you learn the basics about glass, you will be able to identify many early styles of glassware. Free-blown, pattern-molded, and three-piece-molded glassware was researched and categorized by George and Helen McKearin in their 1941 book *American Glass*, which is still one of the best sources.

DECORATION BASICS

There are many ways to decorate glass.

Applied decoration: Glassmakers can add blobs of hot glass to shaped pieces. Lily-pads, looping, and threading prunts (pointed blobs) have been used.

Offhand or tooled decoration: Ruffled edges, air twisted or knopped stems, pinched waists, and neck rings are added by hand with tools.

Molded decoration: Glass can be impressed with a design during shaping. (See PRESSED GLASS, pages 84–88.)

Special finishes: Colors are created by adjusting chemical composition or covering the item with oxides. (See Amberina, Burmese, Iridescent, and Peachblow in ART GLASS, pages 99–104.)

Exterior decoration: Designs can be added after the item is finished. Acid etching, cutting, enameling, or engraving are used to decorate the surface. Camphor finish, satin, and casing are allover effects created with vapors, acid, or another layer of glass. (See CUT AND ENGRAVED GLASS, pages 93–95, and ART GLASS, pages 99–111.)

Stiegel-type Glass

Henry William Stiegel, a German immigrant, operated a glasshouse in Manheim, Pennsylvania, from 1763 to 1774. The glass was made in styles popular in Europe at the time. Most of the items were colorless with enameled or engraved designs. Some colored items were made, too. Because other factories made similar glassware, it is almost impossible to be sure a piece was actually made by Stiegel.

Amelung Glass

John Frederick Amelung, another German immigrant, operated the New Bremen Glass Manufactory in Maryland from 1785 to 1795. Like Stiegel, the glasshouse produced European-style tableware, much of it with engraved designs.

NINETEENTH-CENTURY GEOMETRIC OR THREE-PIECE-MOLDED GLASS

The introduction of the full-size three-piece mold increased production, so many glass items made between 1815 and 1845 are available today. Collectors often refer to three-piece-molded glass as *geometric* because the patterns include diamonds, concentric rings, and sunbursts.

PRESSED GLASS

Until the 1820s, decorations on glassware were limited to applied pieces of glass, applied color, or engraving, which removed part of the glass with a cutting wheel or tool. Cut glass was popular but labor-intensive. The facet-cut crystal of Irish Waterford was known throughout the world because of its design and beauty, but it was too expensive for most households. Three-piece molds imitated the diamond-point patterns of cut glass, but production was still tedious.

Machines to manufacture pressed glass were invented in the mid-1820s. The molds used for pressed glass were made in one or more pieces, sometimes hinged, from brass, iron, or other metal.

Pressure was applied with a plunger to force the glass to take the shape of the mold. Shallow items, like cup plates, open salts, and nappies, could be made with single-piece molds. Deeper items, like sugar bowls and small pitchers, were made with hinged molds that allowed easy removal of the shaped piece. The glass press simplified the production of complicated items like lamps, candlesticks, and compotes, which were traditionally assembled from handmade segments. The segments, now more decorative, were pressed in small molds and joined together with thin *wafers* of hot glass by hand.

The Lacy Period, 1825–1845

Pressed glass was designed to make the best possible use of the new technique of shaping glass. Too much or too little glass in the mold made a finished piece that was either too thick or not clearly impressed. Early pressed glass pieces, such as cup plates and open salts, were quite heavy and had many bubbles and imperfections. *Lacy* pressed glass was an early attempt to camouflage these blemishes. The surface of the finished lacy glass was impressed with an intricate dotted background, called *stippling*. The more stippling, or dotted indentations, pressed into the glass, the more light reflects in the finished piece.

Although similar glassware was made in England and Europe, the Boston & Sandwich Glass Company of Sandwich, Massachusetts, is credited as the earliest American and best-known maker of lacy glass. Lacy glass was also made at the New England Glass Company of East Cambridge, Massachusetts; in Pittsburgh, Pennsylvania; and in West Virginia, New Jersey, Maryland, and the Midwest. Early lacy pressed glass items are usually small, like open salt dishes or cup plates. Complete sets of dishes were not made.

The Height of Production

By the 1840s, American glasshouses were *fire-polishing* their wares, which was originally an English technique. The glass piece was reheated briefly in the furnace after shaping, thus melting the seams

This peacock-shaped tray in Hairpin pattern pressed glass was made by the Boston & Sandwich Company of Massachusetts about 1835. (Photo: Green Valley)

a little and smoothing the surface. Stippling was no longer necessary to hide flaws. Another breakthrough substituted lime, a far less costly raw material, for lead in the glass. Hundreds of patterns of pressed glass were made in complete table settings. It is this later period of pressed, or pattern, glass that is of most interest to collectors.

Heart, Lyre, and Balloon is the name of the pattern of this pressed glass creamer. The maker is unknown, but it was probably made in the Pittsburgh area. It is 3⅞ inches high.

Thirty or so factories were making pressed glass between 1830 and 1850, and still more between 1850 and 1900 (seventy-five in Pittsburgh alone). Boston & Sandwich Glass Company; Bryce, Higbee & Company; Dalzell, Gilmore & Leighton; George Duncan's Sons & Company; Hobbs, Brockunier & Company; McKee & Brothers; New England Glass Company; Riverside Glass Works; Tarentum; and the U.S. Glass Company combine (a group of several factories) are some of the bigger producers. The same pattern was sometimes made by several firms at the same time. Similar patterns were made, including many variants of popular patterns such as Ashburton, Bellflower, and Daisy and Button.

Examine pressed glass items at shows, shops, and online. Dealers often label their pieces with pattern names. Books picture and price many of the patterns. Look for *Early American Pressed Glass* by Ruth Webb Lee; *Early American Pattern Glass: Collector's Identification & Price Guide* by Darryl Reilly and Bill Jenks; and *A Field Guide to Pattern Glass* by Mollie Helen McCain. The popularity and prices of pressed glass fluctuated during the twentieth century. It was popular until 1930, lost favor in the 1950s, started a comeback in the 1990s, and regained its fame and high prices by 2000.

Reproductions and Look-alikes

Many early clear and frosted glass patterns have been reproduced since the 1920s because they are so desirable. The pattern Westward Ho, first made about 1879, includes a wounded deer, a bison, a log cabin, pine trees, and an Indian. It was reproduced in the 1930s, in the 1980s, and again in the 1990s. Many collectors will pay as much for the 1930s copies as for the originals, because the copies are very good quality. If you want to buy original Westward Ho glass, you

Dating Your Pressed Glass— Looks Count

Knowing pressed glass styles will help date a piece of pressed glass. There are exceptions to every rule, but patterns typically went in cycles, just as skirt lengths do.

1820s–1830s: Early patterns were simple, with heavy loops or ribbed effects. The glass itself was heavy, with a translucent appearance.

1830s–1840s: Lacy patterns had stippled backgrounds and allover designs. Hearts, feathers, lyres, sheaves of wheat, eagles, and thistles were popular motifs. BEWARE, there was a later lacy revival. Flick the glass with your fingernail and listen. True lacy-period glass will ring because of the lead content. The later version will make a dull sound, not a ring, because glass factories switched to lime glass.

1850s: Simple patterns, like Argus (thumbprint), Ashburton, and Thousand Eye, became possible because of fire-polishing and improvements in pressing machines. Patents were not common at this time, so factories imitated competitors' patterns.

1860s: More elaborate geometrics and stylized flowers appeared. Popular lines included Bellflower (and its many variations) and Horn of Plenty (Comet). Many of these patterns were made in colored glass after the Civil War.

1870s: Naturalistic patterns, like Grape, Rose in Snow, Daisy, and Thistle, were introduced. Patterns with figural details, often frosted, were in style, such as Actress, Classic, Lion, Three Face, and Westward Ho.

1880s–1890s: Allover geometric patterns, like Daisy and Button, imitated cut glass. Other popular patterns, such as Delaware, Hidalgo, Ruby Thumbprint (also known as Excelsior or King's Crown), and X-Ray, were stained, trimmed with gold, or enameled with flowers. Novelty items, like figural toothpick holders and Victorian shoes, became popular.

1885–1900: Porcelain gained popularity, so glass styles imitated it. Opaque glass, like milk glass, opal, custard, and slag glass, were introduced. By the beginning of the twentieth century, few new pressed glass patterns were introduced.

Frosted Lion is a favored 1870s pressed glass pattern. This covered compote is a hard-to-find piece.

Ruby-stained Heart in Sand water set (Photo: Green Valley)

FLASHED OR STAINED?

For decades, collectors have used the terms *flashed* and *stained* interchangeably. But these terms are not synonymous. The flashing process adds a second thin layer of glass to the item. Glass is stained with a paint-like coating. Stained items are often refired to harden the stain. Another staining process, called *goofus* decoration, coats the glass with paint that is not thermal set.

must learn the very slight differences between the original and the copy, including the size of the bison's legs or the clarity of the pine tree. Companies like Fenton Glass Company and importer L.G. Wright sold many look-alikes in the 1960s and 1970s. Fenton continues to produce older patterns today, and new reproductions are imported into the United States from Asia every year. Companies like Mosser Glass in Cambridge, Ohio, purchased original molds and continue to reissue older patterns in both original and new colors (see "Colored Glassware" below).

Canadian Pressed Glass

Some pattern glass made in Canada is similar to the pieces made in the United States, but many patterns are different enough to be identifiable. Companies that made pressed glass in Canada include the Burlington Glass Works of Hamilton, Ontario (1875–1909); Napanee Glass House, Napanee, Ontario (1881–1883); the Sydenham Glass Company, Ltd., Wallaceburg, Ontario (1895–1913); the Excelsior Glass Company, St. Johns (1878–1880) and Montreal (1881–1885), Quebec; Nova Scotia Glass Company, Trenton, Nova Scotia (1881–1892); and Humphreys Glass Works, Trenton, Nova Scotia (1890–1914). Although a few of the patterns are pictured with histories in *American and Canadian Goblets*, two volumes, by Doris and Peter Unitt, much is still unknown.

COLORED GLASS

Pick a color, any color—glass was likely made in it. However, not all colors are equal in the world of glass. There are two basic means of coloring a glass object: by mixing something into the glass or by applying something to the outside of the glass. Adding certain salts or oxides to the glass and adjusting the amount of applied heat results in colored glass. If you break off the stem of a colored glass goblet, you will see that the color goes through the entire thickness. Applied color, such as staining, flashing, or fired enameling, is added after the piece is shaped. A broken piece will show color only on the exterior of the piece.

The differences between old and new colored wares are slight. Since the 1940s, companies like L.G. Wright, John C. Kemple

Glassworks, and Mosser Glass have made millions of new pieces of glass from old molds or have designed new, similar pieces. Westmoreland Glass Company, which was in business from 1890 to 1994, produced old lines until it closed.

Basic Pressed Glass Colors

Most pressed glass was colorless. After the introduction of lime glass, items were made in amber, amethyst, black amethyst, apple green, emerald green, and sapphire (also called electric) blue glass. Not all patterns and not all items in a pattern were made in color. *Stains* were used to color part of the glass. Maiden's blush or cranberry (pink), ruby (red), and amber (brownish yellow) stains were popular.

Vaseline and Canary: Yellow-Green Glass

Glass was colored yellow-green with uranium oxide as early as the Roman Empire. But yellow-green glassware was not plentiful until the discovery of a less costly process for extracting uranium oxide. The earliest of these newer pieces were English, Bohemian, or French, but the first large-scale

production seems to

This Thousand Eye pattern mug was made of pale blue glass, a fashionable color in the 1870s. Mugs like this were used by children.

have been done by the Boston & Sandwich Glass Company in the 1840s. Many American glass collectors use the term *Vaseline* to refer to yellow-green glass because of its similarity in color to petroleum jelly. The name was not used by the original makers, however, because Vaseline Petroleum Jelly was not patented until 1878. Companies originally referred to the glassware as *uranium* or *canary glass* in their ads and catalogs.

Reproductions of nineteenth-century yellow-green glass have been made since the 1920s. Uranium has been a regulated material since the 1940s, although the ban against its commercial use was lifted in 1958. Reproductions made since then are close to chartreuse in color, and they are almost as expensive as originals.

Opaque Colors—Opal, Milk Glass, Custard, and Slag Glass

Glassmakers have produced opaque white glass for centuries. The Italians called it *lattimo* and used it in lattice and filigree decoration. Eighteenth-century English, French, and German glassmakers used opaque white glass to imitate porcelain. The use of opaque colored glass in the United States coincided with the introduction of the machine press and reached its height during the 1870s and 1880s. Boston & Sandwich Glass Company used alabaster, opaque blue, and clambroth (a grayish white) colored glass for vases, lamps, and open salts in the mid-nineteenth century. *Milk glass* and *opal* are names that have been used to describe opaque glass, but both terms include colors other than white, such as blue, green, and pink. Usually opaque white glass is called *milk glass* and opaque white glass with translucent edges is *opal*.

The factories that made clear pressed glass also made opaque colors. The best-known producers are Atterbury & Company; Challinor, Taylor & Company; McKee & Brothers; and Westmoreland Specialty Glass Company. Originally milk glass was not used to create full sets of dishes. Most nineteenth-century items made of milk glass were accessories, like sugar bowls, creamers, and compotes, or novelties, like plaques, toothpick holders, and animal-shaped covered dishes.

It is easy to recognize milk glass, but it can be difficult to determine its age. Many old milk glass pieces have a C-shaped rough spot on the foot of the glass. Known as a *straw mark* or *lap line*, the spot was formed when the glass cooled after it was snipped into the mold. The plain surfaces of old milk glass items are often marked with concentric circles, a result of uneven cooling in the mold. Old milk glass has less blue in it, the texture is less oily, and the glass is heavier.

Custard glass is known by several names. This pale yellow or ivory-colored opaque glass has been called buttermilk glass by collectors and Ivory and Ivorina Verde by factories that made it. Many pieces of custard glass were decorated with gold and multicolored enameling, especially on the feet. There is some debate about the origin of custard glass in the United States, but it is thought that the Northwood Company of Indiana, Pennsylvania, produced it first around 1896. Chrysanthemum Sprig, Argonaut Shell (Nautilus), and Louis XV are among the most popular Northwood custard patterns. Some pieces are marked *N* for Northwood Glass.

Every piece of purple slag is unique because the two colors used were just mixed together to form a random pattern. An unknown American maker created this 6-inch-high cake stand.
(Photo: Green Valley)

Slag glass, sometimes mistakenly called *end-of-day glass*, is a multicolored opaque glass. Originally called *mosaic* or *marble glass*, it was made at many English, French, and Bohemian factories beginning around 1875. The marbled effect was created by gathering glass from two pots—one a colored and one an opal or milk glass. Challinor, Taylor & Company introduced purple slag around 1886 in the United States. In addition to purple, English and American slag glass of this era was made in blue, pink, and amber (caramel). In general, pressed slag glass items are found in the same patterns as milk glass. Other colors of slag glass—red, orange, green, butterscotch, and a mixture of several colors—have been made since the 1940s.

Bohemian marbled glass items were made in a wider range of colors, imitating gemstones like malachite, jade, and chalcedony. English and European slag glass has more uniform marbleizing than the American version. American slag glass has clearer lines of demarcation between the colors.

Chocolate glass, another opaque colored ware, was made at the Indiana Tumbler and Goblet Company of Greentown, Indiana, and other factories between 1900 and 1903. Chocolate glass has a marbled tan color, like coffee streaked with cream. It is not a true slag glass because it is not a gather of two different colored glasses. The short period of production of chocolate means that a small number of pieces were made and the glassware is rare. Chocolate glass is often confused with caramel slag glass, which has been made by Imperial Glass Corporation and others since the 1960s. Caramel slag, a combined gather of amber and milk glass, is very different from the more blended color of old chocolate glass.

Cranberry and Ruby

Cranberry glass is pinkish red, much the same color as cranberry juice. Ruby glass, named for the gemstone, is a deeper red than cranberry. Both colors are created by adding gold to the glass formula. Cranberry and ruby glass are expensive to produce, and neither is suitable for pressing by machine. The two types of glass are usually applied as flashing or casing over another layer of glass. Reproductions of both ruby and cranberry glass are still being made.

CUT AND ENGRAVED GLASS

Cut glass has been in existence since ancient times. Cutting and engraving were the most common decoration techniques used by Roman and Arabian glassmakers. The techniques disappeared in the tenth century but were revived in Germany in the late 1500s. The English started cutting glass about 1676, when lead oxide was added to glass to make it stronger and more brilliant. By 1760 England was supplying cut glass to most of Europe. Irish glass-

---

AMETHYST OR SUN-PURPLED GLASS?

Most glassmakers used manganese as a decolorizer in their clear glass between 1880 and 1914. Exposed to sun, the manganese oxidizes and slowly turns the glass lavender or purple. Selenium replaced manganese as a decolorizer in 1914 and was used until 1930. Glass made with selenium turns shades of yellow or brown. Colored glass that includes these elements will change, too. Dark amber glass will turn purple; yellow glass turns blue or green; and aqua glass becomes shades of blue or brown.

Since the mid-1970s, bottles, telephone pole insulators, and pressed glass have been mechanically irradiated to change their colors. This method turns antique glass darker shades of purple and brown. Modern glass is made with different chemicals that cannot be colored by sun or radiation.

Chocolate glass was made only in Greentown. This Squirrel pattern water pitcher is 8¾ inches high. (Photo: Green Valley)

Detail of an engraved glass tumbler

CUT OR ENGRAVED?

There are two basic differences between cut and engraved designs: the texture and the style of the design. Engraved designs, also called *intaglio,* have a gray, frosted tone and tend to be floral or figural. A copper wheel is used for engraving, and very little of the glass is removed from the surface of the item.

Cut patterns have deeper, geometric designs and are lustrous because of the polishing process. Graduated sizes of stone and iron wheels, often with an angular edge, are used to remove large areas of glass.

Some cut glass was made with a layer of colored glass over another layer of glass. The cutting revealed the bottom layer and created the pattern. This Bohemian glass vase is 16½ inches high. (Photo: New Orleans Auction Galleries)

makers, especially the Waterford factory, became famous for their cut wares, and many collectors believe most cut glass made between 1780 and 1850 came from Waterford. It is very difficult to identify the maker of early cut glass unless the glass is marked. Most cut glass from this era was made in England, not Ireland.

Cut glass in America is divided into four periods: Early (1771–1830), Middle (1830–1876), Brilliant (1876–1910), and Flower (1905–1916).

Early-Period American Cut Glass (1771–1830)

Early-period American cut glass resembled German thin-walled wares and English heavy flint wares. Like most clear glass of the time, it was a bit gray in color with minor bubbles. The cut and engraved designs helped to disguise the flaws and added luster to the glass. Cut panels and flutes and engraved swags and festoons were popular designs in this period. The most famous makers were Henry William Stiegel and John Frederick Amelung, both German immigrants.

Middle-Period American Cut Glass (1830–1876)

Middle-period American cut glass remained simple in design, still favoring flutes, panels, and printies (concave ovals). Engraved designs of the same period used naturalistic themes, the most popular being grapevines and leaves, and later, mythological scenes. The most elegant cut glass of this period was flashed, or cased with another layer of colored glass. The top layer of color was cut through, and the plain glass underneath could be seen in the design. Ruby red, emerald green, and cobalt blue were popular colors. The designs, both geometric and figural, were influenced by imported Bohemian wares and by immigrant Bohemian glassmakers. It can be difficult to distinguish a Bohemian color-cut-to-clear item from a similar American piece. Many pieces originally thought to have been made in the United States are now known to be European in origin.

American Brilliant-Period Cut Glass (1876–1910)

Cut glass became the rage after the 1876 Centennial Exhibition in Philadelphia, where many American glassmakers showcased their wares and demonstrated the cutting process. The public saw thick, heavy, clear glass cut with deep miter cuts that removed wedge-shaped pieces. Then, a succession of increasingly smaller wheels made more delicate mitered cuts, creating allover or repeating geometric patterns. The finished piece was either polished by hand with wooden wheels or with an acid bath, resulting in a brilliance that gives the glass its name. It could take as long as six months to finish larger items.

Brilliant-period cut glass was made in full sets, including goblets, wineglasses, water tumblers, dishes, and many accessories, from knife rests shaped like barbells to candelabra. Cut glass dishes were used to serve any food that was not heated, and cut glass bottles adorned many women's vanity tables. Most brides were not given silver, but expensive, heavy cut glass bowls and pitchers.

Around the turn of the twentieth century, cutting factories looked for ways to reduce the cost of producing finished glass. Some factories began using fire-polished blanks that had the initial cuts pressed into them. Cutters needed only to add the finer cuts to finish the piece. Factories also introduced designs with engraved floral elements and fewer heavy miter cuts.

Because of the influence of European, English, and Irish designs on the American glass industry and the similarities among American companies' wares, cut glass identification is difficult. Only about 10 percent of old cut glass is marked.

New brilliant cut glass and engraved glass is being made in Europe, especially in the Czech Republic.

Cut glass detail (left). Pressed glass detail (right).

BRILLIANT CUT GLASS OR PRESSED GLASS?

Look: Cut glass sparkles more than pressed glass because it has sharp edges. Pressed glass designs are molded into the glass, making rounded edges that feel dull and do not reflect light as well.

Lift: Pick up a cut glass item and compare it to a similar piece of pressed glass. The cut glass is heavier.

Listen: When you tap your finger against it, cut glass rings with more clarity than pressed glass. (If the piece of cut glass is cracked, it will sound flat.)

Some Major American Cut Glass Factory Marks

Factory and Location	Dates of Operation	Mark
J.D. Bergen Company Meriden, Connecticut	1886–1913	
O.F. Egginton Company Corning, New York	1896–1918	
Hatch & Clark **T. B. Clark & Company, Inc.** Honesdale, Pennsylvania	1884–1885 1885–1927	
T.G. Hawkes & Company Corning, New York	1880–1962	
J. Hoare & Company Corning, New York	1868–1920	
W.L. Libbey & Son **Libbey Glass Company** (Continued as Libbey Glass Manufacturing Company to the present) Toledo, Ohio	1888–1892 1892–1919	
Maple City Glass Company (established by T.B. Clark & Company, Inc.) Honesdale, Pennsylvania	1898–1911	
Meriden Cut Glass Company (part of International Silver Company) Meriden, Connecticut	c.1896–1923	
Mt. Washington Glass Company **Pairpoint Mfg. Company** **Pairpoint Corporation** New Bedford, Massachusetts	1837–1894 1894–c.1900 c.1900–present	
L. Straus & Sons New York, New York	c.1872–1919	
Charles G. Tuthill & Company Middleton, New York	1895–1902	

PAPERWEIGHTS

Paperweights with single flowers, nosegay bouquets, and intricate mosaics have attracted collectors since the nineteenth century. Glass paperweights debuted at an 1845 industrial exposition in Vienna. A Venetian glassmaker, Pietro Biaglia, made spherical souvenirs to demonstrate his abilities. A French delegate told the Saint-Louis, France, glass factory about the idea, and the factory immediately produced a selection of paperweights and desk accessories. Baccarat followed the next year. A few millefiori paperweights may have a signature cane with the company's initials and a date. Experts can identify makers based on individual canes and overall design.

The Saint-Louis, France, glass factory made this fruit bouquet paperweight. The lampwork fruit can be seen on a swirling latticinio basket. (Photo: L. H. Selman)

Millefiori

The earliest paperweights were created using the Italian *millefiori* and *lampwork* techniques. The term *millefiori*, which means "thousand flowers," describes the process of combining segments of glass for a mosaic, flowerlike effect. The glassmaker first creates *canes* by fusing colored glass rods together. The cane is then sliced into thin discs, which can be assembled to create a variety of shapes, including vases, plates, and paperweights. *Lampwork* uses the flame of a lamp to bend, stretch, and otherwise shape the canes. Another technique, *filigree*, uses canes that are usually made of clear and colored glass rods. Instead of slicing the cane into discs, the glassmaker twists longer pieces of cane together.

Clichy is famous for its millefiori rose paperweights like this Clichy rose and garland weight that is 3¹⁄₀ inches in diameter. (Photo: L. H. Selman)

The first Venetian paperweights were groups of millefiori. French glassmakers added a layer of clear glass on top of their lampwork designs. Over time, factories made the clear layer thicker, producing a magnifying-glass effect that showed the complex millefiori patterns.

Nineteenth-century paperweight makers used millefiori and filigree to make swags of garland, trefoils, stars, and allover designs. Lampwork flowers and animals were arranged on top of millefiori, filigree, or solid backgrounds. Cameo paperweights, also known as sulphides, have molded ceramic medallions in them that appear silvery inside the glass. The cameos were usually profiles or busts of famous people, although scenes and souvenir themes were made, too. Classic paperweights were made in three sizes: miniature (less than 2 inches); regular (2 to 3¼ inches); and magnum (3¼ to 4½ inches).

French Paperweights

French paperweight makers are known by the location of the factories. The three most important are: Baccarat (Compagnie des Cristalleries de Baccarat, 1765–present), Clichy (L.J. Maës, Clichy-la-Garenne, 1837–present; merged with Cristallerie de Sèvres in 1885), and Saint-Louis (Compagnie des Cristalleries de Saint-Louis, 1767–present).

American Paperweights

The Boston & Sandwich Glass Company, Sandwich, Massachusetts, produced the first American millefiori paperweights in 1852. New England Glass Company and Mt. Washington Glass Company, both of New Bedford, Massachusetts, were the other two major producers. American glassmakers used the same basic techniques as the French, so the paperweights are very similar. Around 1900, Millville, New Jersey, glassworker Ralph Barber developed a new brass crimping tool that made possible the creation of larger three-dimensional roses, called the Millville rose.

Other Paperweights

Inexpensive advertising and souvenir paperweights were made after the 1860s. The weights often had photographs or printed messages encased between layers of glass. Some included millefiori canes with logos or commemorative dates. Many were domed, like classic paperweights, and others were rectangular, oval, or diamond-shaped. These paperweights are of historic interest, but most do not have the artistic or monetary value of the earlier weights. In the early 1900s, glassmakers introduced pressed glass paperweights in which a photograph or printed message could be displayed.

Snow dome paperweights delight many collectors. Most people can remember shaking the paperweight to see the snow fall inside. The earliest account of paperweights with snowy scenes was from the Paris Universal Exposition of 1878. Old snow domes are made with glass domes mounted on china or marble bases. Newer ones are plastic.

ART GLASS

The popularity of pressed glass waned in the 1880s. As a result of the changes in tastes, companies like Mt. Washington Glass Company and Hobbs, Brockunier & Company in the United States, and Thomas Webb & Sons and Stevens & Williams in England, introduced glassware with new colors, applied designs, and enameled details. Today this glass is known as *art glass.*

Art glass is decorative, and many English and European pieces were not made to be functional. American companies added "useful" pieces to their catalogs. Great-grandmother brought out the Mt. Washington Burmese sugar bowl and creamer and Hobbs Peachblow pitcher for tea parties, but a Webb Matsu-no-ke vase would have been kept in the curio cabinet. Complete table settings were not available.

Shaded Colors

Items made with glass that shades from one color to another are among the most popular and easy-to-spot art glassware. The colors were made by refiring portions of specially formulated glass.

Amberina and Other Shaded Amber Colors

John Locke patented a formula for Amberina, a two-tone glass shading from amber to ruby, in 1883 for the New England Glass Company. The glass was made by adding colloidal gold to amber

IT'S PRETTY, BUT IS IT OLD?

Most people know art glass when they see it. It is colorful, often shaded from one color to another, and embellished with fancy details like ruffles and three-dimensional fruit and flowers. But is it the real thing?

In the 1930s, there was renewed interest in nineteenth-century glass styles. Several factories, including Fenton Art Glass Company, Gunderson Glass Works, and Pairpoint Manufacturing Company, introduced glassware that imitated the styles of the 1880s. Much of it was handmade in the same colors and with similar decorations. Copies are still being made in the United States, Europe, and Asia. It is easy to be confused.

glass. After shaping a vase or a bowl, the glassmaker would reheat sections of the glass, which would turn red. Amberina with a purple-red tone was fired too long. Better pieces have a yellow-red tone. Because it was much easier to reheat the top of a piece than the bottom, most Amberina is red at the reheated top. The pieces shading from amber at the top to red at the bottom are called Reverse Amberina.

The earliest New England Amberina pieces were blown- or pattern-molded. Hobbs, Brockunier & Company and Sowerby, under license from the New England Glass Company, made Amberina pressed glass items. Other companies made shaded amber-to-ruby glass but were prohibited from using the name Amberina. Mt. Washington Glass Company made its own version, called Rose Amber.

The queen of Amberina is the expensive and rare Plated Amberina made by the New England Glass Company after 1886. It shades from yellow to ruby and is always cased to a cream-colored or chartreuse inner layer—never a white one. True Plated Amberina is ribbed.

Glassmakers imitated the shaded coloring of Amberina by applying color. The Painted Amberina process, patented in 1895, involved partially coating, then reheating, the glass. The result was two layers of paint—one yellow and one red. Painted Amberina is recognized easily because a portion of the painted coloring has usually worn off. It also has a more iridescent color than true Amberina. Flashed Amberina is made by adding a thin layer of ruby glass to a solid amber item. This process leaves a slightly raised area where the flashing was added.

Amberina was one of many popular two-tone glasswares made in Victorian times. The New England Glass Company of New Bedford, Massachusetts, made this Amberina pitcher in the Inverted Thumbprint pattern. The 4-inch-high pitcher has an applied reeded handle. (Photo: Cincinnati Art Galleries)

Right: This 8¾-inch Plated Amberina glass pitcher with an applied amber handle shows the characteristics collectors want. It has a cream-colored or chartreuse inner layer, not a white one, and it is ribbed.

Burmese

The success of Amberina started a race among glassmakers to make other two-tone glass. Frederick Shirley registered the formula for Burmese glass for Mt. Washington Glass Company in 1885. Burmese glass is an opaque glass that shades from salmon pink to lemon yellow. The glass was made by the same process as Amberina. The company registered Burmese in England a year later and licensed its manufacture to Thomas Webb & Sons.

Although some pieces are left glossy, most Burmese pieces have a slightly rough satin finish. A few are diamond-quilted, but most are plain. Some Burmese pieces are decorated with designs of ducks, flowers, ships, or Egyptian scenes. The rarest Burmese has three-dimensional applied leaves and flowers that are also made from colored Burmese glass. Queen's Design is Burmese with a beaded enamel decoration, usually daisies. It was named in honor of Queen Victoria, who admired the glassware.

Peachblow

Peachblow describes two-tone glass that resembles a Chinese porcelain glaze. The peachblow craze began with the 1886 sale of a seventeenth-century Chinese vase, now known as the Morgan vase, considered to be one of the best peachblow-glazed items ever made. Glassmakers already had several two-tone pink glasswares in the making, and it is likely they capitalized on the publicity generated by the Chinese vase when they named their new colors.

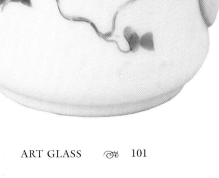

Burmese, a pink and yellow shaded glass, was decorated in many ways. This water pitcher has an enameled decoration of ivy with gold trim. It was made by the Mt. Washington Glass Company. (Photo: James Julia)

Peachblow glass varies in color from one company to another. The name itself changed from company to company. Original trade ads sometimes used Peachblow as one word and sometimes as two. The companies themselves used a variety of names in their ads: Peach Blow, Peach Skin, Peach Bloom, Coral, and Wild Rose.

Mt. Washington Glass Company made Peach Blow or Peach Skin, a single-layer, opaque satin glass ranging in color from pale blue to pink at the top. This glass is not at all the color of a real peach. Pieces were in the same shapes as Burmese. Mt. Washington's production lasted only two years.

The New England Glass Company introduced a similar single-layer glass with color shading from pink to a deeper rose color at the top. Because Mt. Washington registered the term *peach* to describe its two-tone glass, New England marketed its version as Wild Rose. But, to add to the confusion, trade journals then and collectors now refer to New England's product as Peachblow.

Hobbs, Brockunier & Company marketed its double-layer version of Peachblow as Coral when the pieces were left glossy and as Peach Blow for satin-finished pieces. The outer layer is like Amberina, shading from yellow-amber to deep red at the top. The inner layer is a creamy opaque lining.

English companies also made Peachblow. Thomas Webb & Sons made a double-layer peachy shaded glass that it called Peach Glass. Stevens & Williams, another English company, sold a line called Peach Bloom.

Shaded pink satin glass vase.

Bottom: This gold iridescent Tiffany vase, marked L.C.T., has a pattern of green leaf forms. (Photo: Cincinnati Art Galleries)

Rubina and Other Two-Toned Flashed Glassware

Several two-tone glasswares were made by flashing a thin layer of colored glass onto the interior surface of the pitcher or bowl. Color combinations include Rubina, which is clear with ruby; Rubina Verde, a canary base with ruby inside; Ruby Sapphire (also called Bluerina by collectors), sapphire blue with ruby; and Ruby Amber, amber with ruby. Flashed two-tone glass has layers that show at the rim and an abrupt transition from one color to another.

Iridescent Glass

Tiffany is the first word that comes to mind when discussing iridescent glass. This glass is easily recognizable and often signed. Louis Comfort Tiffany began his career as an interior decorator in 1879 and first saw iridescent glass in Europe. Dissatisfied with the colors available for his leaded windows, he hired chemists and glassmakers to develop his own. In 1891 he established Tiffany Glass & Decorating Company in Corona, New York, a town on Long Island. Beginning in 1894, vases and accessories were made in various iridescent shades of gold, green, and blue with pulled designs and applied decorations. Noniridescent pieces were also made, usually in darker semi-opaque colors, also with pulled designs. Tiffany usually signed the glass with the name *Tiffany,* the initials *L.C.T.,* or the word *Favrile.* A very small number of Tiffany pieces of glass are unsigned. The company closed in 1928.

Iridescent glass by Tiffany was so successful that many other factories tried to copy the work. In Europe, the Loetz factory of Austria made a similar type of iridescent glass. Kew Blas, Frederick Carder's

Steuben, Quezal, and Durand were among the other American factories that made iridescent art glass at the turn of the twentieth century. Cheaper imitations, like carnival glass, appeared after 1904.

Cameo Glass

Cameo glass is named after the famous cameos worn as jewelry. Raised designs are created by etching, cutting, or carving away colored layers of glass to make a cameo design. Multicolored designs can be created by leaving portions of different colored layers. Often mottled glass of varying tones is used for the design. Frosted or plain-colored backgrounds set off the overlaid designs. If you run your fingers over the glass, you can feel the raised design.

Cameo glass was made in England, France, Bohemia, and the United States after 1870. English cameo glass usually features classical designs. The finest English pieces by Thomas Woodall, George Woodhall, and John Northwood at the Thomas Webb & Sons factory are in many museum collections. French cameo glass by Émile Gallé, Daum Frères, and others often has art nouveau-style flowers and plants. Mt. Washington Glass Company, Handel & Company, New England Glass Company, and Tiffany were the major American nineteenth-century producers of cameo glass.

Many more companies created cameo glass after the turn of the twentieth century, especially during the art deco era. Cameo glass copies have continued to be made since the 1980s, many marked with fake marks like *Galli*, *Tip Galle*, *Richards*, and *Nancy*.

The signature "Gallé" is on the side of this 14¼-inch-high cameo vase with green berries, leaves, and branches on an amber background. (Photo: James Julia)

Left: Many pieces of cameo glass are signed on the bottom or as part of the cameo cutting. Daum, Nancy is signed on the foot of this 20¼-inch-high vase. The cameo cutting creates a lake scene. (Photo: James Julia)

ABC'S OF ART GLASS

Agata

Agata is an opaque glassware, ranging in color from pink to rose or from rose to white, with mottled spots resembling lusterware. It was made by the New England Glass Company for a short time during 1887. There is also a green version of agata.

Right: Agata finger bowl and underplate (Photo: Cincinnati Art Galleries)

Bride's Basket

Bride's baskets were usually one-of-a-kind novelties made in just about every color of art glass by American and European glass factories. Many baskets have silver-plated stands and handles. They were especially popular about 1880, when the decorated basket was often given as a wedding gift. Cut glass baskets were popular after 1890. Bride's baskets lost favor about 1905.

Crown Milano bride's basket (Photo: Joy Luke)

Coralene

Coralene glassware was made in England, Bohemia, and the United States during the 1880s. Finished glass items, usually made of colored satin glass, were decorated with enamel. Tiny glass beads were applied to the paint before it dried, and the entire piece was heated to set the enamel and fix the beads. Designs included coral branches, seaweed, daisies, birds, and fish. Modern imitations are made with glue instead of fired enamel, so the beads fall off easily.

Crackle Glass

Glass with an allover crackled finish was first made in Venice in the fifteenth century and revived in the 1880s. The small lines were created by plunging hot glass into water and pulling it out quickly. Crackle ware is still made.

Right: Coralene vase with coral branches

Crown Milano

Frederick Shirley formulated Crown Milano for Mt. Washington Glass Company in 1884. The opaque glass has a pale biscuit color and a satin finish. Items are decorated with flowers and usually have gold scrolls. Some pieces are marked.

Findlay Onyx and Floradine

Findlay Onyx and Floradine are two similar types of glass made by Dalzell, Gilmore & Leighton Company of Findlay, Ohio, about 1889. Onyx is a patented yellowish white opaque glass with raised silver daisy decorations. A few rare pieces were made of rose, amber, orange, or purple glass. Floradine is made of cranberry-colored glass with an opalescent white raised floral pattern and a satin finish. The same molds were used for both types of glass. Onyx and Floradine were made for only a few years because the glass was brittle and tended to break during shipment.

Mary Gregory–Style Glassware

The term *Mary Gregory* is used to describe any old or new glass decorated with white enamel painted pictures of boys, girls, and young women. Some pieces with tinted faces and clothes were made, too. Mary Gregory worked from 1872 to 1888 at the Boston & Sandwich Glass Company in Sandwich, Massachusetts. Legend has it that she painted white enamel figures on dark-colored Sandwich glass, but experts now know that Boston & Sandwich did not produce this style of enameled glassware. Mary Gregory did decorate glass, but she did not paint white enamel figures. It is unlikely that any American glass factory produced Mary Gregory–style glass before Westmoreland Glass Company's 1957 line. Research in the 1990s confirmed that all the nineteenth-century solid-color glassware with white figures came from Bohemia and Germany.

Crown Milano vase with Persian design (Photo: James Julia)

Far left: Findlay Onyx spooner (Photo: James Julia)

Mary Gregory–style barber bottle

Matsu-No-Ke

Matsu-no-ke is an applied clear glass decoration patented by Frederick Carder at Stevens & Williams in England in 1884. The decoration is shaped like a pine branch, called a *matsu* in Japanese, with applied flower blossoms. Carder used the decoration at his Steuben Glass Works in 1922. Other companies, especially Bohemian glassmakers, made similar decorations with clear and colored glass.

Mercury Glass

Mercury, or silvered, glass was first introduced in London, England, in the 1840s. It became popular in the United States during the 1850s and again in the 1910s. The silver color is inside the wall of the piece. Clear glass is blown into a vase or globe shape with two walls separated by a small air space. Air is vacuumed from the space, then a mercury solution is poured through a hole in the bottom. The hole is closed with a metal, rubber, or glass stopper and cemented. The silvery mercury clings to the sides of the glass. Gold-colored glass is made by putting mercury in amber glass. Some mercury glass items are decorated with engraved or enameled designs. The finished piece looks like metallic silver and won't tarnish unless the seal at the bottom is broken. A good piece of mercury glass has no signs of worn "silver."

Mother-of-Pearl or Pearl Satin Glass

Mother-of-Pearl is a mold-blown glass with a satin finish. It is made of two or more layers of clear or colored glass. Indentations or ridges between the layers trap air bubbles, which give the piece a pearly effect. The process was patented in England in 1858. Mt. Washington Glass Company received a patent in 1886 to make Pearl Satin Ware, which is also known as Mother-of-Pearl glass. Pieces can be found with herringbone, diamond-quilted, raindrop, and Federzeichnung (a maze-like pattern resembling an octopus) designs.

Similar glassware was made by other factories in the United States, England, Bohemia, and France. The glass items were decorated in many ways, including enameled or applied glass decorations, gold leaf, threading, and cameo techniques.

Pomona

Pomona glass is a clear glass with a soft amber border decorated with pale blue or rose-colored flowers and leaves. The colors are very pale, and the background of the glass is covered with a network of fine lines. Pomona glass was made between 1885 and 1888 by the New England Glass Company. Pieces referred to as *first grind* were made from April 1885 to June 1886. The design was made by applying a wax surface on the glass, then cutting it with a design, then dipping the piece in acid. *Second grind* pieces were made with a less expensive method of acid etching that was developed later.

Rainbow Satin Glass

Glass with pink, blue, and yellow striations and a satin-like finish is called Rainbow satin glass. This type of glass was made by the same process as Mother-of-Pearl glass. Several companies produced Rainbow satin glass in the 1880s, but few pieces were made, and it is expensive today.

Left: Midwestern "second grind" Pomona pitcher with added enamel floral design (Photo: Cincinnati Art Galleries)

Mother-of-Pearl satin vase with zigzag design (Photo: James Julia)

Left: This design on "first grind" Pomona glass is more delicate than designs on "second grind" pieces. (Photo: Cincinnati Art Galleries)

Royal Flemish

Royal Flemish is a thick, clear satin glass with elaborate enameled designs in transparent colors and gold. Mt. Washington Glass Company introduced it about 1889 and patented the process in 1894. Royal Flemish items were made in the same shapes as Crown Milano. Few are marked.

Royal Flemish vase
(Photo: James Julia)

Satin Glass

Satin glass has a dull, velvety finish. The glass is given its satin finish by hydrofluoric acid vapor treatment. Many English and American companies produced satin glass during the 1880s. Pieces usually have a white lining and sometimes applied glass flowers or enameled designs. Vases, rose bowls, fruit bowls, baskets, lamps, pickle jars, and other types of decorative pieces were made. See also Coralene, Mother-of-Pearl, and Rainbow satin glass.

Diamond-quilted satin glass vase

Spangle and Spatter Glass

Spatter glass is made with multicolored irregular blotches. During the shaping of the item, the glassmaker rolls the gather of glass in little pieces of colored glass, and the pieces adhere to the gather. Spangle glass is spatter glass with metallic flakes, also called inclusions, mixed in. Spangle glass, and sometimes spatter glass, is cased glass with a thin layer of clear glass over the multicolored layer. Both types of glass were made in many European countries and the United States between about 1880 and 1900. Some collectors incorrectly refer to these wares as end-of-day glass, implying that the decoration was made of leftovers.

Wavecrest, Kelva, and Nakara

C. F. Monroe decorated opaque white glass beginning in the 1880s in Meriden, Connecticut. Much of the undecorated glassware he used was made by Pairpoint Manufacturing Company of Sagamore, Massachusetts, and some by French factories. Three names were used on the pieces: *Wavecrest,* registered in 1892; *Nakara,* which was in use about the same time but never registered; and *Kelva,* which was registered in 1904. Wavecrest and Nakara can be difficult to tell apart. Both are painted in pastel colors with floral or scenic designs. Nakara often has beaded details and transfer-printed designs. Kelva always has areas of mottled color.

Dresser sets, jewel boxes, powder boxes, hair receivers, humidors, desk accessories, and other such wares were made. Many boxes have elaborate brass fittings and are satin-lined, although the original fabric is often missing. Very few pieces of Kelva, Nakara, or Wavecrest are labeled or signed.

Spatter glass cruet

Wavecrest dresser box
(Photo: Cincinnati Art Galleries)

Chapter 7

BOTTLES

ALMOST ANY EIGHTEENTH- OR NINETEENTH-
CENTURY BOTTLE is of interest to the collector. The best bottles are the oldest, rarest, or the most unusual in shape or color, but
not necessarily those that are the finest examples of glassmaking.
Bottles were commercial containers, not works of art. They were
made to be useful.

MAKING A BOTTLE

The earliest bottles were *free-blown* by the glassmaker, then transferred to a *pontil* (also called a *punty rod*) for additional shaping.
Free-blown bottles have a neck, a shaped body, a flattened base, and
a mark or scar on the bottom called a *pontil mark* where the punty
rod was removed. If the rough scar is ground smooth, it is called a
ground pontil. Decoration, if any, is added by enameling or engraving, pattern molding, or by applying glass adornments. Free-blown
bottles have no mold seams, but they may have some bubbles and
imperfections. No two are exactly the same size.

Dip mold-blown bottles are uniform in size and were created for
commercial use. In this type of glassmaking, glass was blown into a
hollow one-piece mold called a dip mold and took the shape of the
mold's interior. Many case and gin bottles were made this way.

By the early 1800s, hinged molds were used to create bottles.
Early mold-blown bottles have seams on the sides where the pieces
of the mold join, but not on the neck because each bottle was finished by hand.

Top left: Fancy cologne bottles were made in the United States from the 1830s. This 5⅝-inch blue bottle has an open pontil.

Top right: This free-blown inkwell has a pontil mark. It was probably made in Europe between 1830 and 1860.

Bottom left: Case gin bottles like this Dutch example were often made in a dip mold. This gin bottle was made about 1770 to 1800.

Bottom right: The pattern in the glass on this 6¼-inch-high American bottle was made by blowing the glass into a three-piece mold. (All photos: Glass Works)

Bottles made before 1900 may have irregular marks that look like the rough surface of whittled wood. *Whittle marks* were caused by hot glass touching the cold metal mold. This flaw usually indicates a nineteenth-century bottle. For more tips on dating bottles, see "Examining Lips, Tops, and Bottoms" on page 121.

Automatic bottling equipment was developed in 1903. Most bottles are now being made entirely by machine, and no handwork is necessary.

Four types of bottles were used before 1900: flasks and bottles that contained whiskey and other alcoholic beverages (both glass and ceramic), bitters bottles (the 1840–1900 types), household bottles (shoe polish, ink, canning jars, milk bottles, candy containers, perfumes, and other such household items), and figural bottles (any bottle with an unusual shape. The bottle may also be included in one of the other classifications). The Picture Dictionary on page 116 shows basic bottle shapes and describes their uses.

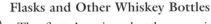

ORDINARY OR OUT OF THIS WORLD?

The chance of finding a rare historic flask that is unknown to other collectors is almost nonexistent. Reproductions of dozens of the flask designs have been made and sold since the 1930s. Many flasks marked *Wheaton* or *Nuline* were made after 1966 and often confuse beginning collectors.

The rare coloration of the mouth and collar of this double eagle flask enticed a collector to spend $56,000 at auction. The very desirable flask, made about 1825–1835, would have been worth about $4,000 in a common color. (Photo: Glass Works)

Bottom right: Weideman Company of Cleveland, Ohio, filled this pottery whiskey jug with Auld Lang Syne Pure Old Barley Malt whiskey. The company was in business from 1861 to the 1950s. This jug was made between 1890 and 1915.
(Photo: Glass Works)

Flasks and Other Whiskey Bottles

The first American bottles to gain favor with collectors and museums were whiskey flasks made between 1750 and 1860. Most of the flasks were pint-size and were made by a pattern or mold-blown method. They had impressed or raised decorations on the glass. Blown bottles varied in size, and consumers worried they might be getting less whiskey in some bottles. Factories developed molds that shaped historic flasks and other bottles of uniform size. Almost any historic flask is identified in the book *American Bottles & Flasks and Their Ancestry* by Helen McKearin and Kenneth M. Wilson. Collectors, dealers, auction houses, and bottle price books identify flasks by the McKearin number, the identification number used in the book.

Bitters Bottles

Bitters, the medicine of the last half of the nineteenth century, were a mixture of herbs, roots, spices, and barks that was blended with alcohol. Some ingredients, like opium or marijuana, are considered dangerous and are illegal today. Bitters were taken by the spoonful—or the full bottle—and they were considered the wonder drugs of their time, in those days before penicillin and medical cures. According to the labels, bitters could cure anything. The label on one bottle claimed the contents would cure "biliousness, liver complaint, fever blisters, constipation, Bright's disease, dyspepsia, malaria, ague, hypochondria, sleeplessness, and others." Bitters were created to avoid the tax on gin in England. It was simple to mix gin with herbs and call the brew medicine. It was also easier to tell your family that bitters helped your digestion rather than admit you were drinking liquor. Bitters remained popular well into the twentieth century.

Most bitters bottles could be classed as liquor bottles, because their contents were high in alcohol. Many bitters bottles were made between 1840 and 1900, or even later. To be classed as a bitters bottle by collectors, the bottle must have either the word *Bitters* in the glass or a paper label that says *Bitters,* or the bottle must have a shape that has already been identified as one that was used for bitters. A labeled bottle with the contents, cork, and outside box explaining the curative powers of the bitters is also desirable. More than four hundred bitters makers have been listed for the United States, and because many of them used several different bottles, there are numerous styles of bitters bottles. Most bitters bottles can be identified by shape, color, rarity, and even value in *Bitters Bottles* by Carlyn Ring and W. C. Ham, or in other books. Collectors often refer to Ring numbers, the numbering system used in the book to identify a bitters bottle.

By 1830 the flask had companions on the store shelf because liquor bottles in unusual shapes were gaining favor. Bininger, a Philadelphia company, made liquor bottles in many sizes and shapes, including canons, barrels, clocks, jugs, and flasks. Bottles with the name *Bininger* in the glass or on the paper label are popular with collectors.

This Bininger's bottle with embossed clock face has an applied top and an open pontil. (Photo: American Bottle Auctions)

This Indian Princess bottle held Brown's Celebrated Indian Herb Bitters. The 12¼-inch bottle, patented in 1868, was made in many colors. The figural shape has been reproduced often because it is so decorative. (Photo: Glass Works)

Picture Dictionary of Bottle Shapes

Collectors and bottle makers have often given shape-inspired nicknames to their bottles.

Flasks

The **calabash** flask is shaped like the calabash gourd, a vegetable that was often hollowed out to hold water.

The **chestnut** flask is almost round and is named for the well-known nut from the chestnut trees that grow in Europe and the United States.

The **Pitkin-type** flask is named for the Pitkin Glassworks of East Hartford, Connecticut. The name is used to describe similarly shaped ribbed bottles made by other factories, too. The blowers used the "German" method of putting a second gather of glass halfway up the post, making the glass walls of the flask thicker. The bottle was then blown into a rib mold to impress ribs. The finished bottle could have vertical or swirled ribs.

Inks

Perhaps because so many ink bottles are unmarked, ink bottle collectors have given them descriptive nicknames. All of the names were inspired by the shape of the bottle.

Igloo

Teakettle

Turtle

Umbrella

Others

The **demijohn** is a large, narrow-necked bottle. Demijohns range in size from one to ten gallons and are often encased in wicker. A carboy is a larger, heavier-walled version of a demijohn.

A **lady's leg** is a long-necked bottle that only slightly resembles the leg of a woman. Boker's Stomach Bitters first used this trademarked bottle shape.

The **case gin** bottle is shaped to fit into a wooden case for shipping. The bottles were more or less rectangular, but slightly smaller at the bottom. They sat flat against each other in a case. The shape was especially favored by the Dutch, who used it for bottles of exported gin. "Dip-molded" gin bottles are the same shape but were molded in boxlike forms.

The black glass bottles used by the English in the seventeenth century were made in several shapes. One, the **mallet**, was thought to resemble a short-handled hammer. The **onion** was named for the shape of the vegetable. The **seal** bottle, used about 1630 to 1750, was named for the extra glob of glass or the seal attached to the outside of the bottle. The seal was impressed with initials and sometimes a date.

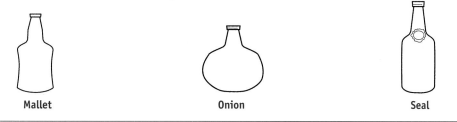

Mallet   Onion   Seal

Zanesville-type bottles are named for the shape of the bottles made by the Zanesville Manufacturing Company in Zanesville, Ohio, between 1815 and 1838 and between 1842 and 1851. Like the Pitkin-type flask, the name is used for other companies' bottles of the same shape.

BOOZ BOTTLES

The cabin-shaped Booz bottle is a famous liquor bottle. Mr. E. G. Booz ran a tavern in Philadelphia. Three versions of the Booz bottle were made for him, and the date 1840 is embossed on the bottles. There is, however, reason to believe these bottles were not made until about 1860. Dozens of recent copies have been produced, some embossed with *Booze* instead of *Booz*.

Customers asked for E. G. Booz's Old Cabin Whiskey, and the name booz *became synonymous with hard liquor. The cabin-shaped bottle with the name and date* 1840 *has been copied often. This 1931 reproduction is one of the earliest. (Photo: Glass Works)*

Household Bottles

Canning jars

Canning jars or fruit jars are popular with collectors. The most famous is the Mason jar with the words *Mason 1858*. The 1858 is the date of the original patent, not the date the jar was made. Variations of the Mason jar were made long after the original jar, and the same date appeared on the jars for more than seventy years. Hundreds of other canning jars can be found. Unusual tops and sealing methods, rare colors, and other uncommon features add to the value. Beware: Many copies of old jars in unusual colors have been made since the 1980s. Collectors identify the jars and their val-

ues with the help of *The Collector's Guide to Old Fruit Jars (The Red Book of Fruit Jars)* by Douglas M. Leybourne Jr. It is published by Douglas M. Leybourne Jr., North Muskegon, Michigan.

Baby bottles

Late eighteenth-century baby feeding bottles were usually made of pottery and shaped like elongated eggs. Liquid was poured into a large opening on one side, and the baby sucked it through a small opening at the tip. In the early nineteenth century, infant bottles were also made of metal, porcelain, or blown glass. Some were decorated with flowers or other motifs popular at the time. By the middle of the nineteenth century, the rubber nipple had been invented, and glass bottles had wider mouths through which they could be filled. The O'Donnell bottle, a glass nursing bottle with a nipple at the end of a long tube, was introduced at the Great Exhibition of 1851 in London, England.

Food containers

Commercial bottles for food were common by the second half of the nineteenth century. Special shapes were popular by the 1860s. The gothic-panel bottle favored by pepper sauce makers is one of the special designs. Paper-labeled jars for foods like pickles or preserves, as well as for brand names like Heinz, are popular with collectors.

Excavations in many inner cities turn up stoneware bottles, many from England or Holland. These bottles, used since the 1650s, held beer, ginger beer, vinegar, cider, ink, or other liquids. By the 1870s stoneware bottles were a standard size: 10 inches high and large enough to hold a quart of liquid.

Carbonated drinks—either natural ones like mineral water or artificially carbonated drinks like seltzer, Coca-Cola, Moxie, Dr Pepper, and Pepsi-Cola—used special glass bottles that changed slightly over the years. An early soda bottle made after the 1830s had a thick blob top and heavy glass to prevent breakage from the pressure of carbonation. The Hutchinson stopper and Codd ball stopper were used before the crown cap was developed in 1891. Milk bottles were first made in 1884 and are easy to identify because they often picture a cow or are embossed with a dairy's name. Mustard was sold in milk glass figural bottles shaped like a house or a hen on a nest. Clear glass bottles in special shapes were used for lime juice, vinegar, preserved fruit, ketchup, and tomato sauce.

Other bottles: ink, poison, cosmetics

The ink bottle with a large base and small neck is a nineteenth-century shape. In general, the shape of an ink bottle will tell its age. Cone and umbrella shapes were used from the early 1800s to the beginning of the twentieth century. Hexagonal and octagonal bottles were preferred from about 1835 to 1865. Igloo or turtle shapes were introduced in 1865 and were popular for schools until about 1895. Barrels were made from 1840 to 1900. Square bottles became popular after 1860. Many inks were

Most bottles with raised, embossed lettering were made after 1858, when John L. Mason patented his famous fruit jar.

Cathedral-shaped pickle jars were very popular in the United States about 1860. This 14⅛-inch-high bottle has an applied ring mouth. (Photo: Glass Works)

Left: J & A Dearborn New York Mineral Water *is embossed on the side of this 7-inch-high bottle. The eight-sided bottle has a graphite pontil.* (Photo: American Bottle Auctions)

The shape of this 2¾-inch-high ink bottle gave it the name teakettle. *It was made between 1875 and 1890. The bottle has a smooth base and a brass neck ring.*

mold-blown. Some ink bottles were made crudely with sealed glass tops. These inks are called *bust-offs* by collectors, because it was necessary to break the neck of the bottle to use the ink.

Another unusual household bottle made to hold poison had many protruding bumps to indicate poisonous contents. Other poison bottles were embossed with a skull and crossbones or were even shaped like a skull.

Cosmetic bottles that contained hair oils, face creams, shaving cream, and other beauty aids came in a variety of shapes. The most valuable have unusual shapes, colors, or paper labels with interesting graphics or famous company names.

Left: Bottles that held poison had to be easily identified. The figural skull-shaped bottle is marked PAT APPL'D FOR. *It was made about 1890–1910.*

Figural Bottles

It is impossible to list the hundreds of types of figural bottles. Any bottle that is shaped like a recognizable person or object is a figural bottle. Some large whiskey flasks—either ceramic or glass—and decorative bottles that held pancake syrup, mustard, ink, or any of the many products sold in fancy bottles, are included. Bottles were made in the shape of clocks, cabins, fish, acrobats, barrels, or houses. Although figural bottles were made before the 1850s, they were especially popular in the late nineteenth and early twentieth centuries.

Figural bottles were made in strange shapes. This 13⅛-inch-high bottle shaped like an Egyptian pharaoh on a throne was probably made in France between 1890 and 1920. It is black milk glass with gold paint decoration.

EXAMINING LIPS, TOPS, AND BOTTOMS

A few rules can aid in dating old glass bottles. The rules are based on how the bottle was manufactured. A search for mold seams, pontils, designs, or whittle marks gives the first clue to the age of the bottle. Most bottles produced before 1840 were made by hand and have no seams. After 1840, bottles were made in molds. Examine the top or lip of the bottle. Between 1840 and 1860, bottles were hand finished, so the neck and lip do not have a seam. Seam marks on bottles made between 1860 and 1880 extend

Opposite page: Barber bottles were made for display on a barbershop shelf, so the color and design were important. This melon-ribbed bottle is 7 inches high.

PATENTED CLOSURES

Soda, mineral water, and beer bottles have closures that kept the gas in the bottle until opened. **Codd** bottles closed with a glass ball that was held in place by the gas, so the bottles had to be filled upside down. Soda pop was nicknamed for the "pop" sound that accompanied the removal of the **Hutchinson** stopper. A lightning closure used a wire bail to seal the stopper into the mouth.

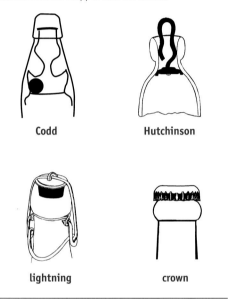

Codd   Hutchinson

lightning   crown

Fruit jar closures sealed tightly with rubber rings to preserve the contents. The earliest jars sealed the rings around the shoulder. Later jars, like the **lightning**, sealed the ring to the lip.

shoulder seal   lightning

most of the way up the neck of the bottle. The seams on bottles made between 1880 and 1890 end just below the lip. Bottles made before 1850 will have a pontil scar or a concave area where the pontil was ground away. During the second half of the nineteenth century, glassmakers used a *snap case* tool instead of a punty rod to hold the bottle for shaping. The bottoms of these later bottles are smoother and do not have a pontil mark. After 1903 most bottles were made entirely by machine, and the seams on these bottle go the entire length of the bottle, all the way through the lip.

HOW TO JUDGE THE VALUE OF AN UNKNOWN BOTTLE

Early bottles (before 1800), historic flasks, free-blown bottles, and early nineteenth-century decorative decanters are judged by the same standards as any fine early glass. Age, rarity, quality, condition, and appearance are the important factors. Nineteenth-century commercial bottles can be very valuable, even if the bottles originally held pickles, catsup, or beer. Nineteenth-century flasks, whiskey bottles, figural bottles, watch- or clock-shaped bottles, bitters bottles, soda and mineral-water bottles, fruit jars, candy containers, and poison bottles all have added value. Even some twentieth- and twenty-first-century bottles are collectible.

When judging old bottles, look carefully at several things.

Condition

Any slight crack, bubble, pitting or cloudiness of the glass lowers the value. But rarity is important, so a bottle may command a high price even if its condition is not perfect. A rare, dark green Bryant's Stomach Bitters bottle with a hole in the bottom sold for a record $68,750 in 1998. Only a few examples of this eight-sided version are known to exist.

Color

Rare colors bring high prices. In general, colored bottles are more valuable than clear ones. Green and aqua are common; browns, odd shades of greenish yellow, and light blue are good; dark cobalt blue is better; dark purple and golden amber are the best. For any particular bottle type or maker, rarity of color varies and so does the value. For example, an 1866 W. H. Ware's Fish Bitters bottle that is clear might sell for five times more than a common amber example.

Shape

Figural bottles are best. Any old odd-shaped bottle or flask is good. Common shapes must have some other feature of note to be desirable.

Age

Machine-made bottles are common. Any bottle with a pontil mark is old enough to save. Two-piece mold bottles with applied tops are good. Three-piece mold bottles are better. Free-blown, pontil-marked bottles with early necks are best, but can be difficult to authenticate.

A tight seal was important for fruit jars, so many closures were invented. This blue jar, embossed Trademark Lightning Registered US Patent Office, *has the original closure and wire bail.* (Photo: Pacific Glass)

Bottle collectors get great bargains because many of them dig for old bottles in dumps, old outhouses, trash heaps, or swamps. Some of them even travel behind bulldozers working on a new freeway. Be sure you ask permission from the owner of the property and follow all the safety rules for digging.

Embossing

Errors and unusual names and logos are best. Bitters bottles and fruit jars are well documented in books about bottles, so any unlisted bottle has a potential for a high price.

Paper Labels

A label is an historic document that identifies the bottle. Any bottle with its original box, instructions, and label is worth owning. Paper labels are often found on bottles made before 1950. Unfortunately, many collectors remove the labels so they can display a plain glass bottle in a window. Today a paper-labeled bottle made before 1920 has a value-added feature and is in the better price range. Nineteenth-century hand-blown bottles with paper labels are best.

TERMS AND ABBREVIATIONS USED TO DESCRIBE BOTTLES

Applied lip. A lip that is handmade and applied to the bottle after the bottle is formed.

Automatic bottle machine or **ABM**. A machine-made bottle.

BIMAL. The abbreviation for Blown in Mold, Applied Lip.

Black glass. Black glass is not black. It is very dark olive green or olive amber and appears black unless it is seen in a bright light. (See page 117.)

Bubbles, teardrops, or seeds. These words describe types of bubbles that form in glass.

Dauber. The slim rod on a perfume bottle's stopper. It is used to apply the perfume.

Dug. Literally, dug from the ground.

Embossed lettering. Embossed letters are letters that are raised on the surface of the glass. In 1867, an American bottle maker patented a process that embossed letters with a special plate inserted in the mold. Medicine, bitters, whiskey, and milk bottles were commonly embossed with slug plates. ISP is the abbreviation for Inserted Slug Plate.

Etched lettering. These letters are cut into a bottle with acid or a sharp instrument.

Free-blown. Glass that was blown by a glassmaker using a blowpipe.

Iridized. Describes once-buried bottles that have an iridescent sheen caused by chemicals in the soil.

Irradiated. Described bottles turned dark purple, green, or brown by a radiation process.

Kick-up. The deep indentation on the bottom of a bottle. Kick-ups are often used in wine bottles.

Milk glass. An opaque glass made by adding tin or zinc to the mixture. Most milk glass is white, but it is correct to call colored glass of this type blue or green milk glass.

Mold-blown. Describes glass that was blown into a mold.

Pontil. A scar on the bottom of a bottle. It was made by the punty rod that held the glass during the shaping process. A pontil mark that has been smoothed out is called a *ground pontil*. An *iron pontil*, or *IP*, has a reddish brown color from the punty rod. A rough pontil scar with broken edges is called an *open pontil*, or *OP*.

Punkinseed or **pumpkinseed**. A flask with a relatively flat shape like the seed of a pumpkin. In the early 1900s, bottle manufacturers called them picnic flasks.

Punty rod or **pontil rod**. The metal rod attached to the glass by the glass-blower to hold it during blowing.

Sheared lip. A lip cut with shears. It is found on bottles made before 1840.

Sun-colored. Glass made between 1880 and 1914 that was left in strong sunlight and turned colors, such as purple, pale lavender, green, or brown. *SC* and *SCA* are the abbreviations for Sun-Colored and Sun-Colored Amethyst.

Whittle marks. Irregular marks that look like the surface of whittled wood. They are sometimes found on bottles made before 1900 and occurred when hot glass touched the cold mold.

BEWARE

Since about 1995 old bottles have been colored by a radiation process that turns the bottles dark purple, green, or brown. Artificially colored bottles have little value for serious collectors but sell to those who want decorative bottles.

This rare pint-size amethyst eagle flask has a sheared mouth and a pontil scar. The exceptional color, mold, clarity, and condition add to the value of more than $40,000. It was made in Keene, New Hampshire, about 1815–1830.

Chapter 8

Furniture

NEW FURNITURE FORMS usually appear when a society needs them. The telephone stand was a twentieth-century invention. It was made after the telephone became a common household item. In the eighteenth century, twin beds, card tables, and upholstered easy chairs were new ideas. Understanding antique furniture requires good sense, as well as an innate sense of suspicion, because old furniture often is refinished,

restored, copied, or embellished. Common sense and a knowledge of history help identify different styles of furniture.

There is country-style furniture, and there is formal furniture. There is furniture from Spain, England, France, Canada, Pennsylvania—in fact, from anywhere and everywhere. This book concentrates on the American, Canadian, and English pieces that might have been used in the United States. A picture is worth a thousand words. Follow the pictures to date and determine the *style* of furniture. To decide if a piece is really as old as it appears, read Chapter 9,

Opposite page: Painted decorations were used on furniture in most countries. This Italian rococo secretary-chest has painted flowers, landscapes, and scrolls with added gilt highlights. (Photo: New Orleans Auction Galleries)

Middle and top: A formal table might look like this 1815 rosewood pier table (left) with columns, a low mirror, and gilt bronze trim. A country table (above) made at the same time might look like this tiger maple drop-leaf table with cherry legs and no trim. (Photo: Conestoga)

AMERICAN FURNITURE PERIODS
1620–1900

Books and experts often refer to Chippendale or Rococo Revival furniture. Often a period is named for a king or queen; however, the dates for a furniture period are not necessarily the same as the years of the monarch's life or reign. The names and dates of American periods of furniture sometimes differ from those used in England and other countries. These are the names and approximate dates most often used for American furniture in books, ads, and auction catalogs.

1620s–1690	**Pilgrim**
1690–1720	**William and Mary**
1720–1750	**Queen Anne**
1750–1780	**Chippendale**
1780–1820	**Federal (Classical)**
	Hepplewhite, *1785-1800*
	Sheraton, *1800-1820*
	American Empire (Regency in England), *1815-1840*
1790–1900	**Shaker**
1840–1900	**American Victorian**
	Gothic Revival, *1840-1860*
	Elizabethan Revival, *1840-1850*
	Early Victorian (Transitional), *1840-1865*
	Rococo Revival (Louis XV), *1845-1865*
	Louis XVI Revival, *1860s*
	Renaissance Revival, *1850-1875*
	Rustic, *1850-1900*
	Greco-Egyptian Revival, *1860-1890*
	Eastlake, *1870-1900*
1876–1885	**Japonisme**
1876–present	**Colonial Revival**
1880–1920	**Golden Oak**
1895–1910	**Art Nouveau**

Furniture designing is much like dress designing: If skirt lengths are long one year, the next year's style tends to make them shorter; and after short skirts have been in vogue for some time, designers drop the length again. If furniture has been light in weight and had straight legs for twenty-five years, then designers will make the legs heavier, curve them, and use dark colors. If massive designs have been the style, then someone will develop simple, lightweight chairs. Furniture design has gone from heavy to light to heavy to light, both in color and weight, since 1600.

Outside influences sometimes vary this pattern. Napoleon's conquest of Egypt in 1798 led to a strong Egyptian influence on French Empire pieces (1804–1815). Sphinx heads, stylized lotus-leaf trim, and other ancient shapes were used during this

At the end of the nineteenth century, designers used a bit of every style. This oak Savonarola chair has a Northwind carving and lion paw feet. It was made about 1890. (Photo: Fontaine's)

time. An exhibit of Egyptian relics inspired American designers in Victorian times. Although bamboo and other Asian features were already found in eighteenth-century furniture, the 1876 Centennial Exposition in Philadelphia inspired a strong Japanese influence on furniture design. It was part of the inspiration for art nouveau design. New methods of production and materials have enabled designers to construct furniture in different ways. For example, coiled spring upholstery was patented in 1828, and the bentwood chairs of Thonet were developed in the middle of the nineteenth century.

FURNITURE PERIODS IN AMERICA

Pilgrim (1620s–1700)

The first period of American-made furniture design was inspired by the English Stuart period (1603–1714). During this period, furniture was heavy and massive. In America this period is sometimes called the Pilgrim Century, and in the 1920s the term *Pilgrim furniture* was coined to refer to furniture of the 1620s through the early eighteenth century. Until about 1700, American styles were simplified versions of English Stuart pieces. Most designs were executed by craftsmen who had recently arrived from England. Rectangular panel construction, along with many other designs, traveled by boat to the new colonies. Trees were plentiful in America, so furniture was made from solid wood with no veneers. Most cabinetmakers preferred oak, ash, or maple, but many other types of usable woods that grew in the area were also chosen. Drawer handles were often made of wood.

Carver and *Brewster* are names used to describe chairs of this period. Traditionally, one type of chair was said to have been used by Governor John Carver and the other type by Elder William Brewster, both original members of the Plymouth Colony in Massachusetts. One chair had more spindles than the other. A word

FAKE BREWSTER CHAIR FOOLED THE EXPERTS

In 1970 the Henry Ford Museum bought a seventeenth-century Brewster chair from an antiques dealer. The prized acquisition was featured in a publication about the museum's furniture collection. Years later the chair was pronounced a fake by the twentieth-century maker, and research—including X-rays of the construction—proved the maker's skill and ability to fool the experts. He had built the chair, aged it, and created a false provenance for it. The museum now uses the chair in exhibitions of fakes and forgeries.

Legend says Carver and Brewster chairs arrived on the *Mayflower* with the Pilgrims. This is probably not true. However, a chair possibly brought by Governor John Carver is in a Plymouth, Massachusetts, museum.

Remove the carved crest on this English chair and what remains is the basis of the Brewster-type chair created by colonial chair makers. This seventeenth-century chair has one row of spindles.

*William and Mary
furniture had balls
and turnings and
many legs. This
gateleg table of turned
and grained walnut
was made in Boston
about 1710. A rare
example, it sold for
over $100,000 in
2003.* (Photo: Sotheby's)

of warning: Thousands of reproductions of Carver and Brewster chairs were made in Victorian times, and it is very doubtful that yours is anything but a copy.

The trestle table is another furniture form that appeared with the Pilgrims. The early trestle table was a long, narrow table that had to be small enough to fit into a house. Probably fewer than eight people could be seated at the table. Keep this in mind when you see illustrations that depict dozens of Pilgrims eating their Thanksgiving dinner at a long table.

William and Mary (1690–1720)

American furniture named for the English monarchs William and Mary is the easiest for the furniture buff to recognize. Dutch influences became popular toward the end of the seventeenth century, and furniture developed a round ball syndrome. Look at a William and Mary table stretcher, chair stretcher, lowboy, or almost

any piece made during the period. Somewhere, somehow, the designer almost always included a fat wooden ball. If the fat ball is included in the design, it is just about a sure thing that the furniture is a William and Mary design. This design element disappeared by the time of the next ruler, Queen Anne. The William and Mary style was in vogue in America from about 1690 to 1720, a few years later than in England. It took several years for designs to cross the ocean in the minds of newly arriving cabinetmakers or in paintings or pictures in design books.

American furniture of the early 1700s had not only the fat ball, but also the Spanish foot that was so popular in England at that time. Inlay, marquetry, and veneer were popular in England, but

Americans settled for burled veneer and fancy grain. Teardrop brass handles were used during this time. Designers liked furniture with many legs, such as the gateleg table. A room decorated with pure William and Mary designs appears to be a forest of wooden legs. This was the time of the first high chests, which were later called highboys. The slant-top desk, the daybed, and the upholstered easy chair were also introduced.

Queen Anne (1720–1750)

Queen Anne designs ruled furniture in England during Queen Anne's reign, from 1702 to 1714. In America, the style was fashionable from about 1720 to 1750. The style reflected an abrupt change in design. Furniture became a bit less bulky and blocky, and slight curves appeared. The Queen Anne chair had pad feet and cabriole legs (curved at the knee). This curved leg also appeared on tables, chests, and almost every piece from that period that had legs. (An old antiques dealers' joke is: "You can recognize a Queen Anne chair because *Queen Anne is bowlegged*.") Curves appeared at the top of a chair, in the crest of a mirror, and in the dome-like "bonnet" of a highboy. Queen Anne furniture had simplicity and grace and was usually made of walnut, cherry, or sometimes maple. The hardware was slightly enlarged, and the bail handle appeared with an escutcheon. Designers also developed new forms, such as the corner chair, the card table, and the tilt-top table. This was also the period when secret drawers were hidden in most large pieces of furniture that contained drawers.

Queen Anne furniture's short bowlegs and curved top can be seen on this 1730–1750 bonnet-top highboy made in Connecticut.

The collector examining an American Queen Anne chair should look for five things:

1. The top of the back is curved.

2. The splat rests on the rear of the seat and does not end above the seat as it does in later chairs.

3. The front legs are cabriole.

4. The front feet are Dutch, club, or ball and claw.

5. There may or may not be stretchers between the legs. Because the curve of the cabriole leg distributed the weight, a stretcher was not required for structural support. The later the Queen Anne chair, the less chance of a stretcher being included in its design.

Chippendale (1750–1780)

Imagine being a furniture maker who is planning to redesign a Queen Anne chair and its narrow curved leg and solid-splat high back. The new design must be different, but not so strange that it seems awkward or ugly. Much thought by furniture designers, plus a sense of what the public would accept and buy, led to the American Chippendale chair.

Furniture designs were named for the ruler of England until 1750. In 1754 furniture designing was revolutionized when Thomas Chippendale of England, a cabinetmaker of some fame in London, published *The Gentleman and Cabinet-Maker's Director.* The book pictured 160 designs from the early Georgian period (1714–1760), Queen Anne-style designs with slight changes, and new designs that reflected influences of French and Chinese pieces (thus the term *Chinese Chippendale*). Cabinetmakers of the day used the book and several other editions that followed, and a new name was given to English and American furniture of the 1750–1780 period— *Chippendale.* Experts are still debating whether the designs were done by Mr. Chippendale or by his employees.

There are Gothic-, French-, and Chinese-inspired styles of Chippendale furniture, but several characteristics are found in all of

the designs. The proportions of the chair changed, and the back was lowered. If you measure a Chippendale chair from the top of the back to the floor, it should measure 3 feet 1 inch to 3 feet 2½ inches. Later chairs are lower, earlier ones much higher.

Two types of legs were used with the ball-and-claw foot—a curved leg or a square, rather straight leg. Stretchers were usually omitted from chairs and other four-legged pieces.

In America, especially in the eastern cities where many gifted cabinetmakers worked, some typically American designs finally appeared. It is possible to look at a Philadelphia Chippendale piece and know it was not made in any other city because of the ornate carving and other design characteristics, such as the Philadelphia peanut that appears on most highboys made in Philadelphia. Unless your family owns ancestral furniture from pre-Revolutionary days, you will probably never find an eighteenth-century Philadelphia highboy. Nineteenth-, twentieth- and twenty-first-century copies have been and are still being made, and even copies cost thousands of dollars.

This inlaid mahogany and cherrywood American Federal chest of drawers was made in New England about 1820. The dark woods, small round drawer pulls, and carved rounded legs are typical of the Federal style. (Photo: Neal)

Chippendale is the period of the big brasses. Look at a piece with drawer pulls. It is obvious that the pulls are not just useful, but are also an important part of the decoration. Designers developed some new furniture forms: the piecrust table, the chest-on-chest, the secretary bookcase, and the large upholstered sofa. Rooms of the time were filled with large, heavy, carved wooden pieces of polished mahogany. Some of the best pieces were made in New England, especially in Boston and Newport, in other eastern cities like New York, Philadelphia, and Baltimore, and in the South in Tidewater, Virginia, and Charleston, South Carolina.

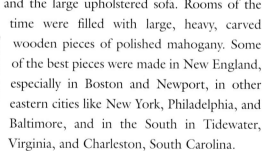

Federal (1780–1820)

The term *American Federal* or *Federal* means anything made during the early years of the Republic. This includes the Hepplewhite, Sheraton, and early Empire styles.

Hepplewhite (1785–1800)

Designers must provide new styles every few years to keep the public buying. In the 1780s, heavy, carved, dark wooden pieces with curved legs and backs had been in vogue for several decades. It was time for a change. The Hepplewhite style of furniture was popular in the United States from about 1785 to 1800. Once again, the period was named for a cabinetmaker. George Hepplewhite, who made furniture in London, England, died in 1786. His wife, Alice, continued the business and published *The Cabinet-Maker and Upholsterer's Guide* in 1788 in England. The volume pictured designs that were in style, most of them inspired by the work of the Adam brothers, James and Robert. The Adams were British architects. After they had designed houses with large rooms with light-colored walls and restrained classical decorations, they decided to design a style of furniture that would complement the design of the rooms. These designs became popular with the general public.

Top and bottom: Sheraton and Hepplewhite tables appear lightweight and have simple designs. One easy clue to tell the difference: A Hepplewhite table (above) has square legs. A Sheraton table (below) usually has rounded legs. Both of these Pembroke tables were made about 1820. (Photo: Charlton Hall)

There are several clues to recognizing a Hepplewhite chair. The top of the back of the chair is approximately 3 feet 1 inch from the floor. The back of the chair does not touch the seat. The design will include an oval-, heart-, wheel-, or shield-shaped back. The chair's lines are more slender than those of a Chippendale chair, with delicately carved, straight, tapered legs, and a general feeling of delicacy that differentiated Hepplewhite designs from heavier Chippendale styles. Special furniture forms were also introduced during this time, including the extension table, the sewing table (a little table with a single drawer and a cloth bag hanging beneath it), the tambour desk, the recamier sofa, the pier table, the center table, and the sideboard. The light feel and appearance of the design made several older forms of furniture impossible to produce, and the large, high chest of drawers was no longer made.

Hepplewhite furniture was usually made from mahogany, satinwood, and other fancy woods. Inlay was popular. The brasses had oval-shaped backs with bail-type handles.

Sheraton (1800–1820)

Thomas Sheraton of England was making furniture at about the same time as the Hepplewhite company. He printed a design book for the use of other furniture makers. It is not known if Thomas Sheraton personally ever made furniture. He published his first design book in 1791, and by 1805 he had written six publications. His earliest printed designs were reminiscent of Chippendale's work, but later pieces showed a decided French influence.

Words sometimes have several meanings. *Sheraton* has one meaning to a museum curator and another to a collector, but both meanings are correct. The traditional description of Sheraton-style furniture includes classical lines and graceful, delicate, and simple design. Straight lines were favored. The chairs had rectangular backs with a minimum of carved decorations, and the legs were often rounded and reeded. Some designs required the use of the stretcher between the legs, which was an old idea that was brought back to add stability to these lighter chairs and tables. Sheraton's later designs featured vase- or lyre-shaped table pedestals, a style that merged almost imperceptibly with the late Federal and early Empire period designs.

This top-quality carved mahogany dining chair was made in Boston about 1820. The saber legs and curved back support were inspired by the Greek klismos chair. It is part of a set of five chairs that sold for $215,000 in 2004.
(Photo: Skinner)

Many collectors do not use the word *Sheraton* to describe early lightweight inlaid furniture. Instead, they use the word to describe the style's later heavier, darker designs. Some books about antiques use—and even misuse—the name Sheraton so much that its definition has become blurred. A study of furniture books shows that Sheraton and Hepplewhite styles can be divided and described in several ways. We have chosen those most commonly used. To most collectors, Sheraton is light in weight and color.

In the United States, if a chair has a rectangular back, it is Sheraton, while a shield-shaped back is Hepplewhite. If the chair leg is square, it is Hepplewhite; if it is round, it is Sheraton. If the sideboard is widest in the center, it is Hepplewhite; those that are widest at the ends are Sheraton. A chair with square legs and a square back would be transitional Hepplewhite or transitional Sheraton. The most important problem for the average collector is to determine the age of the chair. The name *Sheraton* or *Hepplewhite* both refer to furniture designs favored from about 1785 to 1820.

Much nineteenth-century American Sheraton furniture has substantial rounded legs that are reeded, with simple wooden surfaces made of a wood like curly maple. Oval brasses are favorites for Sheraton furniture. Late American Sheraton designs were copied in less sophisticated furniture that was made in rural areas. Books written before 1930 would have called this later style of American Sheraton *country furniture*, but that term has a different meaning now and includes many primitive forms.

American Empire (1815–1840)

The word *Empire* describes furniture designed and made in France between about 1804 and 1815. The French Empire style began with the designs of two French architects who redecorated Napoleon's palace. Their designs were intended to remind visitors of the emperor's military conquests. The style was stiff and formal, with Greek, Roman, Egyptian, and Pompeian motifs. Empire furniture was made for looks, not comfort, and chairs had straight backs and hard seats. The woods were painted or stained black, the fabric colors were dark and muted. Gold appeared as the only bright spot, and gold was in the ormolu mountings and trim on the furniture. Construction joints were often hidden by a piece of ormolu placed as decoration. This French style soon influenced furniture makers in the United States. The American Empire furniture period lasted from about 1815 to 1840.

Victorian (1840–1900)

The heavy, square furniture of the Empire period was redesigned to be very ornate at the beginning of the Victorian era. The Victorian designer continued with the Empire theory that it was not impor-

❧❧

DUNCAN PHYFE

Duncan Phyfe had his own furniture workshops in New York from 1792 to 1847. He worked in several styles, including Sheraton and Empire. What is now called Duncan Phyfe style is based on his later designs. Past authorities thought his early work was fine and his later work inferior, but today it is all considered important. Styles such as the lyre-shaped pedestal table called Duncan Phyfe today were the Empire designs of his day.

❧❧

Empire-style furniture was made in many countries. This 1825 mahogany library chair was made in France. It has splayed back legs, ring-turned front legs, and ram's-head carving at the ends of the arms.
(Photo: Phillips)

❧❧

Sheraton made the first twin beds.

❧❧

tant for furniture to be comfortable. If you sit on a carved Victorian chair, you will notice that the carving often protrudes at some of the same spots you do—a situation that does not add to the joy of being seated. The invention of the jigsaw allowed furniture makers to include scrolls, curls, and intricate designs in their pieces. Designers and furniture makers seemed to become intoxicated with the new technologies.

Handmade and handcrafted furniture almost disappeared as mass production became a reality. Marble tops, heavy furniture, and dark woods (especially rosewood and mahogany) filled every room. New furniture forms included bedroom suites, whatnot shelves, and large side cabinets. Victorians disliked the undecorated surface, and pattern appeared against pattern. Measurements of chairs varied from those larger than Chippendale to those smaller than Hepplewhite, so size alone is of no help in dating a chair. Rather than using dimensions, collectors rely on the general feeling of the period—the ornate wonder of it all—to identify a piece.

The major periods included under the heading "Victorian" in books, sales, and auctions are Gothic Revival, Elizabethan Revival, Rococo Revival, Louis XVI Revival, Renaissance Revival, Greco-Egyptian Revival, and Eastlake.

Gothic Revival (1840–1860)

Gothic Revival architecture was popular in England during the 1820s and 1830s and in the United States by the 1840s. Furniture made to fill the castle-style homes of the time resembled small bits of Gothic architecture. Backs of chairs looked like church arches. Headboards and footboards were made to look like the panels of a Gothic building. Chair backs were high, straight, and carved, resembling church chairs, or they were round with partitions that looked like stained-glass windows. Alexander Roux and J. & J. W. Meeks of New York were the most important American makers of this style of furniture.

Opposite page: These 74-inch-high Victorian corner cupboard étagères were made for the home, not for a church. Rosewood, cherry, oak, satinwood, and pine were used to construct these pieces, made in New York about 1850. (Photo: New Orleans Auction Galleries)

Elizabethan Revival (1840–1850)

Elizabethan Revival was a short-lived style that could be classified as part of the Rococo Revival. Elizabethan Revival-style chairs and sofas featured spiral-turned legs and uprights, plus needlework seats. A few examples of this style remained in favor into the 1870s.

Rococo Revival (Louis XV) (1845–1865)

The French-influenced Victorian furniture of the Rococo Revival included highly ornamented, curved pieces with rococo lines, C and S scrolls, and carved flowers, grapes, and leaves. The style was influenced by eighteenth-century designs that were popular when Louis XV reigned. Rococo Revival designs included cabriole legs, French scroll feet, oval-backed chairs, and white marble tabletops. John Henry Belter of New York City made furniture during this period. His laminated wood construction made some of the ornate designs possible. Other makers of note were Alexander Roux, Charles Baudouine, Joseph Meeks & Son, and Leon Marcotte, all of New York City, and Ignatius Lutz of Philadelphia.

Louis XVI Revival (1860s)

Some Rococo Revival pieces were based on French eighteenth-century Louis XVI styles. Many cabinet-makers working in New York City during the 1860s were Frenchmen who had recently come to America. Names like Marcotte, Roux, and Baudouine were common. This style of furniture was made of ebonized maple or light fruitwood. The designs were neoclassical with wooden trim and narrow legs. The furniture had restrained bits of ormolu, gilded decoration, and perhaps a French porcelain plaque. Brass and mother-of-pearl were used as inlay. Many pieces were reasonably accurate copies of the eighteenth-century style with a nineteenth-century adaptation of color, upholstery methods, and even casters on the legs.

Renaissance Revival (1850–1875)

Rococo Revival furniture was heavy and ornate, but toward the end of the period and into the twentieth century, the style became even heavier, more ornate, and more deeply carved. Today this later style is classified as Renaissance Revival. As in the past, designers ignored comfort in favor of style. Three-dimensional carvings protruded from every possible part of a chair or table, and the pieces became so massive that they were almost impossible to move. The rectilinear look predominated. Sideboards and cabinets looked like massive architectural parts of a room. Fifteenth- to eighteenth-century motifs, such as columns, deep carvings, and cartouches, were borrowed freely. Easy chairs were made with thick upholstery on the back, seat, and arms. Headboards for beds were often over eight feet high. Carved wooden drawer pulls appeared during this time.

Renaissance Revival furniture looks heavy and ornate but has fewer curves than other Victorian styles. This high-backed bed is 96½ inches high, probably too high for a modern home with 8-foot ceilings and a carpeted floor. (Photo: New Orleans)

At first, the furniture style was favored by East Coast manufacturers, but soon furniture factories as far west as Grand Rapids, Michigan, began mass-producing this style. The Cincinnati, Ohio, firm of Mitchell and Rammelsberg sold Renaissance Revival furniture in mass quantities. The firms of Christian Herter, Kimbel and Cabus, Alexander Roux, and George Hunzinger, all of New York City; John Jelliff of New Jersey; and Berkey & Gay and other Grand Rapids, Michigan, firms worked in this style.

Greco-Egyptian Revival (1860–1890)

An important collection of Egyptian artifacts was exhibited in America in 1852. The collection delighted and inspired enthusiastic designers of the time. The Victorian-Egyptian furniture made between 1860 and 1880 was the result of this new interest. Sphinx heads, animal paws, obelisks, and hieroglyphics were incorporated into designs on chairs and tables. The furniture included the curved lines of the Gothic Revival style, but the embellishments were Egyptian. Similar pieces made with hoof feet and chairs and stools with classic shapes were called "neo-Grec." There was another flurry of interest in Egyptian designs about 1889.

Eastlake (1870–1900)

Charles Lock Eastlake was an English architect and author. His book, *Hints on Household Tastes in Furniture, Upholstery and Other Details,* influenced design changes in England and the United States. He emphasized the importance of good taste and suggested that in simplicity there is beauty.

Eastlake furniture that was designed in the United States was quite unlike the style recommended by Charles Eastlake. The overall outline of the pieces was simple, but furniture in this style was far from what the twenty-first-century eye would call plain. The furniture was rectangular with several contrasting woods and incised lines that were often rubbed with gold. Sprigs of flowers or other

Sphinx heads, ormolu mounts, lion's-head brasses, and curved, carved, and gilded legs declare this to be an American Egyptian Revival chair. The mounts are incised P & S *for Pottier & Stymus, a New York furniture firm.*

American Eastlake furniture has rectangular lines and is often highlighted with fancy-grain wood. Unusual shapes were popular, and some pieces were decorated with incised lines rubbed with gold. This Eastlake walnut table has contrasting woods and a marble top. (Photo: Charlton Hall)

shallow carvings were used. Turned spindles were popular. Sets of furniture for the parlor, bedroom, or dining room were in demand. "Eastlake" designs were made by many commercial furniture factories in the Midwest especially Grand Rapids, as well as by some of the eastern manufacturers, such as Herter Brothers, Kimbel and Cabus, and Charles Tisch.

And Then—

In the 1930s a few furniture makers made reproductions of Victorian furniture for use in Southern homes. But the ornate, carved, and usually uncomfortable furniture of the 1840–1900 period did not regain popularity with collectors and museums until the 1970s when a major exhibition of Victorian decorative arts at the Metropolitan Museum of Art generated interest. The exhibit showed collectors and dealers how to differentiate between the great and the ordinary. They began to understand the various periods included under the heading "Victorian." The new interest encouraged collectors to buy Victorian furniture, and manufacturers started making reproductions in the Victorian style.

This 46-inch-high Shaker chair was made of tiger maple in New Lebanon, New York, about 1830. The pommel-topped posts and shaped back pieces are found on many chairs made by the Shakers. Shaker chairs are surprisingly lightweight. (Photo: Skinner)

OTHER NINETEENTH-CENTURY AMERICAN FURNITURE STYLES

Shaker Furniture (1790–1900)

The furniture designed and made by the Shakers reflects their religious beliefs. Shakers lived by strict rules and were expected to strive for perfection. Careful attention was paid to quality. Shaker furniture never had poor finishings or uneven parts. It was designed for simplicity and utility. The pieces were light in weight. Most were made from pine, but maple, cherry, and other woods were also used. Early chairs and tables were painted or stained blue, blue green, mustard yellow, and red. Later a light stain or wash was used so the grain of the wood showed.

The earliest chair seats were made of rush, splint, or straw, while later ones had the characteristic woven-tape seats. The leg of the chair was tapered, and there was no separate foot. An easily identifiable feature of Shaker furniture is the acorn-

shaped finial used on ladder-back chairs. The Shakers made a trestle-type table with a shoe foot during the 1800–1860 period. They also produced a sawbuck table (a table with a crossed pair of legs at each end) that was used in the kitchen and for ironing.

Shaker chests were constructed with simple molded edges. The wooden knobs on the drawers were mushroom-turned. There was never any brass hardware. Sharply angled bracket feet were used.

Painted Furniture

Painted furniture has been made in America since the seventeenth century, but few pieces retain the original painted finish. Use by generations of owners wears the painted surface, removing parts of it. In the late nineteenth century, painted pieces were not in style, and many were stripped down to the wood. Pieces from the seventeenth and early eighteenth centuries often had carving and turnings that were painted black. Some pieces made with less carving and applied turnings were decorated with painted red, blue, yellow, black, and white geometric patterns. Furniture was also given a painted finish that resembled grained wood. These pieces were not painted to fool someone into thinking the piece was an expensive piece of real mahogany. They were grain-painted to be more decorative. Other pieces were painted with fanciful scenes or geometric designs.

A type of painted finish called *Japanning* was used in the eighteenth century on pieces of Queen Anne and Chippendale furniture. Japanning produced a finish that resembled the lacquered finish on some pieces exported to England from China or Japan. The English copied the lacquer using a less expensive and readily available substitute of whiting and opaque varnish. Americans used clear varnish over thick coats of paint. Then birds, houses, trees, and flowers were added to form an allover raised design.

In the early 1800s, when Federal furniture came into fashion, many pieces were made with wood veneer and inlay. Some had painted decorations that looked like small shells or flowers. Others had striping and

Opposite page: New England "fancy chairs" were colorful and easy to move so they were popular as dining room or extra chairs. The seat on this early nineteenth-century painted chair is made of bentwood slats. (Photo: Skinner)

Paint has been used to decorate furniture for centuries. This blanket chest was made in York County, Pennsylvania, about 1800. It has a sponged background and "pinwheel" decorations on the front and sides. (Photo: Conestoga)

HITCHCOCK CHAIRS

Lambert Hitchcock made chair parts in Farmington, Connecticut, from 1818. He specialized in painted furniture. Most items were sold in pieces and assembled by the buyer.

Hitchcock built a factory in 1825. Chairs made between 1825 and 1832 have the signature *L. Hitchcock, Hitchcocks-ville, Conn. Warranted*. In 1832 Arba Alford joined Hitchcock as a partner, and from 1832 until 1843 the signature was *Hitchcock, Alford & Co., Hitchcocks-ville, Conn. Warranted*. In 1843 the Hitchcock Alford partnership dissolved and brothers Arba and Alfred Alford established Alford and Company. They made painted chairs. In 1844 Hitchcock set up a new factory at Unionville, and marked his chairs *Lambert Hitchcock, Unionville, Connecticut*. He died in 1852.

The Hitchcocksville factory stopped making chairs in 1864. It reopened as the Hitchcock Chair Company in 1946 in the town now renamed Riverton. The twentieth-century Hitchcock chairs marked *L. Hitchcock, Hitchcocksville, Conn. Warranted* are also branded with the letters *H. C. Co.*, the reversed *N* and the registered trademark symbol ®.

highlighting. Painting was refined and formal. Some of the best painted pieces from this period were made in Baltimore. Fine Federal furniture had gilded decorations that resembled metal mounts. Some tabletops had painted scenic views that resembled oil paintings. Painted furniture at this time was meant to be showy and obvious. This was also the era of the Hitchcock chair, a less sophisticated painted form, often using stencils, that was inspired by the formal Federal furniture. Thousands of these inexpensive painted "fancy chairs" were made in factories for people with average incomes.

Perhaps the most interesting painted furniture had a grained finish made from several colors of paint. Red and black rosewood graining, orange-red mahogany graining, and colorful painted finishes with combing, swirls, and sponging added to the lighthearted decoration of tables and chests.

Vinegar painting was a special finish made by applying a second coat of paint over a plain color with a piece of leather or putty. Then a top coat of vinegar was added, and the two paints separated slightly to create seaweed-like patterns.

At the end of the nineteenth century, some of the most ornate pieces were trimmed with gilt and paint as well as with carvings, ormolu mounts, and veneers. The incised decoration popular at the time was often highlighted with gold rubbed into the incised lines. Furniture was sometimes ebonized with a special black-paint finish.

Spool Furniture (1815–1900)

From about 1815 to the late Victorian era, *spool furniture* was in style in many rural homes. A lathe was developed to create elaborate turnings, which some say were originally cut to make wooden buttons or spools for thread. Furniture makers realized the turnings would be attractive as parts of chairs, beds, and tables, and this led to the development of spool furniture.

It is easier to make long, straight pieces of spool turnings than to curve the corners. The earliest beds had angled joints, while joints on some of the later ones were curved. About 1850, furniture makers discovered a method of bending the strips of spool turnings.

Bentwood and Michael Thonet (c.1840–Present)

Michael Thonet (pronounced "Tone-it") was a furniture maker in nineteenth-century Vienna. As early as 1830, Thonet was experimenting with different ways of making inexpensive furniture. In 1841 he was granted patents in England, Belgium, and France for new methods of working with wood. The Austrian government asked him to move to Vienna, where he could make furniture for the court. Thonet and one of his five sons established their own business in 1849, and in 1853 they renamed it Thonet Brothers. All five sons were involved in the business, which made special-order pieces. In 1851 they won a first prize at the Crystal Palace Exhibition in London, England. The Thonets opened their first factory to make mass-produced furniture using Michael Thonet's methods and his specially designed machinery in 1856.

Thonet's bentwood furniture was made from prepared beech wood. Poles were boiled in water, bent to the proper shape, and dried in ovens for several days. The finished chairs were shipped in parts and could be screwed together by the storekeeper. The most famous bentwood chair, the Vienna

Opposite page: This Hitchcock chair was made about 1835. It has the stenciled mark "Hitchcock.Alford & Co Hitchcocks-ville. Conn./Warranted" on the back of the seat. (Photo: Isham-Terry House)

Bentwood furniture is, of course, made from bent wood. The technique of curving wood was developed in the 1840s and is still used to make furniture. This classic Thonet rocker, with a caned seat and back, shows off the graceful curves of its wood frame. (Photo: 333 Auction)

Café chair No. 14, was first produced in 1859. More than 50 million of these chairs had been sold by 1910. The first bentwood rocking chair was made in 1860.

Michael Thonet died in 1871, but his sons continued to run the business. Bentwood furniture was so popular that by 1901 more than fifty-two companies were making chairs using the Thonet patents, and hundreds of other furniture factories were producing copies or similar pieces. Bentwood chairs, tables, cribs, benches, hat racks, beds, and other useful objects were made.

Grand Rapids, Michigan, became an important furniture manufacturing city during the Victorian era. Plants equipped with modern machinery made all sorts of Victorian styles in all price ranges. This walnut pedestal with ebonized and gold trim dates from about 1870. It is in what is called the Grand Rapids style.
(Photo: Fontaine's)

Grand Rapids Furniture

The term *Grand Rapids furniture* is sometimes meant as a comment on quality or a description of design, not a reference to a specific style. Furniture companies in Grand Rapids, Michigan, and across the Midwest manufactured mass-produced, machine-made furniture in the last quarter of the nineteenth century, primarily in the Renaissance Revival, Gothic Revival, and Eastlake styles. Grand Rapids furniture ranged from top-quality to the least expensive poorly made pieces. Elaborately carved, custom-made Renaissance Revival and Eastlake designs were reinterpreted for the machine-made products. The carving was flatter, and incised lines were often the main design element. Inlay was rarely used, but large pieces of burled veneer, especially walnut, were added for contrast. Furniture was made from solid walnut, oak, and other woods. The geometric shapes and flat surfaces created the "look" we now call Grand Rapids style.

Furniture makers in the western states made a similar style of furniture, but their version had a painted veneer, not burled wood trim. The western pieces date from the late nineteenth century, and many were made in Utah or California.

Iron and Wire Furniture (1820–1900)

Until the beginning of the nineteenth century, iron was hand wrought, but with the innovations of the Industrial Revolution came the ability to mold or cast iron. Iron furniture soon was introduced for use in the garden. Strapwork wrought iron chairs made in the eighteenth century remained popular into the nineteenth and twentieth centuries. Cast-iron furniture was made in England as early as 1823, but it was the 1851 Crystal Palace Exhibition, which included displays of cast-iron furniture, that created the demand for it. Many benches and chairs were made to resemble branches of trees, ferns, or grapevines. Other furniture was made with geometric patterns, scrolls, and leaves in the Gothic and the Rococo Revival styles. Gardens of the nineteenth century were filled with iron benches, chairs, and tables and matching urns and fountains. There were even iron statues. Companies making ironwork in the United States included Fiske Foundry, J. L. Mott & Co., Hutchinson & Wickersham, Peter Timmes and Sons, and Samuel S. Bent of New York. The most famous British makers were Coalbrookdale Iron Foundry of England, and Walter Macfarlane & Company of Glasgow, Scotland. Some pieces are marked with the name of the foundry.

Iron garden furniture is so stylish and durable, it is popular again. This 46-inch-long Victorian cast-iron bench has a scalloped apron, decorative panels, and even hoof feet. (Photo: New Orleans Auction Galleries)

Wire made of iron and other metals was used in the nineteenth century to make many household goods, from kitchen baskets to clock cases to chandeliers. Most of the wirework pieces seen today were made in France or the United States. Chairs, tables, settees, and plant stands made of wire were popular from about 1875 to the early 1900s. These pieces and other smaller ones were made of steel wire that was twisted and woven. They were lightweight, and the wire could be curved into lacy patterns. The pieces were popular for use in gardens or indoor greenhouses or garden rooms. Marked pieces of wirework are almost unknown.

Rustic Furniture

Black Forest Furniture (c.1880–present)

For many years, collectors were told that the huge carved wooden hall trees held by three-dimensional bears or the all-wooden carved chairs that resembled branches and leaves were made in the Black Forest region of Germany. Research since the 1970s has proved that the carved wooden furniture and many of the famous carved cuckoo clocks were actually made in Switzerland. The carved bear furniture was made by the Trauffer family. They taught at the Brienz carving school and carved the bear furniture at home in the evenings. From the 1880s to the 1950s, three generations of the family manufactured the furniture. Pieces were made from linden or walnut trees. The carved bears were used as arms, legs, or ornaments on chairs, tables, settees, hall stands, blanket chests, and armoires. The furniture was popular with tourists, and many pieces were shipped to the United States. Black Forest furniture was totally out of fashion by the 1960s, but it became popular again in the 1980s. Copies are now being made in Asia, and because the wood is hand-carved, the reproductions can be confusing.

Horn and Antler Furniture (1800–1900)

Horns and antlers were used to create a different type of rustic furniture. The earliest recorded use of antlers for home decoration or furniture dates from the 1400s. Chandeliers were made by artistically joining the horns of elk, reindeer, moose, and other animals with decorative devices such as carved or modeled saints, angels, or dragons. The earliest chairs made from horns may date from the Middle Ages, but they became more common about 1800. Sheraton's 1803 book, *Cabinet Dictionary*, depicts a hunting chair with legs made of antlers. By the 1820s, there were cabinetmakers producing a full line of antler furniture, including sofas, chairs, and tables. The 1851 Crystal Place Exhibition in London included a display by a German firm that made horn desks, candelabra, and full sets of furniture.

Longhorn steers have curved horns in shades of black to light brown. An abundant supply of horns from slaughter houses led to the creation of horn furniture. Horn chairs were popular from the 1880s until Arts and Crafts furniture with straight lines came into fashion about 1900. (Photo: Fontaine's)

The first important maker of horn furniture in the United States was Wenzel Friedrich, who emigrated from Bohemia to Texas in 1853. By 1880 he was making furniture from longhorn steer horns in the Victorian Revival styles. He made not only chairs and tables, but also rockers, ottomans, flower stands, hall stands, and stools. He bought the horns from stockyards and selected the proper size and shape to make the furniture. The horns were boiled, then scraped with a knife, and finally buffed with a cloth. Some pieces had added cutout decorations of horn or inlay. Upholstery was usually made of cowhide or fur. Other people soon made similar furniture, often using fewer horns and sim-

pler upholstery. By the 1890s, longhorns were no longer plentiful, and when styles changed about 1900, straight lines were preferred and horn furniture was out of fashion.

Adirondack Furniture (1850–1925)

Making furniture from tree branches in a natural condition was an idea promoted for country houses during the 1850s. Branches, often with the bark still on them, were joined together by workmen, not cabinetmakers, to make chairs or tables. It was the same type of furniture later made as Boy Scout projects. Vacation homes of the wealthy in the Adirondack area of New York were furnished with this type of rustic furniture, most of it made between 1875 and 1925. Workmen in some areas built pieces of furniture and decorated them with mosaics made from varicolored twigs, but many of these pieces were do-it-yourself projects.

Japonisme (1876–1885)

The Centennial Exposition of 1876 had a tremendous influence on design in America. One of the fair's exhibits featured a fully furnished Japanese house. The new unfamiliar designs inspired designers, artists, and craftsmen.

Chairs that looked like they were made of bamboo had been introduced in Europe by Thomas Chippendale in the eighteenth century and were popular in England during the 1790–1810 period. *Japonisme*, or the influence of Japanese design on European art, was widespread in France after 1853, the year of Commodore Perry's visit to Japan. It soon spread to other countries. The Japanese bamboo furniture at the Centennial Exposition started another rage for imitation bamboo furniture. Hardwoods like maple were turned to resemble bamboo. Actual bamboo pieces were imported. Imitation or real bamboo furniture can date from any time after 1770.

Adirondack or rustic furniture, although made since the 1850s, was not recognized as a distinct style until the 1980s. This rustic armchair has twig mosaic decoration. (Photo: Craftsman Auctions)

Japanese design has influenced European and American decorative arts since the eighteenth century. This drop-front secretary has a lacquered finish with scenes of Japanese people and places. This type of decoration is still being used.

Victorian furniture included other Japanese-inspired styles. Light-colored woods like maple were worked into typical Victorian shapes with just a hint of Japanese influence. English or American tiles with Japanese scenes or flowers were incorporated in furniture designs. Some pieces were more Japanese in appearance and portrayed pagoda-like forms with Asian-type carved latticework.

Colonial Revival or Centennial Furniture (1876–present)

The idea of a colonial kitchen or antique furniture is not new. Copies of earlier pieces of furniture were being made in the 1860s. By the time of the Centennial in 1876, the style was accepted for decorating homes. Colonial-style furniture included copies of any period of furniture from the 1500s to late Sheraton. Many Windsor chairs, Chippendale-style pieces, and William and Mary pieces were made. Reproductions of the Empire-style sofas of the 1840s were made by the 1880s. The reproductions and adaptations of the earlier periods of furniture have now aged over 125 years, and this is adding to the confusion of collectors. It takes a careful study of the methods of construction, the woods used, and the fine points of a particular style to determine which are Revival pieces and which are originals. Collectors are not the only ones facing the problems of identifying originals. Many museums and historical societies are just now discovering that the cabinet they thought was eighteenth-century is nineteenth-century or even newer. At the same time that accurate copies were made, many hybrid styles were produced and called Colonial.

Golden Oak (1880–1920)

Furniture manufacturers named the era of the light-colored oak furniture of 1880 to 1920 the Golden Oak period. This category of furniture includes not only honey-colored oak pieces, but also darker-finished furniture. This was some of the first furniture to be mass-produced in America. Golden Oak was made for use in the office, in the factory, and in the home. All types of furniture were made, ranging from dining room sets and desks to baby furniture. The earliest Golden Oak furniture was made in simplified Victorian styles. Tables had carved pedestals, and chairs had turnings and curved backs with carvings.

During the 1890s a new furniture form was introduced—the china cabinet and desk. This asymmetrical piece had glassed-in shelves on one side with a fall-front desk over drawers on the other side. Above the desk was a mirror. A few bits of applied carving were added. Variations of this asymmetrical design appeared in other dining room or bedroom cabinet pieces.

Golden Oak is the name of a wood finish and a style. This drop-front desk has a shell carving, asymmetrical placement of drawers and doors, and incised decorations typical of the 1890s style. (Photo: DeFina)

The Larkin Soap Company of Buffalo, New York, gave furniture as premiums to customers who purchased enough soap. The Chautauqua furniture line was the company's premium between 1890 and 1905. Desks, chairs, and other Golden Oak furniture pieces were offered. The asymmetrical china cabinet-desk, which was one of the premiums, is still called a Larkin desk.

By the end of the nineteenth century, furniture makers were designing Golden Oak in the Mission style, with straight sides, squared chests of drawers, plain legs, and undecorated surfaces. The furniture was still heavy in weight as well as appearance. With the approach of the 1920s, the appearance of weight diminished until the last Golden Oak pieces looked almost Art Deco.

Golden Oak furniture was made not only of oak, but also of combinations of woods like ash, beech, maple, and hickory.

Art Nouveau (1895–1910)

The French art nouveau movement began to influence American furniture design at the end of the nineteenth century. A few furniture makers decorated their pieces with typical art nouveau patterns, including flowing lines, women's faces and bodies, stylized flowers, and other forms found in nature. S. Karpen and Brothers Furniture Company of Chicago was the best-known art nouveau furniture maker in the United States.

SPECIAL DESIGNS AND MATERIALS

Brass Bed

Brass beds appeared in England in about 1835. They were designed for use on the farm or in a village home, but mahogany was still the only suitable material for an in-town home. The first patented design for an English metal bed was issued in 1849. The idea quickly spread to the United States and the Continent, and English brass bed manufacturers made and exported thousands of beds. The brass bed of the 1850s was in the Renaissance Revival style and was often made with a canopy, hangings, and even cupids that held up the corners. The design of the bed gradually changed. The canopy disappeared, and the decorations became more symmetrical and open. The metal bed offered more air circulation; did not attract woodworms, bedbugs, and ticks; and was supposed to be more hygienic.

Birmingham, England, became the headquarters of the brass bed industry. American manufacturers produced beds, but they could not make them fast enough, so many brass beds still had to be imported.

Several types of brass were used in the beds. The most common was iron tubing that was wrapped with brass sheet metal. There was a seam on the rod where the end of the brass was crimped. A magnet will stick to this type of bed. The brass sheeting is usually so thick it will probably never be polished away.

Some of the best beds were made all of brass. They had no supporting iron core and for structural reasons were made only with straight lines. They are plain in appearance, and no seam can be seen.

The least desirable type of brass bed was made using brass-plated metal. It is not unusual to find one with the plating wearing off. A limited number of beds were made of cylindrical, hollow brass tubing for the main crosspieces and seamed brass tubing for the smaller, decorative parts.

Brass beds were expensive, so manufacturers also made similar beds of iron. These beds were often painted. The iron bed was usually much lighter in weight because the iron rods were smaller than the brass tubing. They were often less than one-quarter inch in diameter. Some iron beds had solid brass ornaments, especially at the corners.

Innovative Chairs

The Victorians were fascinated with machinery, power tools, and the possibility of making something unlike anything ever made before. A flurry of patented chairs appeared during the last quarter of the nineteenth century. Each chair suggests a particular use or special construction idea. One of the best-known makers of these types of chairs was George Hunzinger of New York City, who worked from about 1860 until his death in 1898. He made chairs that looked like they were made from plumbing pipes or with copper-wire upholstery. He also made folding and reclining chairs. Some other chairs that date from the 1875–1900 period are the barber's chair, office chair, platform rocker, tilt-back rocker, adjustable child's chair that became a table, invalid's chair, reading chair, swivel chair, and even the familiar school desk and chair.

Pressed-Back Chair

For some inexplicable reason, the name *pressed-back chair* today refers not only to chairs made with a pressed back, but also, incorrectly, to carved solid-wood chairs that have the same type of designs as the pressed-back chairs.

Furniture manufacturers made these chairs between 1890 and 1910. They were inexpensive, utilitarian wooden chairs that were sold in quantity. Thousands of these chairs in hundreds of varieties were mass-produced in Grand Rapids, Michigan, and other cities. The 1897 Sears, Roebuck and Company catalog pictures pressed-back chairs ranging in price from $2.25 to $12. Rockers,

The simple chair with an adjustable back was designed by Englishman William Morris. The style was adapted to many other chairs. This American mahogany Morris chair was made about 1890 with carved dragon-head armrests. It has a reclining back. (Photo: Charlton Hall)

New materials and new tools made new and unfamiliar designs possible during Victorian times. George Hunzinger created many chairs like this folding X-frame chair with needlework upholstery. He patented several construction methods and designs. (Photo: New Orleans Auction Galleries)

The curved lines of this wicker rocking chair were high style in Victorian times. Wicker chairs were made in styles ranging from Rococo Revival to 1920s Art Deco.
(Photo: Fontaine's)

children's rockers, children's chairs, dining sets, armchairs, desk chairs, and side chairs were manufactured.

Most pieces were made by pressing the wood to create the design. The expensive models were made of solid wood with carved decoration. Oak, walnut, birch, elm, and other hardwoods were used. Seats were upholstered in fabric or were made of wood, cane, or leather.

Rolltop Desk

The standard rolltop desk had a flat top with a tambour front that rolled up into the desk. The earliest examples were made of black walnut. Later ones were made of cherry, mahogany, and eventually oak. Many manufacturers used a combination of woods. The desks were factory-made from about 1875 to the early 1920s. They were used in offices and stores, but not in homes. The rolltop desk with Eastlake decoration and a solid rollback top dates from the 1875–1890 period. It was usually made of walnut or mahogany.

The Victorian rolltop desk made a comeback during the 1970s. It had been a relatively unwanted piece of furniture that sold for under fifty dollars until people began to appreciate the amount of security, space, and convenience that this furniture form offered.

Wicker Furniture

Wicker furniture furnished the homes of ancient Egyptians. Most modern collectors are interested only in pieces made in the 1800s or later.

Some cargoes sent to the United States from China in the nineteenth century were held in place with bundles of rattan. Cyrus Wakefield experimented with rattan and found it suitable for many types of furniture, especially for chair seats. He hired ships to import cane and rattan for furniture makers.

Wicker furniture became popular in America about 1850. The curved lines of the Victorian French Rococo Revival style were easily interpreted with the pliable wicker. Some early furniture was made of bentwood covered with rattan.

There was great interest in wicker furniture during the years just after the Civil War. A combination of materials was used. All types of styles were made, including rococo, classical, Gothic, and many variations of designs. Wicker was ideally suited for porch and garden furniture. It was lightweight and durable. Many wicker pieces were left their natural color or lightly stained. Some wicker pieces were used indoors, and most of those pieces were painted.

The 1876 Centennial Exposition influenced the design of wicker furniture. Chinese wicker furniture was shown, and the hour-glass chair was copied by American furniture makers for several years. Painted wicker furniture made from reeds was seen in many Victorian rooms. There were wicker plant stands, easels, shelves, and tables. Wicker could be shellacked, stained, enameled, or gold-leafed. Chairs were often painted in several colors and draped with fabric. Wicker baby carriages, invalid chairs, wheelchairs, and baby furniture were made. Less expensive wicker was manufactured and sold by Sears, Roebuck & Company and Montgomery Ward.

Windsor Chair—A Style with a Country Heritage

The earliest known Windsor chairs were made in England in the late seventeenth century. The first American Windsors were made in Philadelphia about 1730. American furniture makers developed their own style of Windsor chair, without cabriole legs or splats, and with higher backs and thicker seats. Legs on American Windsor chairs are more splayed than those on English chairs.

Windsor furniture is sometimes called *stick furniture*. A Windsor chair's legs are made by turning a piece of wood on a lathe to form a rounded leg. The legs were inserted into holes in the saddle seat, which was shaped from a two-inch-thick plank of wood. The height of the seat is

Windsor chairs are named for the shape of the back. This chair is a brace back, bow back. Windsors were made from woods chosen for different reasons—to be pliable (the top of the back), easily carved (the seat), or strong (the legs). (Photo: Skinner)

a clue to the age of the chair. Early chairs had seats 18 inches from the floor. Later ones were 16½ to 17 inches high.

Variations on the Windsor chair included arrow back, bow back, comb back, fanback, low back, rod back, sack back, and scroll back chairs. Rocking chairs and writing-arm chairs were first made in America. Right hand–style writing chairs were most common.

Windsor construction was used for chairs for many years, and the style was gradually simplified to the famous captain's chair. Windsor construction was suited to chairs and perhaps benches, but there were only a handful of Windsor tables and no other types of furniture.

Windsor chairs were usually made of several different kinds of wood and then painted. Black, dark green, white, brown, and even yellow were the preferred colors. A chair might have a pine seat, hickory spindles, and maple legs and stretchers. Early chairs were usually painted dark green, but by the late eighteenth century, other colors were also used. The paint covered the different kinds of wood used and also protected the wood from the elements if the furniture was used outdoors.

The Windsor chair with nine spindles is older than a chair with four spindles. Workmen simplified designs and gradually made chairs with fewer and fewer parts. The more spindles on the chair, the older and better the chair. This rule alone can date a Windsor chair. Of course, there are also variations in quality and design. The rule applies only to authentic old chairs.

Wooton Desk

Indianapolis, Indiana, was a center of furniture manufacturing when William S. Wooton came to town in 1870. Wooton set up his own

Bottom and opposite: The most impressive Victorian desk available was the Wooton desk. These are two views of the rare model the Ladies' Secretary, shown at the 1876 Centennial Exhibition in Philadelphia. (Photo: Richard & Eileen Dubrow)

company in Indianapolis to make school, office, and church furniture. In 1874 he patented Wooton's Patent Cabinet Office Secretary, the first of the famous desks. The Wooton desk was made in sections with numerous cubbyholes and drawers. The desk had hinged sides and was made to be closed or even locked at night. It furnished security while the office was cleaned. The desks were very heavy, but they had bracket feet with rollers and could be moved easily.

Four grades of Wooten desks were made: Ordinary, Standard, Extra, and Superior. There were three sizes of each grade, ranging from 4 feet 7½ inches to 5 feet 1½ inches high. They originally retailed from $90 to $750. The desks were made in the Eastlake style, using black walnut with pine, maple, poplar, holly, ebony, Spanish cedar, or satinwood. The hardware was bronze or gold-enameled bronze. The carvings were elaborate.

Company catalogs offered a Ladies' Secretary that was smaller than the others, and there was a Lawyer's Own Desk with a flat top resting on top of two cases that pivoted open. Wooton also made rotary desks with cylinder tops. Other companies made similar types of desks.

The Wooton company went out of business in America in about 1884. The desk was made and sold by both Canadian and English firms after that time.

Ladder-Back Chair

The ladder-back, or slat back, chair can be dated by the number of rungs in the back. The more rungs, the earlier the chair. If the posts holding the rungs were made with turnings, the chair was probably made during the eighteenth century. The workman of the nineteenth century made a simplified version of the eighteenth-century ladder-back chair with fewer parts.

HOW OLD IS GRANDMOTHER'S CHAIR?

There is a rule of thumb for dating family heirlooms. If you know your chair was owned by your grandmother, there is a fairly accurate way to tell the age of the chair. Your grandmother probably got married when she was about 25. Her furniture is about the age of your mother because your grandmother furnished her home and started her family at about the same time. So your grandmother's furniture is about the same age as your mother. There is about a 25-year span for each generation. So take your age and add 25 years for your mother's generation. If you are 55, the chair is at least 80 years old. If it belonged to your great-grandmother, it is at least 105 years old.

But beware. Furniture often picks up a history it doesn't deserve, and it is often thought to be older than it is. The best way to date furniture is to examine its style and construction.

Platform Rocker

The platform rocker was patented and produced in the late 1860s. It was a chair on springs attached to a platform. The chair moved, but the base remained stationary. It was popular because the design kept the rocker from wearing out the carpet.

Rope Bed

Ropes were used to support mattresses until about the first quarter of the nineteenth century, when ropes were replaced by slats. The side rails of all beds had either knobs or holes for the ropes before 1825, while after 1850 almost all of them had slats and no holes or knobs. Many old rope beds have been altered to hold a modern mattress. ⟨∂ₑ

Two strong people and a rope are needed to tighten the ropes that hold the mattress on a rope bed like this nineteenth-century pencil post bed. String the rope through holes in the sides and ends of the bed, and tighten with a rope wrench. A tight rope makes a firm bed so you can "sleep tight." (Photo: Skinner)

Chapter 9

Authenticating Furniture

THE BEST WAY TO JUDGE the age of a piece of furniture is to study how it is constructed. Part of this information is technical, but most of it can be used by any antiques buyer out for a day's shopping spree. This is not meant to verify the age of a museum-quality, eighteenth-century Baltimore piece that might really be a very fine and expensive Victorian copy, but it will help with a medium-priced antique that may or may not be old.

If you plan to buy furniture that costs thousands of dollars, our advice is to find a reliable antiques dealer or auction house that will stand behind the sale. Legitimate dealers will take a piece back if it turns out that it is not what it was represented to be when sold. Mistakes may be made through ignorance, not greed, and most dealers are eager to restore your money and your confidence. The long-established dealer is not the difficulty. The problem is usually the antique that is hurriedly bought at auction, on the Internet, or at a house sale.

THE FURNITURE BUYER'S KIT
The furniture buyer's kit should contain a tape measure or ruler, a magnifying glass, a magnet, and a flashlight. Also helpful are a corsage pin and a knife.

Opposite page: Traditional designs have continued to be made by fine furniture firms. This Queen Anne–style game table from the 1940s is made of hand-carved solid wood. The top opens to form a felt-covered surface for cards.

Top: Wet mops and leaks often left a mark. Look at the bottom of large pieces to be sure they are not water damaged or rotted. Check the lower cupboard doors for wear from kicking the door shut. (Photo: DeFina)

Wood shrinks in only one direction. Antique furniture should not be perfectly round. Look for signs of doctored finish or new cuts that indicate a reshaped leaf. Turn the table upside down and look for anything unusual that might be a repair. (Photo: Sotheby's)

An antiques dealer will usually let you examine the furniture, remove drawers, and even unscrew screws if the piece is expensive. Use the tape measure to check the diameter of any part of a table that appears to be round. This may include the top, the legs, drawer knobs, and pegs. Measure the diameter in several directions. Wood shrinks slightly in only one direction, and a round tabletop should be slightly oval after forty years.

Slide your magnet over the brass hardware. If it clings, the hardware is iron or steel that has been plated, and is not copper or brass. It could be a reproduction. Remove a drawer and check the dovetailing for age (see drawings on page 169); then examine the back of the hardware to see if the screws are old.

The backs of large pieces, such as cupboards and sideboards, were made from wide boards. Check to see whether the boards are wider than usual and of varying widths. The cabinetmaker cut down a tree and used all the boards, and some were wider than others. Measure the thickness of the boards. Seven-eighths of an inch is standard today. Knots might appear in the wood where it does not show, but no good cabinetmaker would ever make furniture from what we now call knotty pine. Knots fall out and leave very undesirable holes after the wood shrinks.

If a raw sawed surface of the wood can be seen with a flashlight, check the saw marks. An old saw left straight marks, while the circular saw, which was used after 1850, left a curved mark. A trained touch or a straightedge rule plus a flashlight will help to check the wood for hand dressing. Early cabinetmakers planed the wood, leaving small grooves that can be felt over the entire surface. Hold a straightedge along the wood and shine a flashlight from behind; the light will show each groove.

Check the inside of drawers, under tables, and other hidden spots for the color of the wood. Wood darkens when exposed to light, so hidden unfinished wood should be lighter.

If there are wormholes in the wood, put the corsage pin into the hole. A worm makes a crooked hole, so the pin will not go far. If it does, beware. Fake wormholes mean fake furniture.

Nails

There is a legend in the world of the antiques novice that a square-headed nail indicates an early piece of furniture. This is only partly true, because square-headed nails are still being made and sold. There are even shops that straighten salvaged square-headed nails to sell to customers who are building authentic reproductions or restoring old homes.

Until the end of the eighteenth century, nails were made by hand by a blacksmith. In the American colonies, the blacksmith took a long, thin, square, iron nail stock, hammered a point, cut the nail length, and pounded the top of the nail to form the rosehead found on handmade nails. This nail leaves a square hole when it is removed from wood.

By the early nineteenth century, nail-cutting machines made nails that still had the hand-hammered rosehead top, but these nails leave a rectangular hole when removed. About 1840, machines produced a uniform flattened nailhead. Machine-made nails were less expensive and soon became standard, but they were more brittle than hand-wrought nails. Hand-wrought nails continued to be made for special uses where strength was important. By the 1880s, the round machine-made wire nail with a circular, stamped head

The search for the truth about the age of a piece of furniture depends on intuition and common sense. It is like learning to tell identical twins apart. With intensive study and experience, collectors develop a sixth sense about furniture. Is the chair worn where a chair should be worn? Are the back legs worn at the back from being dragged on the floor? Are the small finials on a ladder-back chair worn where the chair leaned against the wall? Are the rungs worn from the rubbing of many pairs of shoes? Does the low cupboard door show marks where it was kicked shut by a busy housewife? Is the wood near the brass hardware discolored from years of rubbing and dripped furniture polish? Is the item all one piece or were two dissimilar antiques, such as a table and shelf, married into one strange new piece? Does the finish look old? If an antique has been stored in a barn, it is unlikely it will be in an unblemished condition. Pieces that are purchased from elaborate mansions, however, have often received perfect care.

The hardware that moves the top of a tilt-top table often pulls loose if too much pressure is put on part of the top. Look for signs of new screws, new hardware, or broken joints. This repair lowers the value very little. A new top lowers the value by up to 50 percent. (Photo: Skinner)

∽∾ ✍
HINGES

Carefully examine the difference between the butt hinge made between 1815 and 1840 and the type made after 1840. More metal was used in the early type. Keep in mind, too, that mid-Victorian Canadian hardware was sometimes made like early pieces in the United States.

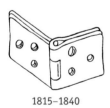

1815–1840

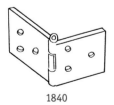

1840

and a sharp, cut point was being produced. This is the same kind of nail we use today.

Screws

The screw is not a recent invention, and screws can appear on an antique of any age. The wood screw was made by hand in the United States and was used by many furniture makers by the early eighteenth century. Because of the design of the screw, it was able to hold hinges and other movable parts in place. Hand-cut screws were used until about 1815, when machine-made screws, which were less expensive and far superior, quickly gained favor.

It is possible to recognize handmade screws by the off-center slot in the head, but there are better methods if the dealer allows you to remove the screw from the furniture. Some dealers will unscrew an inconspicuous screw so you can examine the cuts on the screw shaft or the length of the screw. No two screws will be the same. Machine-cut screws made between 1815 and 1845 had a blunt end, evenly spaced screw threads, and a round, even head. Modern screws may have a pointed end.

When looking at screws and hardware, remember that many were damaged by usage, and screws often fell out and were replaced with later types. This is not an objectionable repair. Finding an old screw helps prove the age of a piece, but a new screw does not disprove age. When a screw is removed and replaced, the hole in the wood is changed slightly. Be wary, therefore, if the dealer removes a new screw from an obviously perfect hole.

Hardware Styles

Look at the hardware on your furniture. If it seems to be original, determine the age from the shape and style. Examples are pictured in books or can be found at antiques shows and auctions, or in museum collections. These are typical forms:

William and Mary drop pull
1690–1720

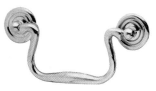

Double swan-neck bail pull
1720–1770

Queen Anne bail pull with pierced backplate
1720–1750

Chippendale bail pull with pierced backplate
1750–1780

Chippendale bail pull with solid backplate
1750–1780

Hepplewhite bail pull with oval backplate
1785–1800

Empire ring pull
1815–1840

Victorian bail handle with pierced backplate
1840–1900

(Photos: Van Dyke Restorers)

Handles and Hardware Styles

It was for the Centennial Exposition of 1876 that hardware was first designed to reflect the decor of a building, or so the story goes. By 1900 catalogs offered hardware in Greek, Roman, Renaissance, Gothic, Louis XIV, rococo, colonial, art nouveau, and other styles. Hardware could be purchased in iron, tin, copper, brass, bronze, silver, and even gold. Knobs were also made in pressed or cut glass, painted porcelain, pottery, or wood. A monogram or emblem could be added to handles that were made to order. Some important manufacturers were Russell and Erwin Manufacturing Company, P. & F. Corbin and Company, Yale & Town Manufacturing Company, Reading Hardware Company, and Sargent & Company.

The style of hardware changed with the style of furniture, and the hardware should match the rest of the piece. It was not unusual for a piece of furniture to have been updated by an owner who added newer-style hardware. Unless the same holes are used, the holes from the original hardware will be plugged, and a quick look should tell you so. The inside or outside surface of a drawer front often shows the old holes. A piece of furniture with its original hardware is best, although it is acceptable to replace hardware with the proper type. Hardware reproductions of all periods or authentic old hardware can be purchased.

Most reproduction hardware is well made and can easily fool the beginner. Check the screws that hold the hardware, and see if they are of the old type. This method is not infallible, because the best reproduction hardware is made the old way—complete with old screw types. Sometimes old hardware has replaced screws that are new.

Dovetailing

There is a rule about dovetailing: the fewer the number of tenons, the older the piece. An early eighteenth-century drawer was joined with one huge dovetail or was pegged together. By 1800 several small dovetails (ranging from three to five) were used on a drawer. Each one was cut out by hand, and the spacing and size of each was uneven. Early Victorian furniture was made with machine-cut dove-

DOORKNOBS

A popular television show of the 1960s featured an eccentric witch who collected doorknobs. She would remove the hardware from a door and leave the home with a problem door and the show with a good joke. But there are also many serious doorknob collectors who search for the brass, bronze, pottery, and glass hardware that was popular during the late nineteenth and early twentieth centuries. They can be found in secondhand shops, at demolished building sites, flea markets, malls, shops, and online sales and auctions.

tailing, often with eight or more small dovetails on a drawer. The dovetails were evenly spaced and symmetrical. Some Victorian dovetailing was made with scallops and pegs, which are an almost positive indication of the piece's late-1800s origin.

Glorification or Its Reverse

In mid-Victorian times, some Queen Anne or early Chippendale furniture was carved and redecorated to make it appear to be the work of a more sophisticated and modern craftsman. The knee of a chair leg or the top of a round-topped table was often recarved to add more interest. Victorians wanted more pattern, and the additional carving increased the piece's appeal to the Victorian homeowner. Sometimes an entire Hepplewhite sideboard was redone with an elaborate veneer and inlay work.

The process of altering furniture by collectors for the past fifty years seems to have been glorification in reverse. Victorian furniture is not primitive enough for the collector of Early American or country furniture. Carvings have been planed from legs, backboards removed from washstands to produce cupboards, and paint stripped or veneer soaked from early twentieth-century pine pieces. Spotting one of these simplified antiques requires a thorough knowledge of the wood, hardware, and furniture style of a particular period. Small details can disclose the secrets of a reworked piece.

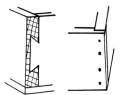

DOVETAILING

One dovetail (left) or several pegs (right) joined early eighteenth-century drawers.

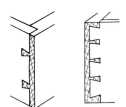

Left: typical dovetailing of the 1725–1800 period

Right: early nineteenth-century dovetailing, sometimes found as late as 1890

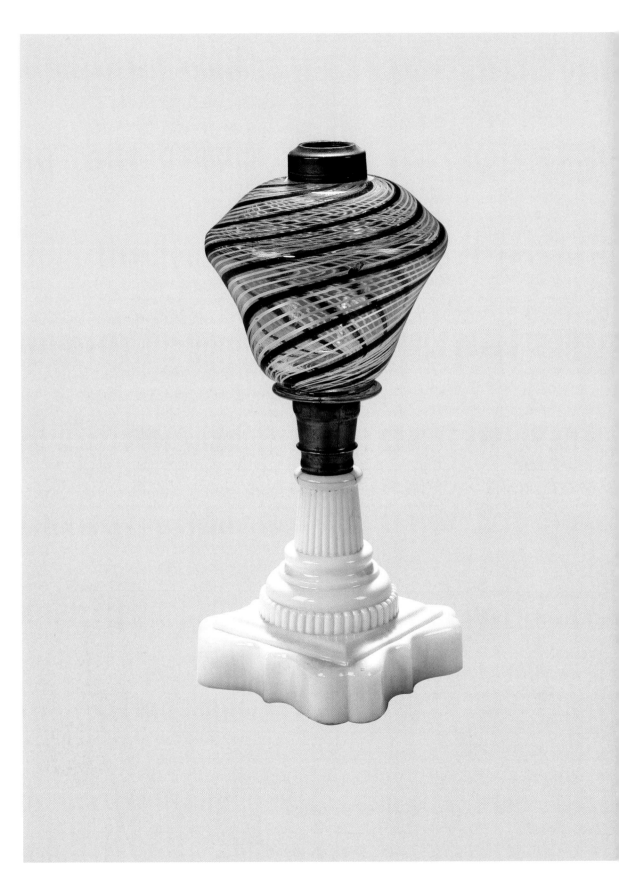

Chapter 10

Lighting Devices

LAMPS OF EVERY TYPE—from early oil-burning Betty and Phoebe lamps, elaborate china oil lamps, candle-burning fairy lamps, art nouveau electric lamps with leaded glass shades, to recent electric lamps with glass or beaded shades—interest the thousands of lamp collectors. A perfectly sane person may have two hundred oil lamps displayed on a shelf in the living room because the collector knows and appreciates old lighting devices. But a few old lamps are usually enough for one home. Any old lamp (even an early light bulb) is of interest to either a collector or a decorator. Antique lamps can be found in homes that are modern in every other detail. The clue to the worth of old lamps is simple. If it looks different, it is valuable.

EARLY LIGHTING DEVICES

The easiest way to date a lamp is to find out which type of fuel it used. Animal fats, vegetable fats, whale oil, kerosene, electricity, and other types of fuel have successfully provided light.

Candlewood

The first lighting devices in America were torches, just long pieces of wood that were lit at one end. Splint lights were fitted with wood

Opposite page: Grease, oils, mixtures of turpentine and alcohol, and other fuels lit the nineteenth-century home. A burner was added to this free-blown glass fluid lamp made in Sandwich, Massachusetts, about 1875. The burner determined what fuel was used. (Photo: Skinner)

slivers that were from eight to ten inches in length. Pine was the wood most often burned for light in the New World, but several other types of resinous trees and bushes were used for candlewood. The term was also used to describe the wood slivers themselves. The pitch in the wood burned brightly, but the tarlike residue dropped to the floor in a sticky mess.

Holders for candlewood are very desirable. Early stands were made of wood or wrought iron. This type of stand also held rush-lights (see page 173). It is easy to tell one of these stands from a candlestand. The holder for a candle had to be either a rounded cup-like holder or a spike to impale the candle. Holders for rushes or splints have clips, clamps, or metal pieces that grip the candle-wood.

Grease Lamps

Grease lamps were the next type of lamp used by the pioneers. The Betty lamp was the first of these lamps. The first governor of the Plymouth Colony is said to have bought an iron Betty lamp in Holland to bring to America. The Betty lamp was a shallow dish that was oval, round, or triangular. The dish ranged from two to three inches in diameter and was made from one of various types of metal, such as pewter, iron, brass, or silver. Each lamp was fitted with a "nose" or spout, which protruded one to two inches on one side of the dish.

A Betty lamp's bowl was filled with tal-low or grease. A wick made from a twisted rag or rushes was placed in the grease and pulled through the nose until a short end was visible. The end was lighted. A handle or chain was sometimes added so the Betty lamp could be hung on the back of a chair. The name *Betty* came either from the word *betyng,* an oil used in the lamp, or from *besser,* the German word for "better."

The Phoebe lamp was developed next. This new style of lamp was a Betty lamp with a cup beneath the wick to catch the oil drip-pings. Most of these early lamps were made with a spike and chain so the lamp could be stuck anywhere on a wooden wall. The Betty

This brass Betty lamp has a hinged lid that covers the grease and holds the wick in place. It also has a pick that was used to raise the wick when it was to be lit.
(Photo: Hesse)

LIGHTING FUEL DATES

Candlewood/pine splint: Colonial America

Grease: Colonial America

Candles: Colonial America

Whale oil: 1800–1840

Argand: 1780s–mid-1800s

Lard oil: 1840–1860

Turpentine (camphene): 1820s

Turpentine and alcohol (burning fluid): 1840–1860

Gas (coal gas): early 1800s–early 20th century; popular 1850–1879

Kerosene: 1860–present

Electricity: 1879–present

or Phoebe lamp occasionally was placed on a stand. These lamps were used in America from the time of the Pilgrims until the Civil War.

Rushlights

The rushlight is another early lighting device that used a flame. Rushlights were made from the pith of cat-o'-nine-tails and other reeds that were peeled, dried, and then soaked in fat or grease. The fatted rush was held at an angle in the tweezer-like end of the rushlight holder. The rushlight burned with a clear, steady flame and was odorless and smokeless and did not drip.

Early European lamps are often more elaborate than American examples. This brass lucerna has three wicks, a candle snuffer, and a wick pick. (Photo: Hesse)

Candles

Candles were first used in Roman times, and they were in use in Europe by about the eleventh century. These ancient candles were similar to the ones we use today. Candles were scarce in the colonies because there wasn't much tallow available. Beeswax and bayberry, which were both sources of candle wax, were found in small amounts. Animal fat tallow (usually beef) and whale spermaceti candles were made after 1750. Spermaceti candles, made from wax from the heads of sperm whales, were the finest because they gave more light than a tallow candle. The term *candlepower* originally described a measure of the light produced by a pure spermaceti candle weighing one sixth of a pound.

Candlesticks

A candlestick is any device that holds a candle. The shape of a candlestick can be an indication of its age. The earliest candlesticks were made from solid cast brass or wrought iron. The spike, or pricket, holder for candles was used in Europe beginning in the fifth century. This candleholder impaled the candle on the sharp spike. The obvious advantage of this design is that any size candle will fit the fixture. It is seldom found on American candleholders and was out of style by the middle of the nineteenth century.

Left: Glass candlesticks were very popular in the mid-nineteenth century. This pressed glass candlestick was made by the Boston & Sandwich Glass Company, Sandwich, Massachusetts. (Photo: Green Valley)

Top: Chambersticks are usually not this elaborate. This brass candleholder with a handle also has a gimbal that kept the candle level. Lamps of this type were used on ships. (Photo: Hesse)

Right: Lusters were made of metal, glass, or porcelain with glass prisms. This pair of late nineteenth-century Bohemian glass lusters was made to be displayed on a fireplace mantel. (Photo: Jackson's)

The hollow-stem candlestick with a sliding knob that could raise the candle was used about 1710. Sheet-iron candlesticks were used in the early 1800s. Most spring candlesticks were used during the middle of the nineteenth century. The candle was pushed down the tube holder and held against a spring. The spring forced the candle up as the candle burned.

Silver and brass candlesticks changed in shape from one decade to the next. (For more details, see Chapter 12, Silver.)

Luster

There are several dictionary meanings for the word *luster* (sometimes spelled *lustre*), but to a lamp collector it is an elaborate candlestick, probably with arms, that is decorated with hanging glass prisms. Cut glass prisms and drops probably were first made in England and Ireland. Some of the lusters that were popular during the first half of the nineteenth century were made by New England glassmakers, but the majority were made in Europe. A luster set is a large candleholder with several branches in the center and two single candleholders. They were displayed on the mantel. The candelabra was made of cast metal, usually brass, or French gilt or marble. Cast metal animals and other figures often decorated the base.

Argand Lamps

By the end of the eighteenth century there were many inexpensive fuels that gave a bright light when burned in lamps. Some mixtures combined turpentine with alcohol and were highly explosive. Several new types of lamps were made to overcome the danger of explosion.

Aimé Argand, a Swiss, invented and patented his lamp in 1782. It burned any fluid oil—whale oil, lard oil, and even camphene. Its hollow wick permitted more oxygen to reach the flame, so it gave a brighter light. After the hollow wick was developed, a glass chimney to protect the flame from a draft was introduced.

By 1840 a burner was designed with a tall, tapered wick tube that was held above the fluid. The tube had a cap so it could be covered when not in use and the fluid could not evaporate or release bad odors.

The Argand lamp, invented in 1782, can be identified by the tall, hollow wick tube. These English double-arm Argand lamps are 28 inches high. (Photo: New Orleans Auction Galleries)

Astral Lamps

Astral lamps, developed in the early nineteenth century, held oil in a shallow ring reservoir below the burner. These lamps were an improvement on the Argand lamp because they burned more evenly and the oil reservoir did not cast a shadow.

Whale Oil Lamps

Whale oil was an important fuel for lamps during the nineteenth century. It was used in homes, for street lighting, in lighthouse beacons, and even for locomotive headlights. The demand for whale oil created the giant whaling industry in America. By the 1860s, the industry was in decline because of competition from petroleum, depletion of the supply of whales, and destruction of much of New England's whaling fleet in Civil War battles.

The common whale oil lamp was developed after the invention of the flat wick burner in 1783. That patent, plus another for an upright wick tube, made the development of the closed reservoir for fuel possible. Whale oil lamps had a closed reservoir and a vertical wick tube. Whale oil is heavy, so the tube had to be inserted far into the reservoir, with a short tube extending above the lamp. If you find a whale oil lamp with a round tin wick tube inserted through a

Left: The whale oil burner could be used in an attractive glass or metal fuel reservoir. This pressed glass lamp in Elongated Loop pattern was made about 1850. (Photo: Skinner)

The Boston & Sandwich Company made many types of glass lamps. This is a fluid lamp that burned camphene or turpentine. (Photo: Green Valley)

Right: Gone with the Wind lamps are often decorated with matching shades and bases. This lamp with painted camels and palm trees may also be called a banquet lamp. (Photo: Fontaine's)

A miniature lamp like this pressed glass kerosene lamp with a handle was made to be carried around the house. This blue lamp was made after 1870.

cork and capped with a tin disk marked *patent,* the lamp dates from about 1810. If the burner of the whale oil lamp was screwed into a metal collar on the lamp with a threaded screw, the lamp dates from after 1830.

Turpentine and Alcohol Lamps

Whale oil became more expensive in the 1840s and people turned to a mixture of alcohol and turpentine known as burning fluid to light their lamps. This fuel was cheap but dangerous, and it was replaced by kerosene as the fuel of choice in the 1860s.

Kerosene Lamps

Kerosene, also called coal oil, was the best of the oils used for light. About 1850, Samuel M. Kier of Pittsburgh made lamps that burned kerosene he distilled from oil that oozed out of the earth and puddled on the ground. When Colonel Edwin L. Drake struck oil in Pennsylvania in 1859, the first economical source of kerosene was discovered. Earlier oil lamps immediately became obsolete. At first, whale oil burners were used with the kerosene, but by 1860 a solid round wick was used. A gadget that turned the wick up and a glass chimney were added later.

Many lighting devices are collected because of their unusual mechanism or age. The *Gone with the Wind* lamp is the most familiar to collectors. The shape and decoration of the font and the shade appeal to the buyer of this lamp. The *Gone with the Wind* lamp appeared in and was named for the famous movie about the Civil War, although it was not used until several years after the war. The lamps were originally called banquet lamps. Millions of them were made in the 1870s and after. The complete lamp has a glass shade with a metal, glass, or porcelain kerosene reservoir and stand. All the lamps had glass chimneys.

Any kerosene lamp with a handle was made after 1870. The handle made it safer to carry the lamp.

Chandeliers

Early taverns and large living rooms of many early American homes had a center light fixture that hung from the ceiling. Smaller rooms, such as the bedrooms or kitchen, did not have a center light.

The word *chandelier* originally described a branched fixture that held candles. A pricket candleholder was often used. Chandeliers were not a convenient source of light. The candles had to be lit with a taper on a long pole, and the candle wax dripped onto the floor or the heads of people seated below.

Early American chandeliers were made locally of tinware or wood. Some wealthy homes had factory-made brass chandeliers. It is believed that the earliest English-made chandelier was produced about 1675 for a church. Wealthy Americans had Dutch- or English-made chandeliers.

The brass chandeliers of Holland and England can sometimes be identified by their method of construction and other small details. Doves were often used as finials on London-made lights, while Dutch chandeliers were heavier and often had eagle-shaped finials.

The large center chandelier hung with many crystal prisms was used in the nineteenth-century homes of the well-to-do. It takes an expert to tell the old from the new, and the very fine from the good. The early prism-shaped drops had four, six, or eight sides. By the late nineteenth century, the drops had three sides. The cost of labor made the many-sided prism too expensive for most nineteenth-century homeowners. Collectors can tell a prism's age from the design cut into the glass. The earliest prisms had small star cuttings. Long, finer-shaped notches were made later. By the mid-1800s prisms ended with an arrow or a heavy round ball. Copies of many of the early styles of prisms are being made, so count the sides and watch the design. Best of all, to be sure it is old, know your source.

A chandelier is a large light fixture made to hang from the ceiling. Multiple candles or lamps were held by the frame so the room could be brightly lit. Glass prisms reflected the light to make it brighter. (Photo: New Orleans Auction Galleries)

Tiffany Lamps and Others with Glass Shades

Louis Comfort Tiffany was a glassmaker of great renown who made lamps in the United States from about 1891 to 1928. Collectors still treasure his glass and lamps. (See Chapter 6.)

Lamps made by Tiffany usually had leaded glass shades and green bronze bases. To be sure you have a Tiffany lamp, you should find the words *Tiffany Studios* on the metal base. The glass shades were also marked *L. C. Tiffany,* or with the letters *L.C.T.* According to the company's records, all lamps were marked.

Other companies made lamps that were similar to the Tiffany lamps. Handel lamps are probably the best known. Philip Handel worked in Meriden, Connecticut, about 1885, and in New York City about 1900. His firm made many types of art glass and lamp shades. After 1903 he made gas and electric lamps. Handel made lamps with leaded glass shades and lamps fitted with glass shades with metal filigree overlay. Many lamps had reverse-painted glass shades that displayed a picture through the shade when the light was turned on. Handel worked until the 1930s. Other important makers of lamps with glass shades include Pairpoint (New Bedford, Massachusetts, c.1880–present) and Bradley & Hubbard (Meriden, Connecticut, c.1854–1940).

MORE LAMPS

Bouillotte Lamp

Many eighteenth-century French gamblers played *bouillotte,* a card game similar to poker. A special lamp was used at the gaming table. It held two or three candles in a brass or bronze doré frame. The lamp was fitted with a metal shade that was usually painted dark green and was topped with a metal finial. The height of the candle-holders and the shade could be changed with a screw key. Several modern American versions of this lamp are available.

Fairy Lamp

A small, squat candle in a paper covering with a plaster base was developed and patented by the Clarke Company of England. This one- or two-wick Fairy light was a great lighting improvement and

Opposite page: A near-record $1,872,500 was bid for this Tiffany Peacock centerpiece lamp made of leaded glass and bronze. The base holds six Tiffany glass bowls. (Photo: Phillips)

was sold worldwide in the 1880s. Fairy lamps with glass-domed tops were made to hold these candles. The base of the lamp that held the candle was made of glass, china, or metal. Clarke marked some of his candles *Burglar's Horror.*

Peg Lamp

A lamp fitted with a small bottom knob that could fit into the top of a candlestick was called a peg lamp. The lamp gave better light because it stood at a greater height.

Sconce

A sconce is a candle or lamp holder with a reflector that is attached to the wall. Sconces were especially practical early lighting devices because the reflectors increased the amount of light cast.

Shoemaker's Lamp

The shoemaker's or lacemaker's lamp is an ingenious device that uses a candle and a globe of water. The light from a single candle is not very bright, so the worker who required more light placed a candle in the lamp where the light was magnified by the water. These lamps were often made with several globes of water surrounding one candle.

Manufacturers of Decorative Lighting Fixtures

Manufacturer and Location	Dates of Manufacture	Comments
Boston & Sandwich Glass Works Sandwich, Massachusetts	1825–1888	Glass lamps
Bradley & Hubbard Manufacturing Company Meriden, Connecticut	1875–c.1940	Pierced-metal, bent-glass, and blown-glass piano and banquet lamps
Consolidated Lamp and Glass Company Coraopolis, Pennsylvania	1894–1967	Glass lamps
Faries Manufacturing Co. Decatur, Illinois	1880–1930s	Verdelite line, similar to Emeralite
Fostoria Glass Specialties Co. Fostoria, Ohio, and Moundsville, West Virginia	1887–1917	Art glass shades
Fulper Pottery Company Flemington, New Jersey	1858–1929	Pottery, lamps
Giannini & Hilgart Chicago, Illinois	1899–present	Leaded-glass shades, windows, mosaics
L. Grosse Art Glass Works Pittsburgh, Pennsylvania	c.1892	Stained-glass windows and ornamental panels
Handel Lamp Company Meriden, Connecticut	1885–1941	Painted, chipped-ice, reverse painted, leaded, and metal-framed glass shades; metal bases
MacBeth-Evans Glass Co. Pittsburgh, Pennsylvania	1895–1937	Lamp chimneys, shades, globes
Edward Miller & Company (The Miller Company) Meriden, Connecticut	c.1866–present	Oil lamps
Pairpoint Manufacturing Company (Still working as Pairpoint Glassworks) New Bedford, Massachusetts	1880–c.1937	Pressed, cut, Puffy (blown-out glass), and decorated shades; metal lamp bases
Pittsburgh Lamp, Brass, & Glass Co. Pittsburgh, Pennsylvania	1901–1926	Glass oil lamps, painted glass shades
Rochester Lamp Company New York, New York	1884–c.1905	The "Rochester lamp," an oil lamp designed to burn safely and cleanly
Roycroft East Aurora, New York	c.1895–1938	Mission-style, hand-wrought copper shades and bases; metal and wood bases with glass or fabric shades
Suess Ornamental Glass Company (Max Suess) Chicago, Illinois	c.1886–1910	Leaded-glass shades
Tiffany Studios Corona, New York	1878–1928	Art glass and leaded-glass lamps and shades; metal lamp bases
Vineland Flint Glass Company Vineland, New Jersey	1897–1931	Art glass shades
R. Williamson & Company Chicago, Illinois	1882–1929	Leaded-glass shades

Chapter 11

Clocks and Timepieces

DESIGNING A CLOCK has always been a challenge. A seventeenth-, eighteenth-, or early nineteenth-century clock had a swinging pendulum. The clock's case had to be large enough to allow the pendulum to swing. The nineteenth century was a period of invention and new technology. Totally new clock mechanisms were invented, so new shapes for clock cases developed. Eli Terry of Plymouth, Connecticut, patented a small works for a clock in 1816. Smaller clocks could sit on a shelf or a fireplace mantel instead of standing on the floor or hanging on a wall. By 1840 clock designers discovered how to use coiled springs instead of weights to drive the works. Clocks with coil works were even shorter in height.

Time is of interest to everyone, and clocks, watches, sundials, and other timepieces fascinate many collectors. Even the amateur who is interested only in decorating a house needs a clock somewhere, and an antique clock is often the choice.

There is a simple rule for evaluating clocks: if a clock is in working order, attractive, or unusual, it is a desirable clock. If it has unusual features or chimes, it has added value. A collector's clock should also have age, excellent condition, rarity, and probably a label.

Opposite page: Eli Terry made this thirty-hour pillar-and-scroll clock in Plymouth, Connecticut, about 1817. It has a mahogany case with inlaid birch panels, a painted wooden dial, wooden works, and the original paper label.
(Photo: Cottone)

There are hundreds of different types of American, English, and European clocks, and most clocks made before 1975 are valuable. To decide if your clock is a collector's gem will require study on the Internet or at the library in any of the many books that list clockmakers and clock types. If an important maker's name appears on an American clock, it will be listed in a book or on a Web site, and a complete history of the clock factory can be found.

THE TALL CASE OR GRANDFATHER CLOCK

From 1680 to about 1840, the floor clock known as a grandfather clock was popular in America. It was originally called a tall case clock, and much of the literature lists these clocks only under that name. The clock case could be as tall as nine feet. The name *grandfather clock* was used as early as 1835, but it became popular about 1875 because of the song "My Grandfather's Clock."

Several clues will date a tall case clock. The earliest had square or round dials. The arched dial was designed about 1715. At first the name of the maker was inscribed on the semicircle or arch. By 1720 moving figures that pictured ships, Father Time, animals, or faces were added. The first clocks to show the various phases of the moon were made about 1720. The month, day, and year were shown on some clock faces. Clock dials were made of brass with silver decorations until about 1770. Numbers representing the hours were engraved on the brass dial between 1770 and 1800. The name of the maker and designs were often added to the engraving on the face. Painted dials and white enamel dials were not used until 1790.

Clock faces made of printed paper that could be glued to an iron or wooden panel were used in the early nineteenth century on the least expensive clocks, those with wooden works. Better clocks were made with metal works.

WALL CLOCKS

Banjo Clocks

The banjo clock, first made by Simon Willard in 1802, is the best known of the hundreds of American clock styles that were made to hang on a wall. The name comes from the shape of the clock. Many

This eight-day Aaron Willard Jr. banjo clock was made in Boston about 1820. It has a mahogany case and painted-glass view of a chariot with Aurora, goddess of the dawn.
(Photo: Cottone)

Right: Octagon clocks were popular as schoolroom clocks for many years. This 1924 model was made by the Japanese company Seikosha. Later the company made Seiko watches.

other makers followed Willard's idea, and hundreds of banjo clocks were produced by New England makers. But beware, there has been wholesale faking of Willard banjo clocks. His name has been added to many nineteenth-century clocks made by other makers. Brass eagles or doves were popular decorations on wall clocks made after 1812, and they, too, have been copied.

In time the banjo clock design became more elaborate, and by the mid-nineteenth century the girandole clock case came into fashion. Influenced by the French style of the time, the fancy girandole clock was shaped like the banjo clock but was gilded and had gilt beads or balls surrounding the clock face and the base. Sometimes acanthus leaves or a spread eagle decorated the clock.

Octagon Drop or Schoolhouse Clocks

The octagon-shaped schoolhouse clock was a popular style of wall clock used in offices, homes, and schools from about 1885 until the 1930s. Most of the clock cases were made of golden oak, rosewood, walnut, mahogany, or pressed oak. Some clocks were made of pine, cherry, or other wood. The drop below the face of the clock was either four- or five-sided. The clockworks were eight-day, time only, time and strike, or time and calendar.

Excellent reproductions of many of these clocks made since the 1970s have been imported from Asia, and it is virtually impossible to tell the old from the new unless you are an expert.

MANTEL CLOCKS

A surprisingly large number of styles of mantel or shelf clocks were manufactured from about 1810 to 1860. At first these clocks were made with small, upright, rectangular wooden cases, often with decorated glass doors. Small turrets or steeples were sometimes added to the edges. Many new shapes and materials were developed about 1840 because of the introduction of the coil- or spring-driven clock. Iron, papier-mâché, white metal, or wood were used for cases. Pillars, scrolls, Gothic arches, dancing ladies, flowers, and a myriad of imaginative sculptured or painted decorations appeared at that time.

Marble Mantel Clocks

In the 1860s Victorian design was in fashion in the United States. At that time, expensive European clocks were made of marble and bronze. American makers made less expensive versions of iron or wood painted to look like marble. White metal was coated to look like bronze. Cast-iron handles, feet, and trim were painted to look like brass. The designs were similar but the quality varied. Incised lines, which were often the main decoration, were rubbed with gold or gilt. This type of clock kept accurate time with an eight-day movement. Some even had alarms or bells. Rectangular marble mantel clocks remained fashionable until about 1920.

Mantel clocks came in many shapes. This Acorn clock with rosewood veneer was made about 1845 by the Forestville Manufacturing Company of Bristol, Connecticut. (Photo: Skinner)

Walnut and Oak Clocks

Elaborately cased clocks were offered in catalogs and stores as *black walnut* clocks or *embossed oak* clocks. The clock cases were decorated with curves, scrolls, lines, finials, pillars, and other types of ornamentation. The more elaborate the clock, the better it sold. Walnut clocks, sometimes called *walnuts,* were popular from the late 1870s through 1900. Carved and applied wooden pieces were used on the walnut cases. Decorated glass doors were often added.

Left: The name D. Wood is painted on the face of this eight-day shelf timepiece made in Newburyport. Massachusetts. The 29-inch-high case is made of pine.

Oak clocks—called *oaks*—were in demand from the 1880s until about 1905. They were made by applying the same method used to make pressed oak chairs. Steam pressure and a mold embossed the wood. Clocks with embossed cases had decorations that were impossible to produce by any other means. One unusual type even pictured prominent men of the day.

OTHER SPECIALTY CLOCKS

The Egyptian Revival style became popular at the end of the nineteenth century. Sphinx heads and mummy cases became fashionable decorations for some mantel clocks. Often the clock had matching obelisks that were displayed on each side.

By 1900 the tambour, a simple, round-faced mantel clock with an elongated curved wooden case, appeared.

Alarm Clock

Using a clock to wake you up is not a new idea. Some early alarm clocks even set off gunpowder charges. The wind-up alarm with a bell was made in quantity from about 1880. The most popular shape by 1900 was a round-faced clock set on small feet and topped by a large half-sphere that served as the bell. Later models were made with the bell hidden inside the clock case. Some of the more fanciful examples of early alarm clocks were shaped like trains or had moving figures waving their arms or legs with each tick.

Animated Clock

Any clock with a moving part (in addition to the hands) on the clock face or case is considered *animated*. Clocks with animated dials were made as early as the seventeenth century. A tall case clock might have a ship that rocked or a moon that moved at the top of the clock face. Animated shelf clocks first appeared about 1880 and were made in the United States, England, France, and Germany. The demand for animated clocks has continued, and new designs are available each year. Many animated clocks were made as part of a sales promotion, so the name of the product, not the name of the clock manufacturer, was used. Dial faces may picture a lady strumming a mandolin, the turning of a windmill, an organ-grinder turning a crank while a bear dances, or comic figures with eyes that roll.

Calendar Clock

The Ithaca Calendar Clock Company of Ithaca, New York, dominated the United States calendar clock business from 1865 until about 1914, when that type of clock lost favor. The clock told not only the time, but also the date. Some calendar clocks had to be adjusted by hand when the month had fewer than thirty-one days, while others were made to be accurate for as long as four hundred years. The calendar clock was popular in America, but it was of little interest in Europe. The other companies, all from Connecticut, that made most of the calendar clocks included the Waterbury Clock Company of Waterbury, the Seth Thomas Clock Company of Plymouth, E. Ingraham and Company of Bristol, E. N. Welch Manufacturing Company of Forestville, and the New Haven Clock Company of New Haven.

Cuckoo Clock

The cuckoo clock dates from about 1730, when the pendulum striking mechanism and the cuckoo idea were developed in Switzerland and Bavaria. Cuckoo clocks were never popular with American manufacturers, although some American families liked these novelties. Cuckoo clocks are still popular.

Electric Clock

Battery-powered electric clocks became available in quantity in the United States during the 1870s. Alarm clocks, figural clocks, mantel clocks, and many other types were made to accommodate the new type of works. It was not until a reliable power supply was available in most homes, around 1930, that the electric clock was made to plug into a wall.

Regulator Clock

During the eighteenth century, clockmakers refined the construction of pendulums so clocks could keep accurate time. By the next century, high-quality tall case clocks stripped of striking attachments and other nonessentials were being marketed as regulators. These clocks sold especially well to observatories, men's clubs, and clockmakers, who used them to set other timepieces. By the late 1800s, clockmakers felt free to label some wall and shelf clocks *regulators*, although many were not particularly accurate.

The Ithaca Calendar Clock Company made this double dial calendar clock about 1870. The extra dial has a day and a month cylinder on the face and numbers telling the date around the edge.
(Photo: Cottone)

This cherry-cased clock is an Ansonia Regulator clock, model number 18. The 88-inch-high wall clock with a lyre-shaped pendulum was made about 1895.

Wag-on-the-Wall Clock

The wag-on-the-wall clock was popular in Europe during the mid-1800s. These clocks were sold with a dial movement, weight, and pendulum, but they did not include a case. The wag-on-the-wall clock had a hood at the top to protect the works from dirt. Thrifty people often bought the wag-on-the-wall clock and then cased it at home at a later date.

Other Novelty Clocks

The idea of putting a clock into a case shaped like a person seems to have been an 1870 inspiration. Cases were made to resemble both men and women. The clock was placed in the stomach of the figure. Some of these clocks had animated features with eyes designed to roll back and forth with each tick of the clock. Clocks of this type are known as *blinking-eye* clocks. Most of them were made of black cast iron and were manufactured by either Chauncey Jerome, who worked in many cities in Connecticut, or Bradley and Hubbard of Meriden, Connecticut. The idea has survived into the twenty-first century. Modern examples include Walt Disney figures with rolling eyes and a clock set in the stomach.

Another unusual American clock was the *bobbing-doll* clock, which was made about 1886. A tiny doll on a swing was suspended from a spring that moved up and down as the clock ticked. A similar French clock had a cherub swinging under an alabaster clock case.

Other types of fantasy clocks included clocks with pendulums topped by figures of women swinging back and forth, glass clocks with no obvious mechanism, skeleton clocks, and water clocks. Clocks were also made to look like sunflowers or animals. The tall, thin Hickory Dickory Dock clock had a mouse that ran up and down the clock to indicate the time. Clocks run by unusual power sources or clocks with unique casings are all eagerly collected. Rarity is important to the clock collector, if not to the homeowner who just wants to know the time.

~~~
To be valuable to a collector, a clock should work and have all its original parts in good condition, including the glass. If you buy a refinished or repaired clock, be sure you know what pieces are not original. It is very important for a clock to have its original works. Clocks that have been electrified are worth very little.
~~~

If you are looking for information about a clockmaker, also look in listings of American silversmiths. Silversmiths were also jewelers, clockmakers, or watchmakers, and some clues about the clock's date and city of origin may be found.

A clock is most valuable if it includes its original label or has the maker's name on it. Any working clock by a famous maker or in an unusual shape that is more than fifty years old is valuable. Eli Terry, Chauncey Jerome, Simon Willard, and Seth Thomas are important names in the American clock industry. Each man made thousands of clocks, but they are not all worth the same amount. Learn to identify the best clocks by each maker.

POCKET WATCHES

Unusual antique pocket watches are the most desirable. Watches with moving figures on the dial, watches that play music or have alarms that ring, or watches with elaborate gold cases have great value to collectors and historians and can be worth thousands of dollars. Any early watch signed by an American maker before he had a large factory or any Hamilton, Elgin, or Waltham watch numbered below one thousand is valuable (if it works or can be made to run).

A valued part of a watch can be the old watch paper sometimes found inside the back of the timepiece. If you find an antique watch, don't discard that round piece of paper inside the watchcase! The paper was an ad for the clockmaker or repairman who worked on the watch. The papers were engraved, printed, lithographed, or handwritten. Some collectors search for old watch papers. If the original key used to wind the watch is available, it, too, adds value.

SUNDIALS

The sundial has been in existence since the beginning of measured time. Pocket sundials have been recorded since the thirteenth century. The pocket sundial, used by travelers, was set with the aid of a compass. The permanent sundial is harder to use. The sundial must be set on April 15, June 15, September 1, or December 24, because on those dates your watch will agree with the time on the sundial. The sundial will vary as much as sixteen minutes from the actual time on all other days.

The well-dressed Victorian gentleman had a pocket watch on a gold chain with a fob or watch key. This gold Waltham hunting case watch has a white enamel dial. A foliage pattern is engraved on the case. (Photo: Antiquorum)

Chapter 12

SILVER

ஃ◯ WE HAVE COME a long way from eating with our hands to
using the variety of silver flatware and serving pieces popular in the
late nineteenth century. The fork, knife, and spoon were the earliest forms of silverware, but as time went on all sorts of equipment
for serving, heating, and cooking drinks and food were made.

HISTORY OF SILVER IN AMERICA, 1640–1900

The history of silver in America began in Boston, Massachusetts,
with Richard Sanderson (1608–1693) and John Hull (1624–
1683). Sanderson trained as a silversmith in England and
arrived in the colonies in 1638. Hull was trained by his
half-brother, Richard Storer. Hull and Sanderson
worked together and made the earliest American silver
pieces known to exist. The first American-born silversmith was Jeremiah Dummer, who was born in 1645.

John Hull became famous when he was chosen to
start the mint in Boston. England had forbidden the
colonists to mint their own money, but in 1652 the
general court of Massachusetts ordered the first silver
money to be minted for local trading. Hull designed
and made the now famous pine tree shilling.

*Opposite page: Silver
has been a sign of
wealth in America
since the 1600s. This
Victorian napkin ring
on a stand with a
pepper shaker, salt
cellar, and butter
plate piece was made
by Wilcox Silver Plate
Company of Meriden,
Connecticut.* (Photo:
M. S. Rau)

*American colonial
silversmiths made
pieces with simple lines
and little decoration.
This castor was made
by Zachariah Brigden
of Boston about 1760.*
(Photo: New Orleans
Auction Galleries)

Few families in seventeenth-century America had enough money or leisure to desire wares made from silver. Most early silver was made for churches. The lines were simple and the pieces undecorated. New England (Boston), the state of New York (especially New York City), Pennsylvania (especially Philadelphia), and later Delaware and South Carolina were the centers for the silversmithing trade. Each city developed its own designs and characteristics, which were influenced by the heritage of the colonists. Silver design in Boston echoed English styles, while New York silversmiths received their inspiration from the Dutch.

The silversmith was a successful businessman, well respected in the community. He handled the wealth of the community and was trusted to give a fair accounting of the amount of silver he used. The colonial years were a period of time when it was difficult to keep money safely hidden. A family of means quickly learned it was safer to have a silversmith melt coins and make a large teapot than it was to keep money hidden. A thief had more trouble disposing of a teapot than coins. Each teapot or sugar bowl was unique in design and marked by the maker so it could be easily identified.

Coin silver cups were popular gifts between the 1820s and the 1890s. This 6-inch-high cup was made about 1824. The pedestal foot matches the design of the tea sets of the day.

Coffee, tea, and chocolate were important beverages in the colonies by the early eighteenth century. Pots, sugar bowls, creamers, and other utensils were made to serve these beverages. The design of these utensils changed to reflect the style of the period. Silver shapes changed from colonial to classical, then Federal, Empire, Victorian, and art nouveau.

By 1840 silver pieces could be made by machine, but some silver makers continued making silver pieces by hand.

Designs of the Victorian era were inspired by the Greek Revival of the earlier decades and the repoussé (raised) decorations newly in vogue. Classical forms were decorated with cast bands of trim, sculpted figures, floral patterns, and Oriental and Indian motifs. The silver reflected the rococo patterns of the furniture in the 1850s and the Gothic Revival and Renaissance Revival rectangular patterns of the 1880s. Ideas were borrowed freely, and a tea set might have repoussé roses, ram's head handles, deer's feet and legs, plus an engraved initial.

Silver plating was introduced in 1840, and inexpensive plated wares became available in quantity. New technology changed the way silverware was made after 1850. The drop hammer, the rolling mill, and other improvements reduced the amount of skill and time required to make a spoon or a bowl.

Silver or silver-plated grape scissors are unfamiliar today, but they were used at the table to cut the bunches of grapes in Victorian times. Griffins decorate the handles of these 6¾-inch scissors.

Jabez Gorham apprenticed for seven years, worked with four partners for five years, then formed his own company in 1818. The company eventually became Gorham & Company and later Gorham Manufacturing Company. This was one of the first silver manufacturers to use mass-production methods to make silver.

Silverware, hollowware, and jewelry were made by many companies by the mid-nineteenth century. Baby cups, tea services, pitchers, goblets, and many different serving pieces were popular. Elaborate silver-plated figural napkin rings, tilting water pitchers, and other large pieces were made of silver plate. Souvenir spoons were made in sterling and in silver plate.

The traditional eighteenth-century flatware patterns of Plain Thread, Shell, Grape, and Tip't continued into the 1850s. Ribbon pattern was introduced about 1865. Medallion pattern was made by the 1860s. Many elaborate floral patterns soon followed, and in the 1870s Japanese styles became popular. The famous Audubon pattern by Tiffany & Company was first made in 1871.

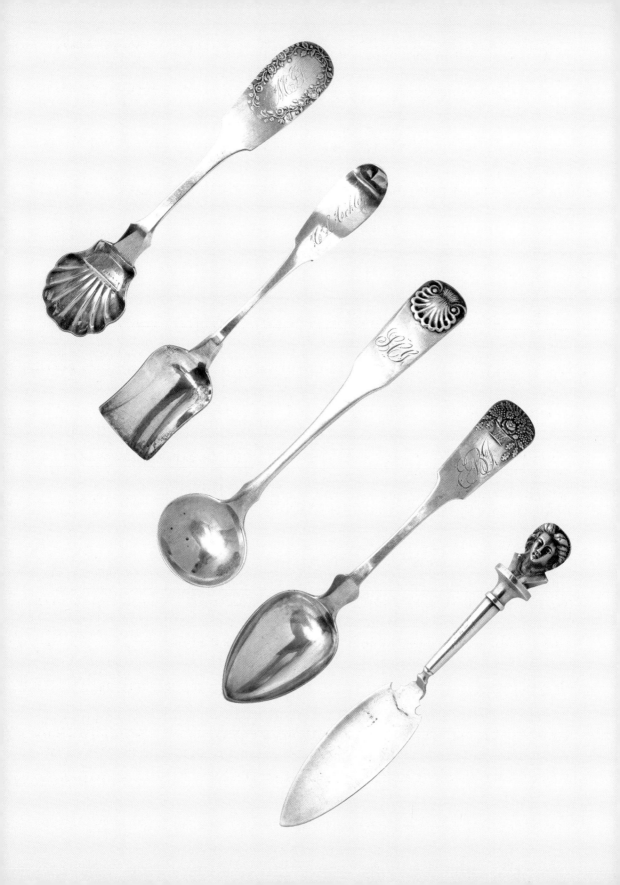

Art nouveau designs were introduced in the late 1880s. The handmade Martelé silver by Gorham and the commercially produced sets by Tiffany & Company and Gorham were sold in all parts of the country.

Although Victorian tastes and the machine age had converted simple silver designs to a mass of decoration by the 1870s, plain lines and simple decorations gradually reappeared in the twentieth century.

SILVER PLATE

If a piece of silver is large and heavy, with ornate designs or engraving, it could be an eighteenth-century or early nineteenth-century piece. It may be sterling silver, but it is more likely to be an example of Victorian silver plate. Victorian silver plate was made from either copper or a white metal called Britannia, which was electrically coated with a thin layer of silver. (For the history of Britannia metal, see page 218, Chapter 13, Pewter.)

A special type of hand-rolled silver on copper was made in the town of Sheffield, England, during the eighteenth century. It is called *Sheffield silver* or *Old Sheffield Plate*. Many other types of silverware, including the plated wares now made, have been produced in the city of Sheffield and are referred to as *Sheffield silver*. The collector of old Sheffield is looking for the old hand-rolled silver-plated copper, not the nineteenth-century electroplated pieces.

Most plated silver found today is not old Sheffield, but instead newer Victorian plated ware. It was marked in England with combinations of shields, designs, and names. The letters *EPNS* (Electroplated Nickel Silver) or *EPWM* (Electroplated White Metal) indicate a Victorian silver-plated piece. Other marks, like

Opposite page, top to bottom: This small spoon with shell-shaped bowl and garland pattern handle, made about 1825, is stamped B. Fries *on the back.*

The shovel was used to serve loose sugar from a bowl. This American coin silver sugar shovel was made about 1850 in Connecticut. It is marked O. D. Seymour.

This 3½-inch-long salt spoon has a handle that tips down. It was probably made before 1830, although the shell pattern remained popular after that date.

Basket of Flowers pattern was popular about 1825. The raised basket is on the handle of this coin silver teaspoon marked Steele & Hocknell.

Medallion head pattern was popular in Victorian times. This jelly server, made by Albert Coles & Co., has a head, possibly Minerva, at the top of the handle. The blade is inscribed Dec. Class '69.

This page: Brownies, characters with round eyes and skinny legs, decorate this silver-plated bonbon basket made by James W. Tufts.

company names, can indicate the piece is plated. All solid English silver was marked with quality hallmarks and the familiar lion.

American plated silver is easy to spot from the marks. Insignias were favored, especially circles with the maker's name inside. The words *triple, quadruple, A1,* or *plate* all indicate that a piece is plated silver. Most maker's marks are listed and can be found in libraries or on the Internet. A few hours of examining solid silver and Victorian plate will make you expert at telling them apart.

QUICK TIPS FOR IDENTIFYING OLD SHEFFIELD

To spot the old hand-rolled (and rare) Sheffield, scratch your fingernail underneath the border of the platter, candlestick, or tureen. Because a thin sheet of silver was rolled on over the copper, your fingernail will catch the edge of this sheet of silver.

Sometimes the silver layer has worn off, and copper shows through. This is called *bleeding.*

Hold the platter near where it is engraved, and huff at it until your breath clouds the silver. Old Sheffield has an inset piece of solid silver for the engraving (so the copper won't show through), and the block of silver should be faintly outlined by your breath.

SILVER PLATE VOCABULARY

4, 6, or 8: appears on some spoons and forks that were double plated.

6, 9, or 12: appears on some spoons and forks that were triple plated.

A1: appears on silver-plated flatware to indicate it is standard plate.

Quadruple plate: indicates 8 troy ounces of silver per gross (144) of teaspoons.

Double, standard, and *half plate* indicate thinner silver plating.

SHOULD IT BE REPLATED?

There is an easy answer. Modern silver plating destroys the charm and color of the old hand-rolled plated ware. Do not replate your old English Sheffield silver, but enjoy the worn patina even when the copper is evident. If you object to the copper, don't buy old Sheffield. Instead buy later Victorian silver plate that has been electroplated. Replating later pieces will not hurt the value.

SILVER MARKS

The marks on the bottom of a piece of silver can be an indication of the age, maker, and origin of the piece. A single mark usually indicates that the piece of silver was made in America, although there are some Irish and Scottish pieces with just the maker's name. Four or five small pictorial marks usually indicate England as the country of origin. A standing lion (called a *lion passant*) is the *standard quality mark* for English silver and indicates that a piece meets the sterling standard of 925 parts silver out of 1,000. Become familiar with the English king's and queen's head marks as indications of age. If the king's head faces right, the piece was made before 1850. Silver made between 1850 and 1890 is marked with Queen Victoria's profile facing left. Silver was stamped with a city mark, a leopard's head for London, a castle for Edinburgh. The crowned harp mark indicates the piece was made in Dublin. Glasgow silversmiths used a fish or tree mark. Ornate capital letters or the fleur-de-lis were used as marks in France. A hand indicates Antwerp, and a spread eagle represents Germany or Russia.

The word *Sterling* indicates an Irish piece made after 1720 or an American piece made after about 1860. *Coin, dollar,* and *standard* were usually American terms, but some Irish makers also used them. The words *quadruple, triple, EPNS,* and *EPWM* indicate that the ware is silver plated. The number *800* is usually found on Continental silver.

The marks used by the earliest silversmiths in the colonies were the maker's initials. Most pre-1850 American silversmiths used their last name, or initials, or first initial and last name. Letters or names were usually stamped inside one of many shapes.

About 1800, American makers began to use other marks that resembled the guild marks used by English silversmiths. A head, bird, hand, star, arm, or letter often appeared in these pseudo marks, along with the maker's mark. They were meant to mislead the public into believing that the silver was of English origin. Many pieces were unmarked or marked later with the name of the store that sold them.

By 1830 the words *Coin, Pure Coin, Dollar, Standard, Premium,* or the letters *C* or *D* were placed on silver to indicate that it was 900 out of 1,000 parts silver. The word *sterling* was frequently used on silver by 1860, and in 1906 it was legally required. *STERLING* means that 925 out of 1,000 parts are silver. This is still the standard for sterling silver. Gorham Silver Company used a special mark for their Martelé silver from 1899 to 1912. Martelé was made of silver of better than sterling quality, some with 950 parts silver to each 1,000 parts.

Numbers such as 800 or 900 indicate the quality of the silver in some European countries. Pieces marked 800 are considered solid silver and are usually German, Italian, or Russian. At least 925 parts out of 1,000 must be silver to be considered solid or sterling silver in the United States or England.

ENGLISH MARKS

Standard quality mark

City mark London

Sovereign's head Before 1850

COLONIAL AMERICAN MAKER'S MARK

John Hull 1645

Silversmiths in Baltimore, Maryland, had a maker-date system from 1814 to 1830. An assay office was legally established in 1814, and marks were placed on all silver sold. The silver had a head of Liberty that indicated the quality of metal, a date letter, the arms of Baltimore to indicate the city, and the maker's initials or name. The dating system was discontinued in 1830, when the silversmiths developed another system. Numbers like *10.15, 112,* or *11/12* were stamped on the silver to indicate the percentage of pure silver in the metal.

Most marks on silver are listed in books on the subject or online. Just be careful to use the proper vocabulary when you search. A book or list published in England called "Hallmarks on Plate" will be about solid silver only. The term *silver plate* in England means the same as *sterling* in the United States. In the United States, the term *silver plated* describes a thin layer of silver electroplated on another metal.

DATING SILVER

American spoons offer several clues to their age. Before 1800 most spoons looked as if they were made from two pieces of silver. The bowl of the spoon was hammered to shape and the handle was soldered to the bowl, or a single piece of silver was cut, hammered, and shaped to look as if it were made of two pieces. The seam where the two pieces were joined is easy to see. Most spoons were made from one piece of silver after 1800. To make the spoon, the silversmith cut a piece of silver shaped like a lollipop from a flat sheet. He then shaped the bowl and finished the handle. Later spoons were cast in a mold.

The shape of a spoon's bowl also dates silverware. Early seventeenth-century spoons first had fig-shaped and then later elliptical bowls. Early eighteenth-century spoons had large bowls. The nineteenth-century spoon was shaped like the ones made today. Spoons the size of today's standard teaspoon were rarely made before 1700. Earlier dinner spoons were much larger.

The handle of the spoon was straight at first, but by 1730 the tip of the spoon's handle bent down. The tip of the spoon handle turned up about 1830. Fiddleback patterns are examples of spoons with an upturned tip.

Forks were first used in France in the thirteenth century. The custom traveled to Italy by the sixteenth century and to England in the seventeenth century. Forks originally had two tines and were used only for serving. Individual forks were used in England by the 1630s, and these forks were smaller and had more tines. Three or four tines were popular in the eighteenth century. Most forks today have four tines.

Bone-handled steel knives had steel blades and pistol-shaped handles. The modern knife became popular after the middle of the nineteenth century.

If the words *England* or *Made in the USA* or some other indication of the country appear, the piece of silver or silver plate was made after 1891.

You can also determine the age of a piece by estimating how old a piece is *not*. The large, porcelain-lined, silver-plated pot often referred to as a coffeepot is really a Victorian ice-water pitcher and can never be older than mid-nineteenth century. Large teapots came *after* the smaller two-cup-size pots. The tea-caddy spoon almost disappeared after the eighteenth century, when tea was no longer expensive. It helps to know what the piece was and how it was used. Once again, common sense is your best guide to determine the age of some antiques. The chafing dish made to hold a can of Sterno can't be older than the introduction of the can in 1887, but the chafing dish that burned alcohol may be from the eighteenth century.

SPECIAL SPOONS AND FORKS AND OTHER SERVING PIECES

Mote Spoon

When loose tea was brewed, small bugs, twigs, and other unappetizing items hidden in the leaves floated to the surface. These undesirable bits were strained from the tea with a mote skimmer. The handle of the spoon was small, straight, and pointed. It was used to

A perforated spoon was used to remove specks of leaves floating in a cup or pot of tea. The pointed handle was used to open leaf-clogged holes at the base of the spout. This English mote spoon is 9½ inches long.

poke the tea leaves from the inside of the teapot spout. Small, decoratively placed holes in the bowl of the spoon strained the tea. The eighteenth-century mote spoon was the size of a very small teaspoon.

A larger type of perforated spoon was used in the nineteenth century to remove berries from their juices, and even today small condiment spoons are made with holes.

Orange and Grapefruit Spoons

The oddly shaped serrated spoon bowl that tapers near the end so it is pear-shaped was made to remove fruit sections from oranges and grapefruit. It was a popular Victorian spoon.

Sucket Fork

An odd piece of silver with a fork at one end of the handle and a spoon at the other is called a sucket fork. The name *sucket* refers to a sticky, preserved grape or plum mixture that was often eaten with the fingers. People used the sucket fork and ate the fruit with the fork end and the juice with the spoon end. The sucket fork was never a common piece of tableware, even in England. A few are known to have been made during the seventeenth and eighteenth centuries. Victorian copies were made.

Wood and Hughes, New York silversmiths, made this medallion pattern sterling silver fish slice about 1875. It is 11½ inches long. (Photo: New Orleans Auction Galleries)

Tea-Caddy Spoon

The tea-caddy spoon is a short-stemmed silver tea scoop that was first used about 1770. The caddy spoon had a short handle and was kept inside the tea canister. Some caddy spoons were shaped like shells, grape leaves, shovels, feathers, jockey caps, eagles, flour scoops, and leaves. They were made until the end of the eighteenth century and then went out of style. They have been reproduced since Victorian times.

Fish Slice

The earliest silver fish slices, or fish servers, were made in the late eighteenth century. The first ones were shaped like a bricklayer's trowel. By the nineteenth century, the silver server was shaped like a triangle (similar to a cake server) or a fish or resembled a large table knife. Often they were pierced so the extra liquid would drain off the piece of fish.

Sugar Tongs

During the eighteenth century, sugar was sold in large, cone-shaped loaves. Sugar nippers were used to cut the large lump of sugar into usable pieces.

The early eighteenth-century sugar tongs were used to serve small pieces of sugar. They resemble scissors with a spoonlike end. The bow-shaped tongs that resemble two spoons joined by an arch were made after 1750. Many varieties of nineteenth-century tongs were made to match patterns of silver tableware. Tongs in old and new patterns are made today.

Left: Hester Bateman was a famous eighteenth-century English silversmith. She made this sugar tongs about 1790. It is decorated with bright cut engraving.

LET'S HAVE TEA—OR TAKE A COFFEE BREAK

Tea, coffee, and chocolate were introduced to Europe in the early seventeenth century. They were popular in England by the mid-seventeenth century and in America by the 1690s. Chocolate was preferred at first. Then coffee, which was less expensive, became the most popular beverage. Tea originally was valued mainly for its medicinal properties. It became popular as a beverage by the end of the seventeenth century. Coffee was usually drunk in coffeehouses, and tea was drunk at home. As tea became less expensive in America, its popularity as a beverage increased. However, following the Boston Tea Party in 1773, when colonists protested the British tax on tea by dumping shiploads of tea into Boston Harbor, it was considered unpatriotic to drink tea. Many people gave up drinking tea until the United States won its independence from Britain.

The teapot, creamer, and sugar were made to serve tea to one or two people. The set was made by John C. Moore for Tiffany, Young & Ellis about 1851.

Silver Tea Service

At first tea was served plain. Later sugar, cream, lemon, or spices were used. The tea service became part of an elaborate ritual. By

1800 the complete tea service contained a teapot, sugar urn, creamer, and perhaps a tray. It could also have sugar tongs, a tea caddy, a tea scoop, a tea strainer, and small trivets to hold the teapot and tea caddy. Some sets even included a coffeepot, hot-water pot, chocolate pot, or waste bowl.

The pieces of early tea services did not necessarily match. Because the proud buyer of a silver tea set usually ordered one piece at a time, a set often had pieces made by several makers.

Teapots

Tea was a scarce and expensive drink when it was first introduced in England during the seventeenth century. Early teapots were designed to hold just one cup of tea. By the mid-1700s the teapot had been enlarged, and it held several cups of tea. After 1800 the teapot became the large six-cup size we know today.

The tiny eighteenth-century teapot not only grew in size with the passing years, it also changed in shape. The pot was round from about 1720 to 1780. The pear-shaped teapot was popular from about 1720 to 1760. Between 1750 and 1800 the inverted pear shape was used. The pot had straight sides between 1790 and 1810. From 1810 to 1835 the body of the pot became rounder and fatter and included a base. After 1835 the old shapes as well as many different new shapes were used. Victorian teapots were larger and more ornate, with no single fashionable shape. (See porcelain teapot shapes on page 7.)

Opposite page: This sterling teapot made in London, England, is very similar in design to American teapots made about 1830. It has an unusual spout that resembles a hand holding a shell.

At afternoon tea, strong tea was poured from a teapot into a cup. Then hot water was added from a special urn to dilute the tea. This beehive form Old Sheffield Plate urn was made about 1800.
(Photo: New Orleans Auction Galleries)

There are other clues that can be used to date teapots, silver or ceramic, such as the shape of the spout, the type of handle, or the way the lid fits.

The Tea Urn

The tea urn became popular at the end of the eighteenth century. The urn originally held hot water, but it was later used to serve strained tea. The urn replaced the kettle. The tea urn usually had a spigot similar to a spigots on a beer keg. The teapot had a pouring spout.

Coffeepots

The body of the coffeepot corresponded to that of the teapot, although the coffeepot was taller. The early ones made about 1715 were tall and had straight sides. After that, the pear shape became popular. Later came the inverted pear, then the straight-sided pot and the urn-shaped pot of 1790. Finally, in the early 1800s, fatter, rounded pots that usually had feet appeared.

If your coffeepot or teapot has an all-metal handle, it was probably made after 1850. Before then, almost all silver and silver-plated teapots had carved wooden or bone handles because metal handles were too hot to hold. In 1849 Henry Reed, a founder of Reed & Barton Silver Company in Massachusetts, made silver handles with discs of oyster shell as insulation. Later, ivory or wood insets were used to insulate the metal handles of a coffeepot or teapot.

Cream Pitchers

"Lemon or milk?" is still the question when the English serve tea. When tea was first introduced to England from China in the early 1600s, it was served plain. A French woman introduced the custom of drinking tea with milk in 1680. It is said that she wanted to cool the tea with milk to protect her fragile teacups. Silversmiths designed new utensils to serve the milk and sugar. The first silver cream pitchers were made in England about 1725. Early pitchers were hammered (or *raised*) from a flat sheet of silver and had no seams. The rim and lip were added to the hammered body.

Pitchers made during the reign of George II (mid-1700s) had a deeper rim and often included feet that reflected the furniture styles of the period. A chair leg was often the model for the small, silver cream-pitcher leg.

Early cream jugs were pear-shaped, and by 1770 the pear shape had a leg with molded feet instead of the three small feet that were used earlier. The classic urn-shaped creamer with a square pedestal base came into vogue about 1800. Larger, fat cream pitchers were used in the nineteenth century. The nineteenth-century creamer was larger than the early eighteenth-century teapot.

Silversmiths in the United States copied English designs.

Sugar Bowls

Sugar in the eighteenth century was not as refined as ours is today. A large bowl was needed to hold the bulky lumps of sugar that were available at the time. Sugar was imported from Cuba about 1724 and was sold in large cone-shaped sugar loaves. The loaf was snipped with sugar nippers, and the pieces were placed in a sugar bowl.

The sugar bowl changed shape in the same manner as the other pieces of a tea set. The bowl evolved from a rounded bowl to a classic urn shape in the late 1700s, and then became a large, fat bowl in the 1820s.

Some imaginative sugar bowls were made in Victorian times. This electroplated English sugar bowl in a coal scuttle shape is 5 by 7½ inches. There is a hook for the sugar scoop.

OTHER SILVER PIECES

Bottle Tickets and Decanter Labels

Until the eighteenth century, most wine and spirits were sold in and served from glass bottles or stoneware jars. The name of the liquor was part of the container's design or was written on a parchment label. After glass decanters came into style in the early 1700s, a label was necessary to identify what was in the bottle. Silver *bottle tickets* were first made in the 1720s. At first they were quite simple, but soon they became more elaborate, with fancy engraving, beaded edges, and enameling.

By the 1790s bottle tickets were called *decanter labels*. They were made from silver, bone, leather, wood, and many other hard, durable materials. A paper label was used on most commercial bottles after 1860.

Braziers and Chafing Dishes

Keeping food hot in a drafty eighteenth-century home required ingenuity and special equipment. The wealthy English or American family had their breakfast eggs cooked at the table in water heated over a special brazier.

Large pieces of meat or roasts were kept warm in hot metal serving dishes, but gravies and sauces were served in separate small dishes that cooled quickly. To solve the problem, silversmiths designed gravy saucepans that were usually made of silver. These were kept on the table over a brazier or small stove heated with a special burning charcoal that did not give off sparks. Later, small spirit lamps furnished the heat. Eighteenth-century American examples of these heaters are known, but they are very rare. The silver brazier had a wooden handle, pierced silver sides, and scrolled feet.

The chafing dish with an alcohol burner as a heater was developed in the United States. English chafing dishes were usually heated with hot water. A fad for chafing-dish meals swept the United States about 1885. Most of these chafing dishes were made from plated Britannia ware. A smaller number were made from sterling silver. Copper chafing dishes in the Arts and Crafts style gained favor after 1900.

Candlesticks

The seventeenth-century candlestick was made with a square base and fluted column. Gambling was widespread by 1695, and a smaller candlestick base became popular because it required less space on the gaming table. In the eighteenth century, candlesticks had a variety of hexagonal or ornamented bases, and candelabra became popular.

In the nineteenth century, candlesticks became larger and more ornate. By the middle of the century, oil lamps replaced the candle as a main source of illumination. Candles and candlesticks were used more for decoration than for light.

These 1840 candelabra can be transformed into candlesticks by removing the top section with the curved arms. The 1840s silver was made in the Adam style.

Castor Sets

Standing salt and pepper castor sets were used during the seventeenth century. The sugar castor, mustard pot, spice dredger, bottles for vinegar and oil, and other spice holders were all introduced within a few years of each other. The containers were made from silver, gold, pewter, china, or glass.

It became stylish in the early eighteenth century to have a silver stand that held oil and vinegar. A matching set of silver castors

for several types of spices and sugar was also used. The two sets were joined together in one large silver frame as early as 1705.

Most of the stands held five bottles or shakers in a frame. The design of the castor set changed about every ten years. Sets were made from silver or Old Sheffield Plate during the late eighteenth and early nineteenth centuries. The condiment jars rested on a heavy footed tray. The center of the tray had a handle that supported the rings that held the jars in place. The set often included small open glass bowls called *salt dips*. Some of the later sets had pierced bands that surrounded the bottles. They were made to hold six bottles.

By the middle of the nineteenth century, castor sets were often made from silver-plated Britannia metal. Castor sets became more ornate each year, and by 1860 some were elaborate cathedral-like creations with small doors that opened to expose the bottles. The designs became heavier, and the sets became taller. The shorter designs returned to popularity by 1880. The lazy Susan–type castor set, a fad for almost ten years, went out of style, and smaller sets that contained three or four bottles came into fashion. By 1890 the racks were just wide frames designed to hold the popular colored glass bottles. A small number of fanciful castor sets were made with cruets and spice holders plus figurines, wagon-like bases, and even a bell to ring for a servant.

Epergne

The epergne is a table centerpiece that was usually made of silver and glass. The large center bowl or basket and several smaller bowls or baskets were placed together to hold flowers, fruits, sweetmeats (usually sugared fruits or candy), or cookies. It is a seventeenth-century design that was also used during the eighteenth, nineteenth, and twentieth centuries in many countries.

Mustard Pot

A small silver dish with a lid was used to serve mustard during the eighteenth century. The lid was notched so a spoon could be kept in the dish. The dish or mustard pot had a glass liner that kept the mustard from tarnishing the silver.

The earliest mustard pot dates from 1737, but other types of mustard holders were used prior to that time. During the nineteenth century, the mustard pot was often included in a castor set with cruets and salt and pepper containers.

The first sauceboats were literally boat shaped. By the late eighteenth century, many looked like an elongated pitcher with a curled handle and long spout. Sauceboats in this practical shape are still made.

Porringer

A porringer is a bowl with a flat, earlike handle. They were made from wood, pewter, silver, or other metal. The porringer was an eighteenth-century utensil. It was used for porridge, thick soup, and other types of thick liquid food. People who used a porringer either ate with a spoon or drank the liquid while holding the porringer's large handle.

Sauceboat or Gravy Boat

The first sauceboats were silver dishes made to resemble the hulls of boats. The dish was fitted with a lip at each end and a handle across the top. They were first made in the early 1700s. Later sauceboats kept the name *boat* but discarded the shape. A piece resembling today's small cream pitcher but with a ring of silver for the base soon came into style. The pitcher rested on three small feet after 1745. Today's sauceboats usually resemble the eighteenth-century examples. Gravy is still served in special dishes.

Right: Soup and other foods with gravy or liquid were served from a covered tureen to keep them hot. This sterling tureen was sold by Tiffany & Company in 1883.
(Photo: New Orleans Auction Galleries)

Soup Tureens and Other Large Bowls

The custom of serving soup from a tureen, or large bowl, developed during the late seventeenth century in England and France. The tureen was placed on a side table or in the center of the dining-room table. The idea of a large, attractive, covered bowl for soup has changed very little during the past three centuries.

The silver punch bowl was developed by seventeenth-century silversmiths. Hot punch, which was introduced about 1790, was served from a bowl that stood on a tray that protected the table. The monteith bowl, a large punch bowl with notches around the top rim, was popular in the seventeenth and eighteenth centuries. Cup handles or glass stems were hung in the notches. Legend says a Scotsman named Monteith was known for his delicious brewed punch. He always wore a coat with a scalloped bottom. The design of his coat was so similar to the design of the punch bowl's rim that the bowl was called a *monteith*. Some bowls were fitted with a notched rim that could be removed from the bowl, leaving a plain punch bowl. A few monteith bowls were made in Victorian times, but most of them were made in the eighteenth century.

Tankard

The original tankard, made to hold drinking water, was made from a hollowed log bound with iron. The word *tankard* came to mean any tall, one-handled wooden or metal drinking vessel, especially one with a lid. The tankard has been used since the sixteenth century, but it reached the height of its popularity during the eighteenth century.

Water Pitcher

The silver water pitcher was first made in the late eighteenth century. A favorite nineteenth-century New England pitcher was shaped like a barrel with two bands around it. The pear-shaped pitcher was popular in Pennsylvania, and a similar pear-shaped pitcher with a deeper neck was popular in the South.

Left: Mugs were made of silver, which kept the beverage hot. This American mug by Leonard & Wilson, Philadelphia is decorated with a cottage scene and Odd Fellows symbol.

VICTORIAN SILVER AND SILVER PLATE

Double-Wall Water Pitcher

The first silver-plated ice-water pitchers had two metal walls with an air space between the walls that kept the liquid cool. Later the pitchers were fitted with a porcelain liner. Several patents for double-wall pitchers were granted about 1850. James Stimpson received the most important patent for a double-wall pitcher and permitted four companies to use it after 1854. No matter how old you think it is, any silver pitcher with a porcelain lining was probably made after 1854, most likely after 1865. Because the ice water pitcher resembled a coffeepot, it is often called by the wrong name by collectors.

Pickle Castor

The pickle castor, a colored or clear glass jar about six inches in height, became popular in 1890. The castor was set in a metal frame, which was usually silver plate, with a base and tall handles that formed an arch above the jar. A pair of tongs or a fork hung from the frame. The pickle castor was usually made from glass and silver-plated Britannia metal. Its top was usually made from silver or silver plate. It remained popular for only about ten years. A pickle castor can date only from the end of the nineteenth century, unless it is a reproduction.

Napkin Rings

The first American napkin ring patent was issued in 1867. By 1877 the silver catalog of the Meriden Britannia Company devoted six pages to napkin rings. Napkin rings remained popular until about 1886, and by 1900 the figural napkin ring was almost completely out of vogue. The elaborate napkin ring is strictly a late Victorian piece.

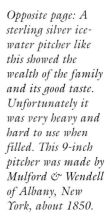

Opposite page: A sterling silver ice-water pitcher like this showed the wealth of the family and its good taste. Unfortunately it was very heavy and hard to use when filled. This 9-inch pitcher was made by Mulford & Wendell of Albany, New York, about 1850.

The figural napkin ring was popular by the 1870s. This silver-plated ring by Meriden Britannia Company has eagles on each side.

Souvenir Spoons

The silver souvenir spoon was a fad during the 1880s and 1890s. Teaspoons, orange spoons, sugar spoons, demitasse spoons, and even large spoons were designed and sold to commemorate important places or events. The handles of the spoons and the insides of the bowls pictured various buildings, exhibitions, or people. Some spoons were enameled, and others were given a gold wash or left as plain silver or silver plate.

Souvenir spoons are still being made, and the supply of old and new spoons is almost unlimited.

And the Thousands of Other Pieces . . .

A complete silver service in Victorian times included many types of spoons and forks. Victorians used a different spoon for coffee, demitasse, soup, cream soup, ice cream, and dinner. No one would ever use a cold-meat fork for hot meat. The sets also had dozens of different serving pieces, including fish servers, crumbers (to remove crumbs from the table), stuffing spoons, sugar scuttles (which were popular from about 1875 to 1900), cheese scoops, marrow scoops, tomato servers, nut picks, and many other special utensils. Also found in every well-to-do Victorian home were card holders, sardine boxes, mustard jars, covered butter dishes, spoon holders, syrup pitchers, toothpick holders, knife rests, biscuit boxes, egg steamers, cigar boxes, toast racks, toast forks, asparagus servers, cake tongs, pepper mills, place-card holders, and pincushions. ☙

St. Paul's Church is shown on this 5-inch silver souvenir spoon from Norfolk, Virginia. The handle is shaped like a young boy eating a watermelon.

Few table settings today include a specially shaped fork to serve tomatoes. This 9¾-inch-long tomato fork with the curved tines was made about 1890.

Cheese like Stilton was served with a cheese scoop. It loosened small pieces in the center of the cheese. This mid-nineteenth-century American scoop was made by Bigelow, Kennard & Company of Boston.

Chapter 13

Pewter

GOLD AND SILVER HAVE ALWAYS BEEN EXPENSIVE, so many of our ancestors bought pewter and other less costly metal serving dishes and spoons. American pewter was made as early as 1639. The first colonists from England brought their molds with them, and American-made pewter identical to the English wares was soon for sale in the colonies.

Early pewter has become one of those antiques that are sold upside down so the marks are visible. The English, British, and Continental marks can be identified. An eight-inch eighteenth-century English plate does not have a dollar value anywhere near as high as that of an American-made plate of the same age and size, even though they appear identical except for the maker's mark. Almost all old pewter, if marked, is marked on the bottom, not on the face of the piece. Beware of some twentieth-century English-made pewter that appears old—and has a mark on the front of the plate.

Nineteenth-century pewter teapots were often made with wooden handles. This teapot by William Calder (1817–1856) of Providence, Rhode Island, also has a black cast-metal knob on the top of the lid. (Photo: Skinner)

Joseph Danforth
Pewter touchmark
(1758–1788)

Flagons were used to pour wine or liquor. This 9¼-inch-high early nineteenth-century example was made by Thomas Danforth Boardman and Sherman Boardman of Hartford, Connecticut. (Photo: Skinner)

Pewter is made from a mixture of tin, lead, copper, and other metals. Some pewter is dull, while other pieces are almost silver in appearance, and the metal's appearance depends on how much tin was included in the mixture. A simple trick will determine the grade of pewter. Rub a piece of pewter on a sheet of white paper. The heavier the mark it makes, the more lead is in the pewter. The lighter the mark, the more tin in the mix, the more silver-looking, and the better the quality of the pewter. No mark on the paper means 90 parts tin to 10 parts lead; faint marks come from 75 parts tin to 25 parts lead.

Marks on Pewter

Marks on pewter are called touchmarks. There are general rules about these marks but they are only 75 percent accurate: The thistle mark is found on Scottish pewter, while French makers from Paris used an angel with the word *Paris*. Other French pewter may be marked with a fleur-de-lis. Pewter from England, France, the Low Countries, Germany, Austria-Hungary, Scandinavia, and America is marked with a crowned rose. St. Michael and the dragon in a circle or a Gothic *B* indicates pewter that was made in Brussels, while an arm with a hand was used by makers in Antwerp. English and American makers almost always used names and letters. Makers in the United States sometimes marked pieces *London* to fool customers who wanted to purchase British-made pewter.

Pewter marks can be deciphered with the help of reference books and Internet sites that picture the marks in detail. The easy way to look up a mark is to try American makers first, since there are fewer of them. If the mark is not on that list, then try English makers. Some of the finest examples of English and American pewter were never marked.

Shape

The characteristic shapes of silver or porcelain teapots and bowls are almost identical to the shapes of pewter pieces. There are two exceptions.

The pewter coffeepot changed shape from small to large, from round to pear-shape, then to the inverted pear. Then came the famous pewter shape called the lighthouse. The lighthouse pot was a mid-nineteenth-century shape often copied in tin and toleware.

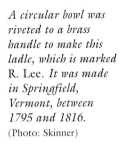

A circular bowl was riveted to a brass handle to make this ladle, which is marked R. Lee. It was made in Springfield, Vermont, between 1795 and 1816.
(Photo: Skinner)

Porringers are the only other pewter pieces that cannot be grouped with the traditional silver shapes. Porringer handles have changed through the years. The handles can reveal the period, region, and sometimes even the maker of a porringer.

After 1850

Museum collections usually concentrate on pewter made before 1850. However, individual collectors buy well-designed pewter no matter the age, especially pieces in the art nouveau style of the late 1800s. Any marked American pewter made before 1875 is rare.

Luther Boardman of Connecticut was a member of a famous family of pewterers. This teapot, made about 1830, is marked with his impressed eagle touchmark.
(Photo: Skinner)

Experts give various explanations of the difference between Britannia and pewter. Actually, there is no difference. Pewter and Britannia were both used to make an everyday ware that resembled silver. *Pewter* was the first name used for the metal, and most early pieces were made by hand. When pewter sales slowed, clever English manufacturers renamed their product *Britannia*. Later Britannia pieces were often spun on a lathe. The percentage of tin, copper, antimony, and other metals in pewter and in Britannia varies with each piece and each manufacturer.

James Vickers of Sheffield, England, bought the formula for the manufacture of Britannia metal from Nathaniel Gower in England in 1769. Vickers then worked for eighteen years to perfect the formula and start the actual manufacture of the ware. By the early 1800s, another Sheffield Britannia maker named James Dixon was exporting large quantities of the ware to the United States.

Britannia ware became fashionable in the United States in the nineteenth century and was being manufactured there by the 1820s. The Babbit and Crossman Company, founded in 1824 in Taunton, Massachusetts, made Britannia ware. The company later became Reed & Barton, a silver company that is still operating.

John O. Mead, a Philadelphia manufacturer of Britannia, traveled to Birmingham, England, in the late 1830s to learn the newly discovered method of electroplating a layer of silver onto the surface of Britannia ware. He returned to the United States in 1845 and is credited with being the first American to successfully electroplate silver.

Before resettling in Philadelphia in 1846, Mead formed the partnership of Rogers & Mead in Hartford, Connecticut. Mead and his partners, brothers William and Asa Rogers, manufactured electroplated silverware. Although Mead left within a year, the Rogers brothers continued in business and formed the Rogers Brothers Company about 1847. The firm made quality silver-plated flatware that brought the firm immediate success.

TO SOUND LIKE A COLLECTOR, YOU MUST KNOW THESE TERMS

The *eight-inch-plate era* lasted from 1750 to 1825 in America. During those years, undecorated plates measuring eight inches in diameter were made.

The *coffeepot era* was from 1825 to 1850. During that time, pewter was made in shapes that imitated the shapes of silver pieces.

Sadware refers to heavy pieces of pewter, like plates and trenchers hammered out of a single sheet of metal.

Hollowware was cast.

A pewter mug kept the beverage hot or cold for a long time. This mug held a quart of liquid, not too much in an era when water was not always safe to drink. It has the touchmark D.M. (Photo: Skinner)

Britannia ware was often silver plated after 1850. The
Meriden Britannia Company,
established in 1852, produced
silver plate as well as Britannia
ware. Meriden bought the
Rogers Brothers Company in
1862 and made silver plate at the
Meriden plant. The ware is marked
1847—ROGERS BROS.

Nickel silver, an alloy made of copper, zinc, and nickel, took the place of
Britannia ware about 1857. By 1879 there were only fifty-five
factories still making Britannia ware. Seventeen independent
Britannia factories, including the Meriden Company, joined in
1898 to form the International Silver Company, which is still
operating.

Britannia's Dark Feet

Some Britannia ware has a dull pewter color. A teapot's spout, feet,
and handle were often made of a harder metal than the body and
were slightly darker in color. The entire pot was then silver plated,
and the dark metal did not show. If the silver has worn off, no
cleaner will make the metal lighter. If you have a pot like this and
the difference in color is objectionable, have the pot replated.

Victorian Britannia coffeepots were fanciful creations made in unusual shapes with applied decorations, then engraved and embossed. This piece, made by Reed & Barton, was probably once silver plated. It is engraved with the owner's name, Zoe.

Chapter 14

Tinware
and Toleware

◦◦◦ TINWARE WAS MADE FROM TINPLATE, a sheet of iron or steel that had been dipped in molten tin so it was covered with a thin plating of tin. Early American tinsmiths used tinplate imported from England. By about 1830 some tinplate was made in America, but most of it continued to come from England until changes in tariff laws in 1890 made imported tinplate too expensive.

Tinsmiths cut and soldered tinplate to make kitchen utensils, cookie cutters, tea sets, boxes, pans, funnels, roasters, apple corers, scoops, mugs, trays, shakers, wall sconces, candlesticks, and small toys. Unpainted tinware was sold across the country by traveling peddlers. The tinware business slowed somewhat during the American Revolution, but the industry was booming by 1800.

Punched Tin
Much of the unpainted tinware used in America was plain, but some was made with punched decoration. Most *punched tin* dates from 1830 to 1860. The dents in the tin were made with a hammer and a nail or with a small die but did not break the surface. If the design went through the tin, the tin was called *pierced tin*. Pie safes, colanders, strainers, lanterns, foot warmers, and nutmeg graters were pierced.

Painted tin was made with sophisticated stenciled and freehand decoration or simple folk art designs. This nineteenth-century tole tray with the popular cornucopia and eagle stencils is 16 by 22½ inches.
(Photo: Conestoga)

Painted Tin

The names given to painted tin are confusing, but the confusion clears when you realize that toleware, japanned ware, painted tin, and Pontypool all mean practically the same thing. *Toleware* is painted tinware, usually with a black varnished background and designs that are hand painted or stenciled. *Pontypool* describes two kinds of tinware: painted tinware made in Pontypool, England, and tinware that was made elsewhere in the style of Pontypool. Toleware made before the nineteenth century was often called *japanned ware*. The designs were sometimes inspired by Japanese lacquerware and the varnishing process was called *japanning*.

Toleware was made of tinplate that was coated with asphaltum (a coal by-product) mixed with varnish and baked. This process produced a black background on which designs in colors—often deep red, yellow, green, and tan—were applied. When the asphaltum was diluted, the finished piece appeared golden brown. Other materials were added to the varnish to produce a red background color. Red varnish was often used instead of asphaltum by 1840.

The earliest toleware was hand painted with designs on the dark brown or black tin. Stencils were used about 1820. Toleware was often painted with scenes, fruits, flowers, and birds. By the middle of the nineteenth century, decorations became simpler, less realistic, and more primitive.

A variety of tole household items, including teapots, coffeepots, trays, cake and bread boxes, document boxes, canisters, and candlesticks, were made in New England, New York, and Pennsylvania. Most had black or dark brown backgrounds. Pieces made in

Pennsylvania were more apt to have a red background and tended to use brighter colors.

Toward the end of the nineteenth century, toleware went out of fashion. In the 1930s there was a revival of interest. Women stripped and repainted old, peeling tinware and redecorated the pieces using the methods and styles of eighteenth- and nineteenth-century toleware. Some of these 1930s reworked pieces are now wanted by collectors.

After 1850 canisters and spice boxes were japanned and stenciled with the name of the products they held. By 1880 names and designs were printed directly on metal cans and boxes.

**TRASH
TO TREASURE**

Tin cans left behind by soldiers in New Mexico and nearby areas during the 1840s and 1850s were often transformed into wall shrines for saints or other decorative pierced-tin pieces.

The red background of this 11-inch-high gooseneck coffeepot was popular in Pennsylvania in the 1850s. The yellow and black flowers and leaves are typical hand-painted decorations. (Photo: Conestoga)

Chapter 15

Music Makers

✒ "MY GRANDFATHER LEFT ME A REAL STRADIVARIUS VIOLIN" is a claim commonly heard, but experts know this is practically impossible. Many farm families living in the northern part of the United States or in southern Canada have carefully guarded the valued Stradivarius violin that has been passed down through the family. Family members often recount the story that sometime between 1880 and 1930, an ancestor bought a violin from a peddler who sold his treasured instrument because he needed money. Inside the violin there is often an old label that reads ANTONIUS STRADIVARIUS CREMONENSIS FACIEBAT ANNO 1734. But the family also has to face the unwelcome information that, according to the experts, there are no unlisted Stradivarius violins, and there is little chance that any unrecorded Stradivarius violins will be found.

There is a slim chance a violin said to have been stolen during World War II might surface. When a legally owned Stradivarius does come on the market, it commands a high price. In 1990 a Stradivarius violin sold in London for $1,760,000.

The forged Stradivarius violins found in the United States and Canada were made and sold in great numbers during the last part of the nineteenth century. Some copies were made with a label that

Opposite page: The violins made by Antonius Stradivarius are valued for their exceptional tone and workmanship. This is the Windsor Weinstein Stradivarius violin, now in the collection of the Instrument Bank of the Canada Council for the Arts. (Photo: Geo. Heinl & Co., Toronto)

reads *Made in Germany* or some other English or German words. The original Stradivarius label was printed in Latin, with the last two digits of the date written by hand. It said, for example, *Antonius Stradivarius Cremonensis Faciebat Anno 1714.* The forged label says exactly the same thing and is written on aged paper. Many other later violins were labeled as Strads to indicate the model, not the maker. A true Stradivarius violin is an exceptional musical instrument. Any experienced violinist can tell a fine violin from a poor one by inspecting it. If you believe yours is a Strad, take it to a professional violinist for an expert opinion.

Forged labels were also pasted into copies of instruments by such famous makers as Giovanni Paolo Maggini (c.1580–c.1632); Nicolò Amati (1596–1684), the teacher of Stradivari; Giuseppe Guarnerius (1687–1745); Carlo Bergonzi (1683–1747); and Jakob Stainer (Steiner) (c.1617–1683). Original violins by these makers are valuable today. So are many other musical instruments of the eighteenth and nineteenth centuries.

Don't ignore the violin bow. Rare old bows made by well-known makers sell at auction for thousands of dollars.

Right: This Swiss cylinder music box by Paillaird was made about 1883. The crank on the left wound a mechanism that turned the brass cylinder so the combs hit the steel pins to make music. (Photo: Auction Team Breker)

A music-making machine was an important piece of parlor furniture. This elaborate Polyphon music box, style 104, was made about 1890. It plays metal discs. (Photo: Auction Team Breker)

Music Boxes

Music boxes first became popular in the 1800s, and the mechanisms were gradually improved during the century. The early music box had a revolving brass cylinder set with steel pins. The pins hit a

metal comb that had between fifteen and twenty-five teeth.

After 1820 the pins and cylinder were made from a single piece of steel. Small quills that improved the tone were added about 1825. A two-comb music box that could play loudly or softly was made in 1838. More combs were added, and by 1840 as many as five were used. The cylinders also became longer.

Bells and drums were added about 1850, and by 1854 interchangeable cylinders were used.

Elaborate tune changers and springs improved the music box after 1875. Large, circular disk cards that looked like a modern CD were made in 1885. The metal disk replaced the cylinder box by 1890. The improvements help to date a music box.

The Talking Machine

Thomas Alva Edison's phonographs were first manufactured in 1878 and are sought-after collectors' items. Edison's phonograph first used tinfoil-covered cylinders that played for only two minutes. By 1885 Alexander Graham Bell, his cousin Chichester Bell, and Charles Tainter had applied for a patent for a *graphophone* that used wax-coated cylinders, which provided better sound. In 1887 Emile Berliner developed a *gramophone* that used hard rubber discs and then later discs of a plastic material. By the early 1900s, discs had become more popular than cylinders. Some very rare recordings, either cylinders or discs, are extremely valuable.

In 1887 Edison introduced a battery-driven motor that replaced the hand crank on his phonograph. He added a large horn to his phonograph in 1895. Any Edison with a horn, especially the type with a large *morning glory* horn, will always find an eager buyer. The larger the horn, the more valuable the machine. Wooden horns and decorated metal horns are very desirable. The Victor Talking Machine Company, which later became RCA, first concealed the horn inside the cabinet of its Victrola in 1906.

Early phonographs had no volume control, and the loudness of the sound depended on the phonograph's needle. Needles with sapphire heads were very durable, but steel needles had to be changed frequently. Needles made of wood, bamboo, and other soft materials could be sharpened and reused. Needles were sold in small tins that often have attractive designs lithographed on the top and sides. These tins are collected today.

Collectors like objects that move and make noise. The more features like bells or drums or singing birds, the more tunes, the more elaborate the case, the higher the price of a music box.

There were many Edison phonograph models. This 12-inch-long by 12-inch-high fireside Model A has a removable brass horn. The records were cylinders. The 1896 model ran on electricity or a battery. This is a later clockwork version.
(Photo: James Julia)

Pianos

Nineteenth-century player pianos, nickelodeons, and large music-making devices are very popular with collectors. These fun collectibles are loved for the joy they give, not just for their artistic or historic value. The early ones were expensive, and today only a very limited number are available.

A player piano can produce music without a pianist touching the keyboard. It has a mechanism that turns a roll of perforated paper and produces notes of a song on the piano. An ad in a local paper is usually enough to attract a buyer for an antique player piano. The Internet and several national collecting publications post ads requesting and offering old and new player-piano rolls.

Old pianos and organs are not as popular with collectors as the less sophisticated nickelodeons and player pianos. Formal pianos were often passed down within families, and there is a good supply today. Many old pianos, especially the *square* pianos, are not very good musical instruments because they do not hold a tune and are difficult to repair. Modern pianos and organs have many advantages over old ones. If you are considering buying an old piano to use as a musical instrument, you may find it better to purchase a new piano. If you are interested in the historic design of the case or the unique sound, then an antique piano might be best. Melodeons or reed organs are considered to be of historic value. Some collectors rework the cases of old pianos that are worthless as music makers and make desks.

It is surprisingly easy to date your piano or organ if it has a maker's name. On the Internet, the Piano Technicians Guild's Web site (www.ptg.org) has links to many piano manufacturers' Web pages that list the model years of their instruments. Some libraries have *Michel's Piano Atlas* or *Pierce Piano Atlas*, which list the manufacturing dates of most American pianos and organs made before 1960.

This rosewood Steinway fancy "D" concert grand piano was built about 1875. It has a rosewood case with shaped legs and a pierced music rack.
(Photo: Antiquarian Traders)

Other Music Makers

The rule for valuing other types of musical antiques is simple: If it is odd enough, someone will want it and treasure it. There are many collectors of old instruments, and they are always searching for rarities. The Internet and special publications devoted to music and musical collectibles are the best sources of information on these oddities. To find or to sell a dulciphone will usually take time and patience. Research at a library or on the Internet is the best way to learn more about instruments. Very little has been written about the many types of unusual musical instruments developed during the late nineteenth century. It is a safe guess that if your instrument looks like a Rube Goldberg invention and makes some sort of music, it is a product of the delightfully inventive minds of the 1850–1900 period, when many unusual instruments were created.

Homemade musical instruments like this dulcimer and fiddle show the inventiveness of country musicians. The three-string dulcimer was made of walnut and poplar with painted decoration. The fiddle was made from a "New Currency" brand cigar box, galvanized tin, oak, and pine.

Chapter 16

Textiles

✥ IF YOU WANT ADVICE about textiles or embroidery, the best place to get it is from an expert—perhaps from a friend who knits sweaters, embroiders pillowcases, or needlepoints chair seats. Anyone who is experienced with a knitting needle or crochet hook can tell you if a piece of needlework is good or bad, simple or complicated.

There are dozens of types of textiles, and the same rules apply to all of them. Like many antiques, textiles are collected for their historical interest. But a textile is also desirable because of its fine workmanship or decorative use, or for some sentimental reason. Since the 1970s there has been interest among collectors in all types of women's work, and any textile worked by hand or decorated with an interesting printed design is now valuable. Take your treasured quilt or rag rug to an expert who will tell you the truth about its maker's ability as a needleworker. Keep the quilt or the rug even if it isn't very good. After all, you own it because of the design or color or perhaps because the amateur needlewoman was Great-Aunt Helen and you are her namesake.

Opposite page: The overall design of this nine-block appliqué quilt was popular in the mid-nineteenth century. This quilt was made with a border on only three sides. (Photo: Brunk)

American Quilts

Patchwork or pieced quilts are different from appliquéd quilts. The top of a patchwork quilt is made of many different pieces of material stitched together to make one big piece. The top of an appliquéd quilt is a large piece of cloth to which many small pieces of material have been sewn. To assemble both types into quilts, the finished top piece is placed on an interlining and a backing fabric, then the layers are quilted together.

One of the easiest ways to tell if your quilt was made more than eighty-five years ago is to hold it in front of a sunny window or shine a strong light through the fabric. If you can see dark spots in the quilt, then your quilt contains cotton seeds that were never ginned out. Many collectors claim that the seeds prove the quilt was made before 1793, the year the cotton gin was invented. Actually, many quilt makers in rural areas did not use clean cotton until years later. Dark spots, or seeds, are found in quilts that were made as late as 1920.

There are many kinds of quilts, but there is a general rule you can apply to determine the age of each type. Quilt designs changed over time, so it is possible to guess the age of a quilt from the design with about 90 percent accuracy. There is, however, room for error, because some quilts were made in styles that had been out of vogue for many years.

All-white cotton quilts were in fashion in the late eighteenth and early nineteenth centuries. They were quilted with elaborate designs—often a large center design with a series of borders—and very fine quilting stitches. The cotton interlining was thin. American quilts almost always were quilted with a simple running stitch. English and most Continental quilts were made with a backstitch. All-white quilts came back into fashion at the end of the nineteenth century, but these were not as elaborately quilted.

Early eighteenth-century quilts, appliquéd or patched, had tree-style designs that were symmetrical from the base up. These quilts had no borders, or almost no borders. By the nineteenth century, quilt patterns were more formal and had a center design with symmetrical borders. The design in the center of the quilt began to

Opposite page: Colored blocks in a pattern called Caesar's Crown or Grecian Star variant were pieced together to form this quilt. It is 77 by 61 inches and was owned by a Kentucky family. (Photo: Brunk)

change by 1825. It was no longer just one big design like a tree, but several repeated squares of designs. By 1860 the center designs were all small squares, and the quilt had a series of little patterns within a border pattern.

Appliquéd quilts were common by the end of the eighteenth century. The quilter cut flowers, birds, or other designs pictured on printed chintzes and then quilted along the lines of the cut designs. Nineteenth-century appliquéd quilts were made with plain or over-all printed fabric that was cut into silhouettes, which were sewn on a white background. Quilts made with green and red cotton appliqués were in style from 1830 to 1850. White quilts with solid red or blue appliqués and embroidered squares were popular from about 1885 to 1925. Sometimes many friends would work on one quilt. Each friend would make one block and sign her name on it in ink or outlined in stitches. Later a party was held, and all the blocks were joined into one large quilt. This type of signature, or friendship, quilt was most popular from 1840 to 1860.

There are numerous designs for appliquéd quilts. New designs often appeared in several parts of the country within just a few days. During the Victorian era, some designs were published in ladies' magazines; before that, word-of-mouth made quilt designs available to housewives in all parts of the country.

Some late Victorian quilts had an irregular overall pattern and were known as crazy quilts. These quilts, popular from about 1870 to 1890, were made by piecing together small, irregular pieces of fragile, glamorous materials like velvet, silk, and satin. Then the quilter added decorative embroidery at the seams and inside the patches, attached the pieced fabric to a lining and a backing, and joined them together. The embroidery did not go through the backing. Quilts with thick lining were tied or tacked together with large knotted pieces of thread or yarn. Crazy quilts were also made in smaller sizes for use as throws on chairs and couches or as pillow covers.

The quilted woolen bedcover often called a linsey-woolsey quilt had three layers. The top layer was made of blue, green, or brown linsey-woolsey, a fabric made of wool and cotton or linen; the middle layer was a filling of carded wool; and a bottom layer was made of yellow or buff wool. The three layers were quilted together with linen thread. A few woolen coverlets date from the eighteenth century, but most were made between 1800 and 1850. The earlier a woolen quilt was made, the thinner its stuffing and the more elaborate its design.

Another clue determines the age of a quilt. The first bedcovers in this country were made from imported textiles, usually printed chintz or linen. Cotton was a hand-woven and homemade fabric until 1815 when the first cotton cloth from an American factory became available. After 1815 most covers were made of cotton. Printed cotton made in the United States was popular by 1840, but by 1870 the colored cotton quilt had gone out of fashion. Colored quilts returned to favor in the 1930s and are easy to recognize because of their geometric, overall fabric designs and bright colors, which are very different from those of earlier quilts.

Quilt sizes have changed slightly since the eighteenth century. Eighteenth-century quilts were very large because they were used as bedspreads. They ranged from nine to twelve feet square. The beds of the period were high four-poster beds that were stacked with pillows. Many eighteenth- and early nineteenth-century quilts were square in shape with two cutouts in the bottom corners that left room for the high posts at the foot of the bed. The nineteenth-century quilt was a smaller blanket-size cover.

One more tip: Sewing machines appeared about 1850. Many quilts were still hand-sewn after that date, but this tip will help you date a machine-made quilt with characteristics of the pre-1850 period.

Coverlets

Woven coverlets of blue and white, or brown, red, green, yellow, or other colors, were made during the eighteenth and nineteenth centuries. In the early years the housewife furnished her own materials for a coverlet. The wool of black sheep was used for the black wool. For other colors, white wool was

This plaid overshot wool coverlet has a center seam that indicates it was made on a small loom. The coverlet is 88 by 94 inches and has fringe on three sides. (Photo: Skinner)

dyed in large kettles. Most dyes came from plants: Indigo produced a blue dye; red came from madder root; goldenrod and sumac made yellow dye; alder bark made tan; hickory or walnut hulls dyed wool dark brown. The exception is the scarlet cochineal dye, which was made from the bodies of Mexican insects.

After wool was dyed and spun on a wheel, the yarn was woven on a loom. The home loom could weave a strip of fabric ranging from only 2½ to 3 yards long and up to 42 inches wide. Therefore, all the early coverlets were made with a center seam. Housewives did their own weaving until 1800, when itinerant weavers began working in New England, New York, Pennsylvania, and Ohio. Families found it was easier and faster to buy the woven product. By the 1870s, most coverlets were woven in factories.

There are four kinds of coverlets, and each was in style for only a short time. *Overshot*, the simplest type of woven coverlet, had a plain weave with colored designs. To form geometric designs, the weaver skipped the colored wool over threads in the lighter background. Overshot was made on the four-harness home loom. The coverlets were made of linen and wool during the eighteenth century, and of cotton and wool in the nineteenth century. Most overshot coverlets found today were made between 1800 and 1850.

Professional weavers made *double-cloth block* or *double-woven geometric* coverlets. Two different threads, plain-woven colored wool and plain-woven natural-colored cotton, were woven at one time on the loom, and the design was made by interweaving the threads. The coverlet was reversible. Most popular from 1820 to 1840, this type of coverlet was made on a narrow loom, and two strips were joined together to make a coverlet.

Summer-and-winter weave was a closely woven coverlet with a honeycomb appearance. If the design was blue against white on one side of the cloth, it was white against blue on the reverse side. Most summer-and-winter coverlets were made in New York and Pennsylvania from 1800 to 1830.

The Jacquard loom was invented in 1801 and was in use in America by 1820. Using the complicated device, weavers were able to produce fabrics with elaborate patterns. The earliest known dated *jacquard* coverlet was made in 1821. Early coverlets had geometric designs but the Jacquard loom made it possible for the new coverlets to have designs with flowers, animals, birds, and even buildings. The loom allowed weavers to create complicated three-color patterns, which were impossible to make before the loom's invention. Another advantage to the Jacquard loom was that it was much larger than earlier home looms, so weavers could make coverlets from one piece of fabric. Most jacquard coverlets were made by traveling weavers.

Nineteenth-century hand-woven coverlets came in many sizes. The most common size was made to fit a single adult bed. Most coverlets were about 72 inches wide, with lengths that varied from 90 to 108 inches. The widest coverlet was an 84-inch seamless bedcover. The smallest coverlet was made for a child's crib and measured 36 by 42 inches.

Many woven coverlets were marked with the name of the weaver and sometimes the name of the owner, the county or city where the owner lived, and the date the coverlet was made. This information was woven into a corner block or the border. Some weavers used logos or special motifs—perhaps a sailboat, a flower, an eagle, or a star—or wove slogans, like UNITED WE STAND, DIVIDED WE FALL, in the corner block or border.

The easiest way to date a coverlet is to look for the weaver's name. If a date appears alongside the name, the problem is solved. If just a name appears, you can consult one of the many books that list coverlet makers. *American Coverlets and Their Weavers* by Clarita S. Anderson includes a list of more than 700 weavers. If you own a coverlet that has a maker's name not listed, you may still

The complex woven design makes a Jacquard coverlet easy to recognize. This American coverlet with fruit and flowers has a name and date woven into two corners. The detail shows the date 1837 and a name, probably the owner's. (Photo: Skinner)

discover the coverlet's history. Send the name and a photograph of the coverlet to the Abby Aldrich Rockefeller Folk Art Museum, Box 1776, Williamsburg, VA 23185. For Canadian weavers, see *"Keep Me Warm One Night," Early Handweaving in Eastern Canada* by Harold and Dorothy Burnham.

Samplers were made by very young girls. This linen sampler, worked with silk and wool threads, was made by an eight-year-old girl in 1823. It shows the expected alphabets and also a motto and a picture of a house. (Photo: Skinner)

Samplers

A sampler is exactly what the name suggests: a sample of the skills of the maker. Samplers have been made for hundreds of years. They reached the height of their popularity during the seventeenth and eighteenth centuries in Europe, but the best American samplers date from 1790 to 1840.

One of the earliest samplers that includes a date as part of the design was made in 1630 in England. It was made on linen with silk thread stitches. Seventeenth-century American samplers are very scarce, and only about five samplers dating from before 1700 are known. Samplers were usually the work of young girls, and the best-known American sampler from this period was made about 1653 by Lora Standish, the daughter of Miles Standish, who was the military leader of the Plymouth Colony in Massachusetts. This sampler is in the Pilgrim Hall Museum in Plymouth.

Most early samplers were made from materials found at home. Smooth or coarse linen, muslin, or canvas was used. Loosely woven material was selected because it was easier to embroider. Early samplers were narrow (ranging from eight to nine inches in width) because looms that made homespun were not very wide. Later samplers were wider because they were made from fabric that was woven on larger looms. By the late eighteenth and early nineteenth century, the sampler was wider than it was high, which is the shape familiar to most of us. Eighteenth-century samplers were usually embroidered with wool thread. Silk thread was used after the Revolutionary War.

The easiest way to date an old sampler is to look for the maker's name and a date, which were often worked into the design. Early samplers were also decorated with the alphabet, examples of types of stitching, and perhaps a worthy motto. Alphabet designs were used after 1720. Mourning and memorial samplers were popular in the early 1800s. Maps embroidered on linen were common in England. Only a few examples made in America are known. Nineteenth-century samplers pictured military campaigns, historical events, hobbies, family portraits, and simple designs. Cross-stitch samplers were made starting in the early 1800s. The cross-stitch type was popular again in the 1930s.

Where a sampler was made can sometimes be determined from its design. After 1820 some samplers pictured actual buildings. For example, crow-step gables known only in early New York were stitched on samplers from that area. Ships appeared on New

England works, while sugarcane appeared on southern samplers. Eighteenth-century samplers often included the name of the girl's school, and this information can pinpoint the origin of the piece.

Berlin Work

In the early nineteenth century, printers in Berlin, Germany, published hand-colored needlework patterns that were printed on a background that looked like today's graph paper. When the patterns reached England, they became known as *Berlin work*. The patterns called for many shades of brilliantly colored wool. The yarn was thick, so the needlework went quickly. Several types of stitches were used, including cross-stitch, needlepoint, and a raised stitch that created a wool pile. Glass beads were sometimes used in the designs. This type of needlework was popular in Europe and the United States from the 1820s to the 1870s.

Left: Berlin work patterns were published on paper, then stitched on a fabric backing. This is a hand-colored Berlin work pattern from the 1850s.

Glass beads were worked into the design of this Berlin work upholstery. It was made in the mid-Victorian era. (Photo: New Orleans Auction Galleries)

Crewelwork

Crewelwork is an embroidered fabric. Colored yarn was sewn in designs on a piece of natural-colored linen. The designs often showed an Asian influence and pictured imaginary flowers and birds.

Most crewelwork was made in India and sent to all parts of the world. It was used for draperies, to cover chairs, or as bed hangings.

Fabrics were expensive and scarce in the American colonies, and many women made their own crewelwork. To save time and the scarce colored yarn, American housewives made widely spaced designs. Many New England pieces were embroidered in the economy stitch, which exposed the maximum amount of thread on the top surface and used less thread.

Deerfield Blue Embroidery

Deerfield, Massachusetts, was settled in 1669. During the eighteenth century, blue and white crewel embroidery was popular. In about 1896 a group of interested women rediscovered the blue and white crewel embroidery and organized the Deerfield Society of Blue and White Needlework. Its members made copies of early American embroidery using the old methods and patterns. Needlework kits based on the Society's patterns are still available.

This needlework picture is in memory of Emma Corbett. The sky and the mourner's face and arms are painted. The rest of the picture is stitched.

Needle Painting

Needle painting is a special type of art. The technique uses a sewn stitch of colored silk thread to produce a picture. The stitches are placed in all directions, and the stitch texture and color variations make the picture. Needle paintings were made as early as the fifteenth century.

Needlepoint

Needlepoint describes counted-thread needlework that covers the entire canvas. It includes petit point, gros point, and flame stitch (bargello). The canvas may be silk, cotton, or linen. The average collector today thinks only gros point is needlepoint. It is often used to upholster furniture.

Early needlepoint patterns were marked in black and white on graph paper, but later canvas and linen with designs already drawn on them became available. Designs included biblical scenes, pastoral scenes, portraits, animals, flowers, and the tree of life. Needlepoint chair upholstery, fire screens, pillows, and wall hangings were popular.

Needlepoint on canvas was a favorite handicraft for Victorian women. The needlewoman could create her own pattern, or purchase the design and transfer it to the canvas, or buy a printed canvas. Some canvases were available with the center design already worked. The Victorian needlewoman was left to complete the background and add the date.

Mention needlepoint and most collectors will think of a footstool or chair upholstered with a colorful, patterned, hand-stitched fabric like this one.

Stevengraphs

In Coventry, England, about 1860, weaver Thomas Stevens adapted his loom to produce woven bookmarks, fancy ribbons, and other novelties. He developed Stevengraphs, woven silk pictures that were mounted on cardboard and sold to be hung in homes. These silk pictures showed the Crystal Palace, the Houses of Parliament, and other famous buildings; horse racing, fox hunting, and other sports; boats, trains, and other kinds of transportation; and portraits of royalty, sportsmen, politicians, and famous people. Most were marked *Woven in silk by Thomas Stevens.* At trade exhibitions in major cities, Stevens set up his looms, demonstrated his technique, and sold Stevengraphs. Stevens died in 1888, but his silk pictures remained popular until about the beginning of World War I. The Stevengraph Works continued to produce silk items until it was destroyed in the bombing of Coventry in 1940.

Thomas Stevens made woven silk pictures like this bookmark sold at the 1876 Centennial Exposition. The design includes George Washington's portrait, flags, an eagle, a saying, and a building on the fair grounds.

Stump Work

Stump work is a form of embroidery that was popular in England and the colonies in the middle of the seventeenth century. The embroidery was padded, and the stitches appeared to be raised. It is seldom done today.

RUGS, CARPETS, ORIENTAL RUGS, AND OTHER FLOOR COVERINGS

The first carpet was produced in Babylonia about 700 B.C. Carpets might have been made at an even earlier date. A type of Oriental rug was used in ancient Greece and Rome, but wear and time have destroyed them. The earliest existing rugs date from the 1400s.

Few rugs were made like this one that is both braided and hooked. The center design was hooked. The surrounding multicolored area was braided. It is a 28-inch square. (Photo: Conestoga)

Sand and rush matting were the first floor coverings used in the American colonies. The earliest rugs in America were made from scraps of fabric. *Tongue rugs* were made with small tongue-shaped pieces of cloth that overlapped and were sewn to a backing. The background material of the tongue rug was completely covered by the overlapping tongues.

Button rugs were made a few years later. These canvas-backed homemade rugs resembled tongue rugs but used round pieces of cloth. The background fabric of the button rug showed between the circles of material that were stitched to the backing. Sometimes the circles were made from braided material and the canvas area between the circles was covered by sewn wool. The button rug was at the height of fashion during the 1820s. A few late examples were made from blue and gray pieces cut from old uniforms in the 1870s.

Hooked rugs were made in American homes by 1700 but were not in general use until the 1820s. The weaver pulled narrow strips of cloth remnants through a coarse fabric backing, creating flower, animal, and geometric designs. The artistic housewife was able to draw her own patterns, but those less talented could buy a pattern from designers like Edward Frost. He sold thousands of patterns,

and his factory was still working in the early 1900s. Hooked rugs reached the height of their popularity from 1820 until 1850. Cheap factory-made rugs appeared in the 1840s and discouraged the art of hooking.

The *braided rug* was popular along with the button rug and the hooked rug of the 1820s. The braided rug was made from braided strips of worn fabric. The braids were sewn together, round and round, until a large circular rug was made. This type of rug is still popular today.

Embroidered rugs were made by many of the well-to-do American women of the early nineteenth century. Woolen yarn was stitched on a heavy material, and the stitching covered the entire surface of the rug. Early embroidered rugs are very rare. Modern embroidered rugs are made today.

Crocheted rugs were made about the middle of the nineteenth century. They were made by crocheting a single strip of rags with a giant wooden crochet hook. The rug was round, and if it did not lie flat after it was washed, it was starched and flattened to the floor.

Carpets were first used in England about 1750. They were made in factories in the United States by 1791. The first carpet

Pictorial hooked rugs were often very elaborate. This nineteenth-century American rug shows a dog and a bird on a branch in a leafy landscape. It is 25½ by 38½ inches. (Photo: Skinner)

Oriental rugs were used in the eighteenth and nineteenth centuries in America. This Shirvan Prayer rug was made in the late nineteenth century. It is about 4½ feet by 4 feet.
(Photo: Skinner)

factory to make finger-tufted rugs was owned by W. P. Sprague in Philadelphia.

The eighteenth century also marked the introduction of *Oriental rugs* into the English and American home. The term *Oriental rug* means any of the hand-knotted rugs made in southeastern Europe, Turkey, North Africa, Iran, Pakistan, India, or China. The elaborate designs had symbolic meanings for the weavers and were frequently worked into a geometric pattern. Seventeenth- and eighteenth-century portraits often show an Oriental rug used as a table covering.

The floor did not have to be covered with a rug or carpet. It was often painted in the informal homes of the early 1800s. There were spattered floors as well as floors painted with stencil designs. Wide border designs were sometimes painted near the edges, and the center sometimes had a smaller, overall pattern.

Painted *floorcloths* were used in England by 1680. Early floorcloths were made of canvas that was printed or painted with a pattern and varnished. Many early floorcloths were imported to the colonies from England. Sailcloth used as a floor covering was brushed with about ten coats of paint, and decorated with geometric designs or painted to imitate marble flooring. These floorcloths were used in middle-class homes by 1720. Nathan Smith started a factory in Knightsbridge, England, in 1754. He made floorcloths from resin, pitch, beeswax, linseed oil, and Spanish brown, which were pressed into a canvas.

Early floorcloths were expensive, but in 1844 a new product was developed by Elijah Galloway, who applied rubber, cork dust, and coloring to canvas. The rubber was costly, but in 1863 Frederick Walton invented a way to use oil in place of rubber. He was the first person to make an inexpensive linoleum. It was a popular floor covering into the mid-twentieth century. Modern versions of floorcloths can be bought today.

CLOTHING

Each year lucky people clean their attics and basements and rediscover the paisley shawl, wedding dress, or christening gown that an ancestor packed away many years ago. These clothes can be worn or displayed and enjoyed.

Shawls

Great-grandmother may have owned several types of shawls. Embroidered Spanish silk, French Chantilly lace, woven Kashmir, and paisley shawls were popular during the nineteenth century.

Shawls were fashionable in Europe and America from about 1790 to 1870. The history of the shawl dates back to the eleventh century in Kashmir. Very wealthy men wore the expensive weavings as belts or shoulder mantles. European travelers, traders, and military men bought the shawls in the 1770s and brought them back as gifts for wives and friends.

Kashmir shawls were woven by men. It took two men three years to make a shawl that sold for as much as a house. European weavers realized less expensive shawls would sell, and by 1805 French weavers were making "exact imitation" shawls using Indian looms and the weaving methods of the Orient. By 1820 lighter weight, better quality shawls were being made by a different weaving technique and selling in Germany, Italy, England, and even the Orient. The invention of the Jacquard loom meant weavers could create the elaborate patterns in a variety of colors and designs in less time. Weavers in Paisley, Scotland, created a shawl weaving industry and moved weaving from the cottage to the factory.

Kashmir shawls were woven from goat hair and were lighter and smoother than the European shawls. The finished shawl had a sheen. European shawls made before 1840 were made of silk and wool and were much heavier. Paisley weavers did not make all-wool shawls until 1823. Jacquard looms made shawls with few errors in the weave, but earlier shawls had several workers controlling the

loom and there were some flaws. Asian teardrop or pinecone, lotus flower, vines, and other ancient symbols were included in the Kashmir designs. The French adapted these designs and changed them enough that by the mid-nineteenth century European designs were the most popular for paisley shawls and Indian weavers imitated the western patterns.

Dress fashions determined the popularity of the shawl, which was used for looks as well as warmth. The 1820s dress was silk with a high waist and needed a large shawl. The Jacquard loom could weave a large shawl in one piece. In the 1830s the shawl became even more popular because it was needed to cover the huge hoop-supported skirt. Shawls were 5 feet square to 5 feet by 10½ feet. The paisley shawl weighed about 3½ pounds, but the Kashmir shawl was very lightweight, about 5 ounces. Paisley improved the shawl by 1865 and made a reversible shawl that hid any loose threads between two layers. It was very heavy and not popular. Printed shawls that imitated the woven Kashmir and paisley shawls were made for the mass market. Designs were printed on fabric with wooden blocks. The bustle, fashionable in the 1870s, did not look good with a shawl. The Franco-Prussian War (1870–1871) stopped the import of shawls from Kashmir. The Paisley weavers had few customers, prices fell and became so inexpensive they were no longer considered fashionable.

The Spanish *mantón,* or shawl, evolved from Chinese silk embroidery. The mantón is a combination of the *rebozo,* a Mexican shawl, and the Chinese silk embroidery seen by Spanish traders in the Philippines. Chinese designs, including exotic birds, flowers, and buildings, were used on the earliest Spanish shawls. By the nineteenth century, the shawl designs adapted Spanish flowers and Christian symbols. Most Spanish shawls feature long tassels made by knotting the frayed ends of the cloth.

French lace, much of it made in Chantilly, was popular shawl material, too. Black lace shawls were worn to contrast with light-colored skirts or as a summertime covering. Lace was made by machine on an adapted Jacquard loom after 1835.

This detail of a silk Spanish shawl shows the colorful embroidery and elaborate fringe. Large shawls were not only worn by women but also sometimes draped on the piano.

Opposite page: Paisley shawls were made to be worn. These three shawls, made about 1900, are draped on dress forms to show the way they were worn. (Photo: Doyle New York)

Large shawls declined in popularity about 1870. Stoles, scarves, and boas became popular in the late nineteenth century.

Wedding Dresses

Until the late nineteenth century, the average woman was married in her best dress. The dress was not white because it was to be worn to church or for visiting. White wedding dresses came into fashion for wealthy women after Queen Victoria's wedding in 1840. By the 1870s, middle-class women wanted white wedding gowns made in Paris, or at least a copy of a French dress. Dresses were often handed down from mother to daughter, so look for restyled bodices or sleeves and added decorations. The most collectible dresses are unaltered with the original lace, beading, and embroidery.

Christening Gowns

Traditionally, the first time a child was seen in public was for his or her baptism, and the baby was dressed up to be introduced to the neighbors. By the eighteenth century, christening gowns were white to symbolize purity. Many were embroidered, and most had matching bonnets. The gowns were used for more than one child in a family and then handed down, and many have names and dates embroidered on the inside slip.

Accessories—Collars, Handbags, Fans, and Gloves

Small articles of antique clothing are easy to collect. Odds and ends like fancy collars, beaded gloves, and lace fans were too good for everyday use and did not suffer the wear and tear other garments endured. The best examples have lace, beading, or embroidery. Machine-made pieces, like celluloid collars or printed fans, are interesting, but collectors prefer handmade examples with intricate details. Many collectors frame antique clothing accessories under light-filtering glass.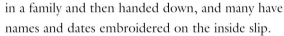

The beaded purse from the 1870s and the three Victorian fans were all carried to parties and important events. The flower-decorated fan is hand painted. The feather-trimmed fan has ivory sticks. The black fan is made of tortoise shell and lace.

Chapter 17

JEWELRY

UNTIL THE EIGHTEENTH CENTURY, gems and jewelry were worn only by the wealthy. That changed in 1730, when *paste*, a glass that could be cut and polished to resemble gemstones, was invented. It was often backed with foil to make the stones look brilliant. Those who couldn't afford genuine stones could now buy jewelry. Some paste jewelry was very fine, and many of the most respected jewelers made paste pieces.

Toward the end of the eighteenth century, the French and American revolutions were under way, and displays of wealth went out of style. Expensive, showy jewelry was not popular. By the beginning of the nineteenth century, European fashions called for the return of jewelry, although in simple forms—draped chains, small brooches, bracelets, hair ornaments, and necklaces with cameos and mosaics. In America, few people wore much jewelry until after the Civil War.

This eighteenth-century necklace was made with old mine diamonds and foil-backed stones the color of topaz. Each "gem" was set in a bezel and backed with foil and gold. The gold-mounted necklace was probably made in Spain.

By the beginning of the 1830s, the Industrial Revolution had introduced equipment to produce jewelry by machine, making it possible for the middle class to afford jewelry. Queen Victoria loved jewelry, and during the early years of her reign sentimental gold jewelry decorated with what the Victorians considered romantic symbols—flowers, a coiled snake, a hand—was popular. Bracelets were fashionable, but earrings were not.

The death of Prince Albert and the outbreak of the Civil War in America both occurred in 1861. The year and its events ushered in an era of darker clothing and heavier, ornate mourning jewelry. Black stones like jet were in fashion. Earrings became popular again, and exotic designs from Egypt and India were stylish.

Clothing became lighter and simpler in the 1880s. Jewelry became more delicate. Silver, rather than gold, was used for less formal pieces. Earrings shrank to a single small stone. Bracelets grew narrower. By the end of the nineteenth century and the beginning of the twentieth century, art nouveau and Arts and Crafts styles began to influence jewelry design.

Buying and Selling Antique Jewelry
Collectors of antique gold jewelry had a heyday prior to World War II. Most stores that sold new jewelry had a box of old scrap jewelry waiting to be melted down for the gold content. Old jewelry often was traded as a partial payment for new, modern pieces or for much-needed cash. Those who wanted to buy old pieces of jewelry paid the value of the melted weight of the piece.

Times have changed. Antique rings and pins are so fashionable that costume jewelry makers are copying them in inexpensive versions. Prestige jewelry stores are selling gold replicas of nineteenth-century jewelry. Today there are many manmade stones. Synthetic rubies and sapphires, cultured pearls, color-enhanced stones, and cubic zirconia are sometimes used instead of real gems. Costume jewelry, especially twentieth-century Bakelite, is collected. It is difficult for a beginner to tell an authentic old piece from a good copy.

Select a trustworthy source from which to buy or sell old jewelry. Any jewelry dealer is able to perform tests to determine the

Opposite page: Blue enamel jewelry was popular in the eighteenth century. This bangle bracelet has irregular pearls and old mine diamonds set in a blue enamel background. It is 18 karat gold.

gold content and worth of a gold pin based on its actual meltdown value. Gemstones can be identified and appraised by any good jewelry store. If you have an old piece of jewelry that looks valuable, take it to an expert for an appraisal. The artistic value of the old piece and the fame of the maker, especially if it is signed, add to its worth.

Before you go to an expert, examine the piece of gold or silver jewelry for a mark such as *sterling, 800, 18K,* or *14K.* Pieces marked *gold filled* are not made of solid gold. Jewelry that is unmarked must be tested by an expert. Look carefully at the clasp on a chain or the back of a pin. A mark may be so small that you may need to use a magnifying glass to see it.

Check your jewelry for hallmarks, small pictures of a king's head, towers, or other symbols. These symbols identify the maker and date and are listed in many books about silver and gold work. Sometimes there is a maker's name or initials or the name of a country or store. (For information on silver marks, see page 198.)

NECKLACES, EARRINGS, AND OTHER NOTEWORTHY JEWELRY

Cameos

Cameos set as brooches were the height of fashion in Victorian times. This 1½-inch-wide stone cameo surrounded by pearls and set in 18-karat gold was made about 1875. It could be the clasp holding a shawl or the center of a ruffled blouse collar.

Cameos were made by the Greeks as early as the second century B.C. The Romans also created cameo jewelry. Cameos became popular in Europe in the sixteenth century. Lava, opals, carnelian, onyx, and other stones, as well as glass and shells, are sometimes carved to make cameos. The artist carves away part of the stone so different-colored layers appear. A stone cameo will usually have an all-white figure against a black background. A shell cameo is usually made with a white figure against a tan to pink background. The back of a shell cameo is often slightly curved because of the natural shape of the shell.

Look carefully for any sign that your cameo is really two pieces of stone that have been cemented together. This is an inferior "cameo." Many cameos were made from two- or three-colored layers of stone. The skill of the artist, the quality of the setting, and the age of the piece determine the value of cameo jewelry.

Choker Necklace

The dog collar, or choker, necklace was first popular between 1890 and 1910. Ribbon or bead necklaces were worn high on the neck like a dog's collar. Pearl, diamond, and jeweled chokers were favored by Queen Alexandra and others, especially women with long necks.

Coin Jewelry

Silver coins have been linked together to make bracelets for years. About 1860 it was the style to engrave the back of a dime or gold coin with elaborate initials or names and join several of the coins into a bracelet. Some engraved coins were made as love tokens. Collectors sometimes find small gold pieces with holes that permitted the owner to wear them as charms. Since the nineteenth century, soldiers in almost every conflict have made linked-coin bracelets to send home to mother or a girlfriend. Any type of coin jewelry is interesting to own and has a value as jewelry, but not as coins.

Top left: This 10¾-inch necklace is a choker that was tied at the back of the neck with a black ribbon. Its stones are "paste," glass with foil backing to imitate expensive diamonds.

Bottom: American coins dated between 1875 and 1883 were engraved with initials, then linked together to form this friendship bracelet. It is 7½ inches long.

Earrings

Earrings for pierced ears were the only kind worn until the end of the nineteenth century. Early earrings hung from a bent wire that passed through a hole in the earlobe. Posts or studs were used after the middle of the nineteenth century. By the end of the century, some people began to consider ear piercing barbaric. Screw backs for earrings were invented in 1894. Clips were patented in the 1930s. Many earrings had their old backs replaced because of the preference of a new owner. By the 1960s, pierced ears and the earrings for them came back into fashion.

Jewelry made from blond hair is unusual. This woven hair bow pin has an 18 karat gold center and ends. It was made about 1880.

Hair and Mourning Jewelry

Beginning in the sixteenth century, jewelry that contained human hair was worn either as a love token or as a remembrance of a loved one who had died. Locks of hair—braided, coiled or flat—were set in a frame to make a brooch, locket, pendant, or ring.

Mourning rings were popular during the late eighteenth and early nineteenth centuries. At a funeral a mourner was given a gold ring with the name, age, and date the deceased died engraved inside. The ring often had hair of the deceased or other memorabilia set on the front. The mourning rings were worn for years in memory of the departed.

Hair jewelry—rings, brooches, lockets, bracelets, watch chains, earrings, and other pieces—was sometimes made from the hair of the deceased. Some commercial pieces were made to order from a living relative's hair or from hair of an unknown donor. It was especially popular from 1820 to the 1880s. Women in mourning also wore pieces of jewelry made with black enamel, jet, or black stones.

Right: Brunette hair was woven into hollow balls, then mounted with gold parts to make these dangling earrings. They have French hooks for pierced ears. Mourning jewelry was worn for at least a year after a death.

Love Jewelry

A popular type of jewelry given as a token of love in the nineteenth century was a pin or ring with precious gems set in a special order to spell out a sentiment like Regard (**R**uby, **E**merald, **G**arnet, **A**methyst, **R**uby, **D**iamond) or Dearest. Other romantic jewelry included lockets that held a picture, heart and key lockets, and Mizpah rings, which were wide gold bands with the Hebraic word *Mizpah* on them. Mizpah means "remembrance or watchfulness," and these rings were given to soldiers before they went to battle.

PRECIOUS AND SEMIPRECIOUS STONES FOUND IN VICTORIAN JEWELRY

Rubies, sapphires, emeralds, and diamonds have been among the most precious gems throughout the ages. They have been favorite stones because of their color, rarity, light-reflecting qualities, and hardness. But many other gemstones, chosen for color or interesting markings, are found in old jewelry. These gems are called semiprecious stones.

Agate

Agates come in many colors, but the most common are brown, black, and white. Most agates have bands or layers of color. Black and white agates are often used to make cameos. Moss agate is a stone that looks as if it has fossilized moss inside. Victorians believed that moss agate protected the wearer from spider bites and thunderstorms. Agate was said to cure insomnia and to bring victory in battle.

Amber

Amber is fossilized resin from a pine tree. Sometimes insects or parts of plants are embedded in it. Amber comes in many colors, ranging from a cloudy light yellow to a clear brownish red that is the most desirable. Amber beads were popular in the 1880s and are still being made. The older beads are more valuable.

This nineteenth-century silver locket and chain is marked with English hallmarks. The 1¾-inch locket has a repoussé decoration of flowers.

Since the 1970s pieces of scrap amber have been heated and fused to form inexpensive new beads and other pieces. Much new Russian and Central European amber has been sold since the 1990s.

TEST FOR TRUE AMBER

Amber is soft and light-weight. To test for amber, mix four teaspoons of salt in an eight-ounce glass of water and place the amber in it. Amber will float, while imitation amber-colored stones or glass will sink.

Small emerald chips are set in these eighteenth-century Spanish earrings. The 1¾-inch earrings are made in a typical style with a bowknot center and dangling parts.

Beryl

The beryl family of gems includes emerald (green) and aquamarine (blue) as well as beryl, which can be colorless or various shades of gold, green, and pink. Emeralds are the most precious gems in this group. Emeralds may be a pale green and have bubbles or cracks, but the finest emeralds have no visible flaws and are transparent and a deep green color.

Carnelian

The brownish red variety of chalcedony, a form of quartz, is called carnelian or cornelian. It has been used for beads and cameos. Napoleon always carried a carnelian, which he believed would protect him in battle. Superstition claims that if the carnelian failed to protect, it would at least stop the bleeding if it was placed next to an open wound.

Coral

Coral was particularly popular in Victorian times. The stone is available in colors that range from white to orange-red to deep coral red. Dark red coral and angel skin (white) coral are the most valuable. Coral was said to protect babies from danger, and many small necklaces of coral beads were made for children. A *coral and bells* was a silver and coral rattle given to teething babies by their wealthy families in the eighteenth century.

Diamond

Diamonds have not changed through the years, but the methods of cutting them have improved. Modern diamonds are more brilliant than the early ones. Early diamonds, before the sixteenth century, were cut to accommodate the original octahedral shape of the stone and keep it as large as possible. In the eighteenth century, French diamond cutters developed a cut that added to the brilliance. It doubled the number of facets on the upper part of the stone. More facets increase the amount of light a stone reflects and its brilliance.

Victorian women liked carved coral jewelry. This pair of 1⅜-inch earrings has cherub heads, flowers, and small dangling parts shaped like Greek vases.

Rose cut and old mine diamonds were often used in Victorian jewelry, and it was only in the twentieth century that the modern brilliant cut diamonds were preferred. Old mine diamonds are worth a fraction of a full-cut stone, but antique jewelry with old mine diamonds can sell for high prices. Collectors look for loose

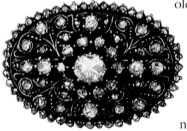

old mine diamonds to replace lost diamonds in antique jewelry. Jewelers who specialize in antique jewelry and repair will buy the old stones. If a Victorian piece is repaired with new brilliant cut diamonds, the replacement stones will be obvious. Watch out for jewelry that once had large diamonds that have been replaced with cubic zirconium or some of the other difficult-to-detect synthetic stones.

Left: This 1½-inch-wide brooch made of 14 karat yellow gold and silver filigree is in a style popular about 1840. It is set with many rose cut diamonds. The solid back is engraved with floral designs. (Photo: Charlton Hall)

Diamonds come in many colors. Most often seen is the bluewhite diamond. Other colors are pink, violet, yellow, brown, and black. Diamonds in shades of red, green, and blue are the rarest. Many diamonds are color-enhanced with heat treatment and irradiation today.

A diamond will scratch glass, but so will many other clear white stones, such as zircon, quartz, white sapphire, beryl, topaz, and tourmaline. It is difficult to determine whether the mark is a scratch or a powder line left by the scratcher.

Emerald
See Beryl.

Garnet

Garnet jewelry was fashionable before 1840, but it was a craze in Victorian times. It went out of style about 1910 and was revived about 1950. Many copies of old-fashioned garnet jewelry have been made in Europe, but the new pieces are usually not as well made as the old ones. New stones are lighter in color and not the deep red that is most desirable. Dark stones reappeared in the 1990s. Some of the faceting on the 1990s jewelry is poorly done. Most garnet jewelry, whether old or new, is made with clusters of small stones set in prong settings made of silver or gold plate. Any solid-gold garnet jewelry is of greater value. Garnets come in many colors, including yellow, orange, brown, violet, green, pink, and red, but the greatest demand is for the red garnet.

Garnet is the lucky birthstone for people born in January. Some people believe that garnets can cure hemorrhages, calm the wearer, or be deadly if shot from a gun like a bullet.

Teardrop-shaped garnets are used in three drops on this 1¾-inch pin. Pearls and other small garnets decorate the piece. It was made in the mid-1800s.

Goldstone

The reddish brown stone that looks as if it is filled with gold grains is called goldstone. It is an imitation stone that was first made about 1840 by spilling copper filings into glass. Many pieces of Victorian jewelry were made with this artificial stone. Aventurine, a type of quartz with sparkling inclusions, is sometimes confused with goldstone. Another type of aventurine is a dull, dark green with metallic spots and is not often used for jewelry.

Jade

Real jade is actually one of two minerals, nephrite or jadeite. Both are usually a pale to dark green color, but they also occur in nature in a variety of other colors, including black, red, pink, violet, and white. Because jade is a hard, compact stone, it can only be carved by abrasives, not cutting tools. Antique Chinese carved jade can be very valuable.

Jet and Look-Alikes

Jet is a form of coal, and the best has been found in England. The first jet necklaces were made about 1800. Dark black pieces were hand carved or turned on a lathe. Jet jewelry was associated with mourning and became very fashionable after the death of Prince Albert of England in 1861. Victorians often wore mourning jewelry—especially brooches, pendants, and rings—in memory of a relative or loved one. Black jewelry was in style from the 1820s until the late 1880s. Jet is a soft stone that is much softer than glass. Glass beads are much harder to scratch. A similar but less expensive black stone used for mourning was bog oak, a fossilized wood preserved in peat marshes.

Moonstone

A moonstone is a colorless, cloudy stone that seems to gleam from within. The moonstone was used in Victorian jewelry from about

1885 to 1900. Some moonstones were carved. The moonstone is considered a lucky stone.

Opal

In ancient times the opal was considered a symbol of hope and prosperity. However, since about the seventeenth century superstitious people have considered this multicolored iridescent gem unlucky. Queen Victoria, who wore opal jewelry

Marcus & Company of New York made this 2-inch-long pendant in the art nouveau style. The stone is a piece of black opal in rough form. The brown parent rock that is the back is decorated with gold and enameled irises.

to help the Australian opal miners, brought the gem back into style. Opals were often used in art nouveau jewelry. There are many types of opals, including white opals, black opals, green opals, and Mexican fire opals and orange opals.

Pearl

Pearls come in many colors, from various shades of white to pink, green, gold, blue, and even black or orange. Their size ranges from as small as a pinhead to as large as a pigeon egg. Until the beginning of the twentieth century, pearls were very expensive jewels and were owned almost exclusively by royalty and the very rich. The development of cultured pearls at the beginning of the twentieth century made pearls affordable for the middle class.

Cultured pearls are real pearls, but they are not natural pearls. A cultured pearl grows inside the shell of a living mollusk, usually an oyster, after a foreign substance such as a tiny bead has been inserted inside the oyster. The bead irritates the oyster, which secretes a coating to cover the rough bead. Natural pearls are made when a foreign substance accidentally makes its way inside a mollusk shell.

Imitation pearls made of glass beads coated with a mixture of silvery crystals to produce an iridescent effect were used in nineteenth-century costume jewelry. Today simulated pearls are made of glass or plastic and covered with a chemical coating.

Baroque pearls were used to form the body of this 1½-inch butterfly pin. The wings are made of mine cut diamonds set in silver and gold. It was made in the 1840s.

Peridot

Peridots are clear yellow-green, olive green, or brownish stones. Sometimes classified as semiprecious stones, they were popular only in the late nineteenth century.

Quartz

Quartz is the most common semiprecious stone used in jewelry. It includes a variety of minerals with a similar composition, such as amethyst, rock crystal, smoky quartz, rose quartz, tigereye, cat's-eye, agate, jasper, onyx, and opal.

This ring, made about 1910, has a ¹/₂-inch square cut peridot and a pierced platinum mounting. It was made in the early 1900s.

Rock Crystal

The term *rock crystal* has several meanings, but for jewelry the term means the clear, colorless quartz that has been dug from the earth. It is as clear as glass if it is of good quality. True rock crystal feels cold in your hand, even on a warm day, while glass will feel almost room temperature. Round and faceted beads were often made of rock crystal in the nineteenth and early twentieth centuries.

Rubies and Sapphires

The sapphire and ruby are varieties of a mineral called corundum. Rubies come in many shades of red. People usually think of sapphire as a blue stone, but there are also pink, orange, yellow, green, lavender, and even black sapphires. Modern stones may be synthetic or enhanced.

Spinel

Spinel is usually a red stone, but it also occurs in violet, blue, green, and black. Until the middle of the nineteenth century, it was classed as a ruby, and even now it is sometimes mistaken for that more valuable gem.

Purple, green, lavender, black, and orange spinel beads form this necklace. Spinel in other colors is also found in nature.
(Photo: Charlton Hall)

Topaz

The clear yellow-brown topaz was very popular in the eighteenth and nineteenth centuries. Natural topaz can also be blue, yellow, orange, light green, pink, and colorless. Pink topaz is the rarest and most valuable topaz. Blue topaz is the most popular. It is also affordable because most blue topaz sold in the late twentieth and the twenty-first centuries is white or colorless topaz that has been heat-treated to turn blue. In the twentieth century, yellow-brown topaz was sometimes heated to turn it blue, pink, or colorless.

The yellow-brown topaz has been so popular through the centuries that the word topaz *is now used for the color. This 3½-inch brass buckle with Japanese-inspired designs has a topaz center stone.*

Tourmaline

Tourmalines are multicolored, layered stones. Their predominant colors are often shades of pink or green, although they can also be yellow, brown, blue, violet, black, or colorless. Most tourmalines were cut for jewelry or made into beads, but flawed stones were sometimes used for small carvings. Watch out for stones that have been dyed a bright color or made from crushed stones.

Turquoise

Turquoise is a porous, opaque stone that ranges in color from blue to a pale blue-green. In Mexico and the American Southwest, American Indians set turquoise in silver for their traditional jewelry.

JEWELRY DICTIONARY

Doublet

To create a larger or more beautiful stone, a jewelry maker can glue a gem to a less valuable mineral to form a doublet. A colorless piece of beryl could be glued on top of green glass to make an emerald-like doublet of little value. A third layer may be added to make a triplet. When carefully crafted, these fabricated stones are difficult to recognize, especially when they are set in a piece of jewelry.

Most opals used in jewelry today are doublets or triplets because opal is found in thin layers and the soft stone is easily dam-

Opposite page: Turquoise with no veining was popular for Victorian jewelry. Pearls surround the domed turquoise stones on this 2¼-inch gold pin. It was made about 1865.

Jewelry Quality Marks

Jewelry is often stamped with words that indicate the maker or the age of the piece. The type of material used will help date the piece. The industrialization of jewelry began in the 1850s after jewelry makers learned how to use gold overlay and gold electroplating. In 1854 it became legal to use karat weights lower than 18K (karat).

25-, 15-, or 10- year warranty: Pocket watches from the late nineteenth and early twentieth centuries engraved with this phrase have a gold-filled case; *25-year* means 14K gold, *15-year* means 10K gold, *10-year* means 9K gold.

800 silver: This mark indicates that 800 parts of the metal out of 1,000 are silver. It is considered solid silver in Germany, Italy or Russia. In the United States and England, at least 925 parts out of 1,000 must be silver for the silver to be considered solid silver or sterling.

Gold-filled or overlay: A base metal covered with a layer of gold at least 1/20 of the total weight. The gold is bonded to the base metal by electroplating and must be marked. Gold-filled, gold-plated, and gold overlay pieces have limited meltdown value.

Gold plate or rolled gold: This metal is similar to a gold-filled metal, but the gold is less than 1/20 of the total metal weight.

Karat stamp: A 1906 U.S. law required that all precious metals include a karat stamp. A 1962 U.S. law required a karat and a manufacturer's stamp. Pure gold is 24K; 14K, 18K, 20K, and 22K marks specify the proportion of pure gold in an alloy. If a piece is 14 parts pure gold and 10 parts of another alloy, it is 14/24 parts gold or 14K. European hallmarks use decimal fractions: .375 is 9K; .625 is 15K; .75 is 18K.

Meltdown: This is the value if the piece is melted and the wholesale price of the raw materials is calculated.

aged. A top piece of clear mineral and a bottom piece for added thickness are sometimes added to the thin slice of opal, making a triplet that is more scratch and crack resistant.

Filigree

Silver filigree work has been made since the days of ancient Egypt. Silver filigree wire was made by drawing a silver wire through successively  smaller holes until a very thin wire was formed. The wire was coiled, bent, and soldered into designs with small silver balls. Gold filigree was made with gold wire. The same technique is used to make filigree today.

Ivory

Ivory refers to material from not only elephant tusks, but also the teeth of whales, mammoths, boars, and other mammals. Elephants are an endangered species, so their tusks can no longer be used for new jewelry.

Platinum

Platinum began to be used for jewelry in Europe and America in the 1850s, but it was not popular until the early twentieth century. Because it has a higher value than gold, it is used only for very fine jewelry.

Top right: Detail of filigree

Most platinum jewelry is 950 parts per thousand pure platinum and marked *950* and *Platinum, Plat,* or *Pt.* If the platinum is 90 percent pure, it is marked *900Pt, Pt 900,* or *900Plat.* Check the marks. Platinum and white gold, which is less valuable, look very much alike.

JEWELRY DESIGNERS
A table in the appendix at the back of this book lists the name, location, date, mark, and other information about jewelry designers of the nineteenth century.

These Tiffany & Company cufflinks and studs have black agate with the intaglio monogram R. They are in the original 1860s box. The box helps identify the maker.

Chapter 18

Toys, Games, Dolls, and Holiday Antiques

❧ FILMS AND ILLUSTRATIONS often picture toy makers working in small village toy shops. This image is just one of the many myths that have been handed down with antiques in America. Many toy makers did have shops, but by the early 1800s, toys were made in factories and sold in quantity. After the Civil War, hundreds of factories produced toys, rocking horses, doll furniture, blocks, and even board games. Handmade toys were the norm in most of western America, where houses were far from towns and stores. But even there, factory-made dolls, wagons, sleds, and whistles found their way into the hands of children.

The early cast-iron, hand-painted tin, wooden, ceramic, or paper toys have always been popular with collectors. Many factory toys were labeled, and any pre-1900 toy with its original label and box is of interest. Empty boxes without the toy sell if the graphics are unusual.

The collector of toys is interested not only in the item but also in the history that it represents. A labeled or boxed toy can be dated and considered in its historical context, and this is part of the charm of the old toy. *The Game of Playing Department Store* board game takes on deeper meaning when you realize that the prices on the

Opposite page: Two boys in matching sailor suits ride on this lithographed tin toy. The wheels and steering column move. The 4 ½-inch toy was made in Germany.
(Photo: Theriault's)

board (such as $2.50 for a pair of shoes) are authentic prices for 1898, the year the game first appeared.

Age alone does not determine a toy's value. The general rule is if the toy was made before 1975, some collector will want it. In some cases, even new toys, such as space-related toys, especially *Star Wars* and *Star Trek*, sell for high prices. There is one other important rule for the collector of toys: Never repaint an old metal or wooden toy because it lowers the toy's value. A professional restoration of an exceptionally rare old toy or a pedal car may add to the value.

METAL TOYS

Tin, iron, lead, pewter, steel, and other metals have been used to make toys. Toy styles and construction have changed through the years, so it is possible to estimate an approximate date for an old metal toy based on its appearance. There is one major problem in dating old toys, particularly lithographed tin toys and cast-iron wheeled toys, such as horse-drawn fire engines. These toys have become so popular with collectors that many firms are making reproductions. Most new toys are not made to fool the collector, but within a few years of use by a five-year-old child, the new toy could easily look like a bargain antique at a garage sale.

This tin toy balloon went up on a string while the aeronaut waved a flag with Lehmann's logo. Mars was the name of a real German balloon. Versions of this toy were made from 1896 to 1935. (Photo: Auction Team Breker)

German toy makers produced many types of metal toys, including dollhouses, kitchens, boats, fire stations, cars, and people working at a trade. By 1900 more than one-third of German-made toys were sold in America. German makers changed the wording on their toys to English names to suit the U.S. market. Many German toys were still being made by hand as late as 1900, and many factory-made toys were still hand painted or hand stenciled.

French toys were often elaborate and expensive, and they were not exported in quantity to America. French toys were not sold in large quantities in the United States until World War I when German toys were unavailable.

Popular Toys and Games Made before 1900

Most of the toys and games that are popular today were invented years ago. This table furnishes the approximate dates some toys and games were first manufactured.

Toys	Starting Date of Commercial Manufacture
Board games	Late 18th century
Cap guns and cap exploders	Mid-19th century (most popular 1885–1915)
Card games (Authors, Old Maid, etc.)	1808
Cast-iron American toys	1825 (most popular 1880–1920)
Clockwork toys	Most after 1860
Friction toys, metal	After 1875
Horse-drawn carts and wagons	1880–1890 (most popular)
Ice skates—all metal with clamp (other types earlier)	1870
Jack-in-the-box	Early 1880s
Mechanical banks	1870s
Rocking horse	c.1780
Rocking horse on a spring platform	1859
Roller skates	1863
Rubber toys	1850
Slot machines	1895
Sports	
Baseball	1840
Football	1870
Golf	Mid-18th century
Steam-powered toys (factory-made)	1870
Steam trains	1830 (limited number)
Teddy bear	1902
Toy soldiers (style of uniform helps to date, but not too accurate)	18th century
Tin toys	1840 (most popular 1870–1900)
Whirligig	15th-century Europe
Windup toys (clockwork toys)	Most after 1860
Wooden pull toys	18th century (factory-made 1860–1900)

Early American Toy Manufacturers

Most toys made by these manufacturers are marked with a name or company logo.

Manufacturer	Dates
Art Fabric Mills New Haven, Connecticut	c.1899–1910
Automatic Toy Works New York, New York	1868–c.1880
R. Bliss Manufacturing Company Providence and Pawtucket, Rhode Island	1832–c.1914
Milton Bradley Company Springfield, Massachusetts	1860–present
George W. Brown and Company Forestville, Connecticut	1856–1868 (merged with J. and E. Stevens)
C.C. Bush and Company Providence, Rhode Island	c.1870
Francis W. Carpenter and Company Harrison, New York	1844–1925
Charles M. Crandall Company Covington (c.1820) and Montrose (1866), Pennsylvania, and Waverly (1885), New York	c.1820–1905
Jesse Crandall New York, New York	1840s–1880s
James Fallows Philadelphia, Pennsylvania	1874–1890s
Francis, Field and Francis Philadelphia, Pennsylvania	1838–c.1860
Gibbs Manufacturing Company Canton, Ohio	1890s–2001 (stopped making toys in 1969)
Gong Bell Manufacturing Company East Hampton, Connecticut	1866–1930s
N. N. Hill Brass Company East Hampton, Connecticut	1889–1930s
S. L. Hill New York, New York	c.1858–1880s
Hubley Manufacturing Company Lancaster, Pennsylvania	1894–1940s
Hull and Stafford Clinton, Connecticut	c.1860s–1880s
E. R. Ives and Company Plymouth and Bridgeport, Connecticut (became Ives and Blakeslee in early 1870s)	1868–1931

Manufacturer	Dates
Kenton Hardware Company (Kenton Toys) Kenton, Ohio	c.1893–1952
Kyser and Rex Philadelphia, Pennsylvania	1880–1884
McLoughlin Brothers New York, New York	1850s–1921
Merriam Manufacturing Company Durham, Connecticut	1856–1880s
National Toy Company New York, New York	1870s
Parker Brothers Salem, Massachusetts	1883–present
Pratt and Letchworth Buffalo, New York (also marketed toys as Buffalo Toy Works)	1880–1890s
W. S. Reed Toy Company Leominster, Massachusetts	1875–1897
C. G. Shepard and Company Buffalo, New York	1866–1892
William Shimer Son and Company Freemansburg, Pennsylvania	1875–c.1890
J. and E. Stevens and Company Cromwell, Connecticut	1843–c.1930
Stevens and Brown Manufacturing Company Cromwell, Connecticut	1868–1870s
William S. Tower (Tower Guild) South Hingham, Massachusetts	1830s–c.1880
Union Manufacturing Company Clinton, Connecticut	1853–1869
United States Hardware Company New Haven, Connecticut	1896–1901
Watrous Manufacturing Company East Hampton, Connecticut	1880s–1930s
Weeden Manufacturing Company New Bedford, Massachusetts	1880s
Welker and Crosby Brooklyn, New York	1880s
Wilkins Toy Works Keene, New Hampshire	1890–1919

Tin Toys

The earliest manufactured American toys were made of tin. Pieces of tin were cut by hand or machine, assembled, soldered, and painted by hand. Tinsmiths used scrap pieces left over from making lanterns or cookie cutters to make toys. The first factory for tin toys opened in Meriden, Connecticut, during the 1840s. Toy makers in Connecticut, New York, and Philadelphia were making tin toys by the 1870s.

The lithographed tin toy was a favorite. Offset lithography was developed during the 1840s, partly for the toy industry. There were several other printing processes that put a pattern on a piece of tin, but by 1860 the offset method was used universally.

Gnomes have always delighted children. This 4-inch lithographed tin toy made by the German firm Meier moves with a lever so a gnome feeds the parrot. It was made about 1900.
(Photo: Theriault's)

Most old tin toys found today were made between about 1870 and 1915, although some were manufactured later. Collectors are interested in any tin toy made before 1915, even if it is only in fair condition. Millions of tin toys were made, and it is only reasonable to assume that the more expensive ones were produced in small quantities. The larger the toy, the more valuable it is. Large toys required more labor and, consequently, were more expensive when they were new. Tin toys are sometimes marked, which adds to the value because a mark identifies the maker and dates the toy. Copies of these toys are still being made, especially in Asian countries.

Tin toy kitchens and kitchen utensils are common, but toy household furniture is scarce. All sorts of wagons, fire engines, stagecoaches, and buses are valuable; locomotives, trains, and horsecars are better; old tin boats are the rarest. Animated groups of animals or people, toys that make noise with a gong, bell, or whistle, or toys that move are desirable.

Tin railroad trains are collected eagerly, especially those made in America. European-made tin trains, even those with American names, can often be recognized because the cars have the numerals *I, II,* or *III,* indicating the first-, second-, or third-class coaches used on European railroads.

Iron Toys

America's first cast-iron toys—pressing irons made with trivets, miniature garden tools, and a few wheeled toys—were produced about 1825. Cast-iron banks, cap guns, and doll furniture were made in the 1870s, and American production of cast-iron toys reached its peak in the 1880s. During the following years until the 1920s, cast-iron toys became larger and more elaborate and were made with more moving parts and greater attention to detail.

Early iron horse-drawn toys were made by at least six American manufacturers during the 1880s and 1890s. Most of these toys were unmarked and cannot be identified, but one maker, Francis W. Carpenter, marked his toys with the patent dates November 16, 1880, and March 20, 1883, on the rod between the horses. Most horse-drawn iron toys that are found today date from between 1915 and 1930, and even these late examples are of interest and value.

The best American iron toys were made by E. R. Ives of Connecticut, who made toys from 1868 to 1931. The word *Phoenix* between the horses, or the dates June 13, 1893, or July 28, 1896, suggest that a cast-iron toy may be an Ives toy. His toys were not marked *Ives* until after 1907.

The largest iron toys are the most desired by toy collectors. Nineteenth-century cast-iron trains are rare, as is fire-fighting equipment.

Moving Toys

Clockwork toys were produced in quantity in America from about 1865 to 1900. The toys were made with brass clockworks inside to move the arms or legs of the toy. Moving toys were manufactured from painted or printed tin, wood, cast iron, or cloth. Dancing figures, walking figures, cigarette-smoking men, circus wagons, merry-go-rounds, boats, and other moving vehicles were made.

Left: One of the most famous early American toy makers was Stevens and Brown. The 1870s doll pedals the iron velocipede with the help of a clockwork mechanism. (Photo: Copake)

Below: The Lehmann clockwork tin toy called Naughty Nephew shows a boy grabbing the steering tiller and receiving a slap from his uncle. (Photo: McInnis)

About 1900 clockwork toys were made with steel works, but tin clockworks continued to be used as late as 1920. Clockwork toys were wound with a crank or with a key. They are very expensive today.

Metal friction toys, which are wound up when the rear wheels are spun against a surface and then move when the toy is placed on the ground, were first introduced during the last quarter of the nineteenth century. Battery-operated toys, space toys, and electronic toys are all twentieth-century inventions.

Toy Soldiers

Lead, wood, and tin figures were known in almost every civilization and in every century. The first lead figures used as toys were made in the third century B.C.

British soldiers in Foreign Service uniforms make up this group of toy soldiers. The set was made by Britains from 1898 to 1901. (Photo: Eldred's)

Until the eighteenth century, the toy soldier was a plaything for royalty and the wealthy. German craftsmen began to make flat tin soldiers in the early 1700s. The victories of Frederick the Great (1712–1786) of Prussia were translated into tin soldier toys for children. In the 1770s, brothers Johann Gottfried Hilpert and Johann Georg Hilpert mass-produced toy soldiers in Nuremberg, Germany. They developed a way to mix lead or copper with tin, making toy soldiers more affordable. The firm created the first soldier on a standing plate and designed about forty different types of soldiers. The company closed in 1801.

Ernest Heinrichsen of Germany introduced standard sizes for tin soldiers in 1839. Through the years, Germany became the leading producer of toy lead or tin soldiers. By 1900 Germany had more than twenty factories making toy soldiers.

William Britain Jr., an English maker of mechanical tin toys, developed the hollow-cast lead soldier in 1893. The technique involved pouring the metal into a mold and then spinning it so excess lead spun out of a hole in the mold, producing a lighter, cheaper cast soldier. This innovation made the Britain family firm, William Britains Ltd., the leading manufacturer of lead soldiers, a field previously dominated by German and French companies. In 1967, because of concerns about lead poisoning and because of advances in the manufacture of plastic soldiers, Britains stopped using lead in its toys.

The first metal toy soldiers produced in America were made in the 1890s by McLoughlin Brothers, a firm that had been making paper soldiers since the 1850s. McLoughlin Brothers and several later toy soldier manufacturers—the American Soldier Company, the Saint Louis Soldier Company, and the Ideal Toy Company—stopped production in the 1920s.

Adult collectors have formed toy soldier societies and museums, and spend large sums of money for new and old toy soldiers.

Banks

Metal banks have been made since the late 1860s. The value of a bank today is determined not by age alone, but also by rarity and condition. Some banks that were made during the 1900s are worth more than those made during the preceding century. Original paint is very important. Collectors want mechanical banks, still banks, and registering banks. The best of the collectors' banks are the metal mechanical types that move when a coin is inserted.

Metal banks that do something when a coin is saved have always intrigued children because it is more fun to save pennies when the penny makes a pig jump through a hoop or if the penny is eaten by a hungry clown. Adult collectors are just as fascinated by moving banks. Much has been written about mechanical banks, and lists of banks, their rarity, and their value can be found in books and online. A rare mechanical bank can sell for thousands of dollars. A mechanical Freedman's Bank sold for $250,000 in 1988. In 1991 a bank with a girl skipping rope (patented in 1890) sold for $55,000, and a bank with a hunter shooting a bird sold for $60,500.

Still banks, first made in the 1870s, became popular with collectors in the 1960s after the prices of mechanical banks rose. Painted or lithographed tin, cast iron, white metal, pottery, porcelain, glass, or wood were used to make still banks. Many were made in the form of a bank building or a safe. Rarity and condition determine the value of these banks.

The horses race around the iron track on this mechanical bank patented by J. & E. Stevens in 1871. It still has its original paint. (Photo: Bertoia)

TEDDY'S BEAR

Theodore Roosevelt went hunting in Smedas, Mississippi, in 1902. During the trip, the president refused to shoot a bear cub. Clifford Berryman, a newspaper cartoonist, drew a picture of the incident and called it "Drawing the Line in Mississippi." The cartoon inspired Morris Michtom, founder of the Ideal Novelty Toy Company, to name his toy bears Teddy's Bears.

A mechanical Teddy and the Bear Bank made in 1907 features Teddy Roosevelt shooting a coin at a hole in a hollow tree stump. When the coin goes in the hole, a bear's head pops out of the top of the tree.

Rocking horses have been popular for centuries. This early nineteenth-century horse was carved from wood but has a comfortable leather saddle.

Opposite page: The ultimate toy, the Teddy bear. Steiff made this cinnamon-colored, curly mohair teddy bear with black shoe button eyes and a stitched nose about 1905. (Photo: Skinner)

Registering banks look like cash registers, and the amount of money deposited is totaled on the face of the bank. Registering banks were first made in the 1870s. The bank you or your parents or grandparents may have owned fifty years ago that was shaped like a cash register is worth more today than it was when purchased new.

OTHER TOYS

Rocking Horses

When the first rocking horse was produced is not known. Many antiques dealers assume rocking horses appeared around 1780, the time of the first rocking chair. Rockers on cradles had been known for centuries, and why it took so long for rockers to be fitted to chairs or toy horses is a mystery. Wooden rocking horses were being made in American homes by 1800.

A homemade German rocking horse made in 1845 inspired Benjamin Potter Crandall to produce a commercial rocking-horse toy. Mr. Crandall's wooden rocking horse, which he called *Cricket*, was so popular that he went on to make a stuffed rocking horse using hides and a tail and mane of real horsehair. In 1859 his son Jesse patented a rocking horse on a spring platform in response to the complaint of many mothers that wooden rockers cut the carpet. This spring horse was so popular that an adult-size version was made. The child's wooden rocking horse and the spring horse remain popular toys and are being made today, although new versions are usually made of plastic or lightweight metal.

Stuffed Animals

Stuffed animals were first made by toy manufacturers in the late nineteenth century. The Steiff Company in Germany made stuffed elephants, pigs, monkeys, and other animals beginning in the 1880s.

The favorite stuffed animal, of course, is the teddy bear. The cuddly American teddy bear was inspired by Teddy Roosevelt's 1902 hunting trip. The teddy bear became so popular that an American who saw Steiff stuffed bears at the Leipzig trade fair in 1903 purchased three thousand of them to meet the demand back home.

Paper Dolls

Paper dolls developed from the *pantins* of the eighteenth century. Pantins were jointed paper doll caricatures of fashionable people. In chic circles in Europe, adults enjoyed the pastime of making a new pantin each day. By the nineteenth century, the more familiar paper dolls for children were sold in stores.

The first American paper dolls were published in Boston in 1854 by Crosby, Nichols and Company. John Greene Chandler was the artist. He illustrated several children's books and made children's games and many types of paper dolls. His first paper dolls included the doll and several sets of clothing in a decorated paper envelope.

Godey's Lady's Book printed paper dolls in 1859. Most other women's magazines, including *Ladies' Home Journal, Pictorial Review, McCall's, Woman's Home Companion,* and *Good Housekeeping,* did as well. Paper dolls still appear in magazines. The dolls were so popular that even newspapers began printing them in the 1890s. Toy and book manufacturers quickly realized that there were profits to be made and began printing paper dolls in many forms.

Girls have played with paper dolls for centuries. These nineteenth-century 5-inch boy and girl dolls have twelve costumes each, one for each month. (Photo: Skinner)

Some thread companies and food-product firms, especially packers of coffees and spices, began giving away paper dolls as premiums.

Raphael Tuck produced several famous series of paper dolls about 1860. The Raphael Tuck paper dolls that were popular in America were made in England. The firm was the publisher for Queen Victoria and had offices in London, Paris, and New York. By the 1890s, paper dolls were at the height of their popularity, and Raphael Tuck was the leader in the field. The company also made many fine color prints, trading cards, *scraps* (small, cut-out, embossed color pictures), and valentines.

Paper dolls were often printed on the back and the front. Many paper dolls made in the 1890s had heads that were made separately and pasted on the doll. The clothes were made to fit under the chin.

Paper doll books were popular dime-store items in the twentieth century, and some are still being made. Collectors prefer uncut books, so figures and clothes that have already been cut out generally command only a low price.

Sunday Toys

Many seventeenth-century households kept a strict Sabbath, but homemade toys such as a Noah's Ark with many animals were acceptable playthings for the children on this day which was otherwise devoted to worship and rest. The practice of allowing children to play only with toys related to religion and the Bible on Sundays continued into Victorian times for some religious families, and these toys were known as Sunday toys. Games and toys with religious themes were also produced commercially. In 1887 McLoughlin Brothers produced *Grandma's Sunday Game of Bible Questions: New Testament*, an educational card game.

GAMES

Board Games

Games provide a window on the interests and values of the times. English board games from the first half of the nineteenth century

The game Teddy's Ride *tells the history of Teddy Roosevelt and his career from soldier to president. The original box, instructions, and playing pieces and the historical subject make this a valuable game.* (Photo: Noel Barrett)

Board games were first mass-produced in England in the late eighteenth century. The first board game made in America was *The Mansion of Happiness,* an 1843 adaptation of an English game.

This is one of four different "dissected" puzzles in a wooden box labeled in French and English. The puzzles show activities in France in the mid-1800s, when the puzzles were made.

were designed to be educational and to promote religious and moral values. Educational games like *Tour of Europe: A New Geographical Pastime* (1794), *Wallis's New Game of Universal History and Chronology* (1814), and *Wonders of Nature* (1818) were popular. Morals and values were promoted by such games as *The New Game of Human Life* (1790), *The New Game of Virtue Rewarded and Vice Punished* (1818), and *The Mansion of Happiness* (1843).

In the second half of the nineteenth century, the purpose of games shifted from teaching about moral rewards to teaching children how to achieve economic success. In 1860 Milton Bradley introduced *The Checkered Game of Life,* a game that emphasized competition. The object of this game was to accumulate wealth, which it most definitely did—it sold 40,000 copies in its first year.

The interest in sports on a national level after the Civil War was reflected in board games like *Game of Baseball* (1886), *Game of Golf* (1896), and *Game of Basketball* (1898).

The value of a board game to collectors is determined by the condition of the board, the box, and the pieces (and that the game includes all its pieces). Good graphics add to the value. With advances in chromolithography at the end of the nineteenth century, many games had colorful boards and boxes. In general, the older the game, the higher the price. Old board games can be very expensive. A *Zimmer's Base Ball Game* published by McLoughlin Bros. about 1895 sold in 1998 for $25,300.

Jigsaw Puzzles
The forerunner of the jigsaw puzzle was the *dissected puzzle,* which was developed in the late 1760s and had hand-cut shapes and few interlocking pieces. John Spilsbury, an English mapmaker, mounted

maps on a board and cut by hand around geographic boundaries to make an educational toy. The jigsaw puzzle we are familiar with today did not exist until the 1870s, when the invention of a jigsaw machine made it possible to cut the interlocking pieces.

Marbles

Glass marbles were made during the nineteenth and twentieth centuries. Workers in many glass factories made marbles for their own children. The Venetian swirl type, with ribbons of colored glass inside clear glass, and End of Day glass marbles, with flecks of colored glass in them, are most desirable. An Indian swirl marble sold for $7,700 in 1995. Sulphides, marbles with frosted white figures of animals, flowers, or faces embedded in clear glass, are rare and expensive. A double sulphide marble picturing a lion and a dog brought $4,200 in 1987.

Stone marbles of onyx, carnelian, jade, agate, limestone, or jasper can still be found, but glass marbles are the most valuable.

Early handmade toy marbles were not round by today's machine-made standards. Clay marbles were used one hundred years ago. Many Ohio, Pennsylvania, Indiana, and Vermont pottery firms also made brown or blue glazed pottery marbles. These marbles sell for low prices.

Look out for damaged marbles that have been repaired by buffing, polishing, epoxy coating, or heating until the outer layer of

CLASSIC COMPETITIVE BOARD GAMES

Many classic games originated in distant places centuries ago: Chess appeared in India in the seventh century A.D., checkers in Europe in the twelfth century, backgammon in China in the second century, and Parcheesi in India in the sixth century.

Handmade game boards are collected by folk art enthusiasts.

Glass marbles were handmade for many years. These marbles have lutz bands that are goldstone or finely ground copper flakes and glass. It is one of the many types of early marbles.

Opposite page: What a clever way to make a walking doll! This early nineteenth-century doll has seven legs around a wheel. Run the legs on the floor and it looks as if the doll is walking. (Photo: Theriault's)

Right: Dolls can be dated by the style of the head and the hair. Top left: The china doll head with deeply undercut curls is from the 1840s. Top right: The doll head with center-part hair and vertical curls is from the 1870s. Bottom left: The china doll head with unusual butterscotch-colored molded hair pulled back from the face is from the 1860s. Bottom center: The Lydia-type china head doll with center-part hair in twelve long curls is mid-nineteenth century. Bottom right: The turned shoulder head doll with the covered-wagon hairstyle is from the 1860s.

Bottom: Some important and expensive French dolls had many changes of clothing. This French portrait Jumeau bébé has her original 1880s wardrobe and other pieces made by later owners. She even has hats, a muff, and a fan. (Photo: Skinner)

glass melts and can be smoothed. The repairs reduce the value of the marble. Also beware that excellent reproductions of marbles have been made since the 1950s, and many are being sold on the Internet as antique marbles.

DOLLS

The china head doll is the most familiar type of antique doll. These dolls usually had a leather or fabric body and a glazed ceramic head with painted hair, eyes, and lips. The doll's neck had holes in its base, and these were threaded and sewn to the doll's body. Machine stitching of the doll's body could not have been done before about 1850, when the sewing machine was invented.

The age of a china head doll can be determined with some degree of accuracy from the hairstyle. The doll with curls on the neck was made about 1840, short curls about 1850, and the chignon style about 1860. Dolls with brown eyes are rare, and blue eyes can be found in various shades. Collectors like blonds because fewer blond dolls were made. A doll head that includes a molded hat is also more valuable.

Doll Types and First Date of Manufacture

Doll	First Date of Manufacture
Baby dolls	c.1850. Before this time, all dolls were adults.
Brownie	1883
China head (European): curls on neck of head	1840
China head (European): short curls	1850
China head (European): chignon or waterfall hair style	1860
Cloth dolls	1880s
Composition head	1800–1850
Closing eyes in head	1800
Glass eyes in head	Early 19th century
Papier-mâché head, kid body	1820
Paper dolls	18th century, pantins; 19th century, made commercially; 1890, height of popularity
Rag dolls	1840 (popular)
Talking	1850s
Tin head	1840
Vulcanized rubber head	1850
Walking	Early 19th century
Wax head	17th century; most found today from 19th century

Bisque is unglazed porcelain, and doll collectors differentiate the types of doll heads, glazed and unglazed, by calling one china and the other bisque. This may confuse the novice, but it is important to learn the proper vocabulary if you plan to collect.

The large (twenty inches or taller) doll with a bisque head and a wig of human hair or mohair was popular during the nineteenth century, and it is one of the most expensive antique dolls. Most bisque and china head dolls were made in Germany or France. Some European dolls were marked with a factory name or symbol. Check the marks on a doll's head in a book of porcelain marks, as well as in books about dolls, because some porcelain factories made plates and bowls, as well as china doll heads.

According to the import laws of the United States, any doll brought into this country after 1891 had to be marked with the country of origin. If a doll's head has the name of a country printed on it, it was most likely made after 1891.

Beginning in the 1850s, doll makers began producing bébés, dolls that represented young children rather than adults. French bébés were especially popular from the 1860s to the 1880s. They were beautifully dressed and expensive. In the 1890s, German manufacturers began to make less expensive (and poorer quality) bébés, and these dolls took much of the market away from the French.

Child and baby dolls made by German firms after 1880 until 1915 looked like perfect children. These dolly-faced dolls had rosy cheeks, a tiny smile, and long, curly hair. They were a product of the Victorian era, when people preferred idealized beauty to reality.

By the turn of the twentieth century, German psychologists were urging society to look at children as real people. The character doll, with a face that looks like a real baby or child, was a result of this new way of thinking. In fact, the dolls' faces were modeled after real children, often the designer's own child. Character dolls were dressed in everyday clothes, not lace and fancy dresses.

Wax Dolls

Wax dolls were made in Germany during the seventeenth century. By the eighteenth century, English and French doll makers were producing wax dolls, but chances are you will never find such an early one. Most of the wax dolls that are collected today were made during the nineteenth century. Dolls with wax heads and glass eyes were created at the beginning of the nineteenth century. By 1826 wax dolls had eyes that could close. Many different types of wax head dolls were made as late as the mid-1930s by factories in Europe. One of the best ways to determine the age of these dolls is to observe the style of the dress. Other hints, such as a label, also help.

Doll Makers

Doll Maker	Country	Dates of Operation
Amberg, Louis, & Son	U.S.A.	1878–1930
Bärh & Pröschild (Purchased by Bruno Schmidt and operated until 1930s)	Germany	1871–1919
Bru Jne. & Cie.	France	1866–1899
Greiner, Ludwig	U.S.A.	1840–1883 (Operated as Ludwig Sons, 1874–1883)
Handwerck, Heinrich	Germany	1876–1932
Heubach, Gebrüder (Bros.)	Germany	1843–1938
Jumeau	France	1842–1899
Kämmer & Reinhardt	Germany	1885–1932
Kestner, J. D., Jr.	Germany	1805–1938
Marseille, Armand	Germany	1885–1950s
Meech, Herbert John	England	1865–1917
Montanari, Mme. Augusta	England	1851–1884
Pierotti	England	1770–1930s
Robins, Joseph	England	1826–1901
Simon & Halbig	Germany	1869–1939
Société Française de Fabrication de Bébés & Jouets (S.F.B.J.)	France	1899–1950
Steiner, Jules Nicholas	France	1855–1891 (After Steiner's death in 1891, the company continued until 1908.)

Top: Thirty-nine different Frozen Charlotte and Frozen Charley dolls—arms up, arms down, joined twins, potty dolls, and others— are part of this collection. (Photo: Skinner)

Frozen Charlottes

Frozen Charlottes, stiff china dolls with unjointed and immovable arms and legs, were made from the 1850s until the 1920s. The boy doll was sometimes called *Frozen Charley*. The dolls were usually made with their arms at their sides or pointing straight forward. A few have been found with the arms folded in prayer. They came in sizes ranging from a tiny, one-inch dollhouse size up to about fifteen inches. Most are about three inches high. These dolls were named for a girl in a New England ballad. The song says that Charlotte rode more than ten miles on a cold winter's night in a lightweight dress and was frozen stiff by the time she reached her destination.

Cloth Dolls

Children have played with homemade rag dolls through the ages. In America, interest in rag dolls increased with the invention of the sewing machine in the 1850s. Women's magazines published directions for making the dolls. Butterick published its first pattern for a rag doll in 1882. The first commercial rag dolls were made in the last half of the nineteenth century. Sometimes manufacturers dipped the fabric in wax to stiffen it. Toward the end of the century, rag dolls were created to advertise products. One of the earliest advertising dolls was made in about 1895 for Northwestern Consolidated Milling Company. The farmer boy doll had the company's trademark printed on his shirt between his suspenders.

Cloth dolls were made from printed fabric that was cut out, stitched, and stuffed. The first American fabric made for stuffed dolls was patented in 1886. It was for a Santa Claus doll designed by Edward Peck. The Arnold Print Works of North Adams, Massachusetts (1876–1925), made many printed fabrics for dolls and animals. Other firms that made or sold doll fabrics were Art Fabric Mills (c.1899–1910) and Selchow & Righter (1867–1986), both of New York City; Cocheco Manufacturing Company of Boston (1827–1912); and Saalfield Publishing Company of Akron, Ohio (1899–1977). Most fabric dolls had the name of the factory printed somewhere on the fabric. Unfortunately, the name was frequently discarded with the fabric scraps after the toy had been cut and stuffed.

Reproductions of several printed fabrics for dolls are now available. They are often offered through museum gift shops.

BROWNIE DOLL

The Brownies were characters in a series of children's stories. This printed fabric, made by Cocheco Manufacturing Company about 1897, can be cut, stuffed, and sewn to make a doll. (Photo: Village Doll & Toy)

HOLIDAY ANTIQUES

Christmas

The first decorated Christmas trees displayed in America were in Bethlehem (1747), Easton (1816), Lancaster County (1821), York (1823), Harrisburg (1823), or Philadelphia (1825), all in Pennsylvania; in Boston, Massachusetts (1832); or perhaps in St. Clair County, Illinois (1833); Circleville (1838), Wooster (1847), or Cleveland (1851), all in Ohio; Williamsburg, Virginia (1842); or Farmington, Iowa (1845). The records are imperfect, and each area claims to have hosted the first tree.

Early Christmas trees in the United States were decorated with paper cornucopias, gilded eggcups or nuts, apples, small dolls, cookies, seedpods, pinecones, ribbons, and candles. Homemade cloth ornaments and paper chains were used by the 1880s.

Some of the earliest glass ornaments to decorate German Christmas trees were chains of small glass beads, which were first made in the second half of the eighteenth century. Later, larger glass balls were made as tree decorations. Fragile glass orna-

Left: German glass Christmas tree ornaments were made in many shapes. This Santa Claus head was a popular shape that was made for many years.

ments were exported from Germany to the United States about 1860 and were manufactured in the United States by the early 1870s. Glass ornaments imported from Germany by 1880 were made in shapes ranging from angel heads to potatoes. In the 1890s, immigrants made glass beads and tubing and strung them on thin wire that was then bent into stars, triangles, and other shapes. By the early 1900s, Christmas trees were decorated with garlands of glass beads up to six feet long.

German tin or tin-and-lead ornaments were made in geometric shapes. Some were colored, and some had added cut glass. Small mirrored or tin reflectors were offered for sale by the 1880s. Wax ornaments were also made in Germany at this time. They were usually angels with paper-and-ribbon clothes and wings.

German Dresden ornaments were made of silver- and gold-embossed cardboard in a variety of shapes, including animals, fish, toys, furniture, and people, between 1880 and 1910. Because they are easily damaged, few remain today. Silver-foil icicles were made by 1878. Lead-foil icicles appeared in the 1920s. Mylar icicles arrived in the 1950s. Angel's hair was made by 1880.

Other collectible Christmas tree decorations include chromolithographed pictures of angels or Santa Claus. Papier-mâché candy containers for hanging on trees were made in Germany by 1900. America stopped importing ornaments from Germany in 1914 because of the outbreak of World War I. During the years between World War I and World War II, Germany was again the major source of glass Christmas tree ornaments. America stopped importing glass ornaments from Germany in 1939. Corning Glass Company then began mass producing lacquered glass ornaments, producing 235,000 that year. After the war, German ornaments that looked exactly like the old ones were again imported.

Glass holders and tin-clip holders for candles were introduced during the nineteenth century. The first electric Christmas lights were used on a Christmas tree in New York City in 1882. By 1901 General Electric was selling a string of lights for twelve dollars, which was more than a week's wages for the average worker. Figural bulbs were developed in Austria in 1909. Shortly thereafter, these

Opposite page: Nativity sets have been part of Christmas celebrations for centuries. This Joies de Noel boxed paper set has a lithographed tree to decorate with paper angels, candles, and toys. There are also figures of the holy family. (Photo: Skinner)

lights were being made in Germany, Japan, and the United States. Character bulbs became an important part of Christmas decorations by the 1920s. Hundreds of styles were made, including comic figures, vegetables, animals, autos, birds, and, of course, Santa Claus. Bubble lights were first made in the 1940s, twinkle bulbs in the 1950s, and plastic bulbs by 1955. The cool lamp made for plastic trees was first sold in 1958.

Some collectors search for yet other Christmas antiques. The first Christmas card was sent in England in 1843, or possibly as early as 1839. The first American card was made by Louis Prang in 1873. Christmas seals were first used in 1904. The first Christmas plate was made by Bing & Grondahl of Denmark in 1895. The first Christmas spoons were made by Michelsen Silversmiths of Denmark in 1910.

Valentine's Day

Valentine's Day traces its roots to a Roman mating ritual and to a Christian saint, Valentinus, who was martyred in the third century. There are many legends about St. Valentine, but most agree he was a friend to young lovers and he was put to death on February 14. By the fourteenth century, the Roman festival celebrating spring had spread to England, where young men and women exchanged handmade gifts and cards. By the mid-1700s, valentines were commercially produced in England. Early valentines were puzzles, pinpricks, and cutouts. Comic valentines of the 1840s were not the funny cards we know today. They had cruel messages and were sent, often anonymously and with postage due, to someone the sender disliked.

Collectors were not serious about collecting old Christmas ornaments until the mid-1970s. Before that, old ornaments sold for less than a dollar, and collectors often found them in attics or at garage sales.

DANGER!

If you plan to use the strings of Christmas tree bulbs you have collected, check that the cords are not frayed. Old wiring can be a fire hazard.

Lacy pop-up paper valentines were the deluxe, extravagant card of Victorian times. They are still being made. This late nineteenth-century card has roses and a child with wings.

In Massachusetts, Esther Howland began designing colorful, paper lace valentines in 1847, and by 1860 her business was producing 100,000 cards each year. Flowers, birds, and cupids were popular designs. George Whitney, one of Howland's employees, started his own successful business and eventually bought out Howland's company. Three-dimensional foldout and pop-up valentines from Germany were popular by the turn of the twentieth century.

Other Holidays

One can never tire of Christmas and Valentine's Day, but there are other holidays and holiday items that attract collectors. Today collectors look for collectibles from Halloween (candy holders, costumes, masks, decorations, jack-o'-lanterns) and Easter (eggs, papier-mâché bunnies, candy containers), as well as Thanksgiving decorations, Fourth of July postcards, and hundreds of other holiday-related items. Some of these holidays may date from hundreds of years ago, but most collectible items used in these celebrations date from the twentieth century. 🌀

Chapter 19

Prints, Pictures, and Photographs

⤷ PERHAPS YOU OWN an old picture of a clipper ship, a balloon ascension, or an early baseball game. Any picture of an unusual or historic event is some collector's dream antique, so if you aren't eager to own it, someone else will be happy to buy it. If the picture or print depicts a subject that interests you, it will also interest others. If the picture's subject is so unusual that you've never seen it depicted before, the picture is probably of even greater interest.

Early prints can be identified easily if the maker's name appears on the print, but if there is no name, you can judge the picture by its subject matter, beauty, or quality. Nineteenth-century prints of flowers, people posed for portraits, and religious subjects have a disappointingly low value. Pictures of rare breeds of cows, chickens, or horses; sporting events; ships; Civil War battle scenes and other historic events are of value even if the maker is virtually unknown or not especially talented. Unusual types of pictures, some early ads, homemade pastel or crayon pictures, and primitive watercolors and oil paintings are also valuable.

When collectors look at a picture, their natural reaction is to look for the signature. Some artists sign the picture itself, usually at the bottom in a corner. Printed information usually appears in the

Opposite page: In the nineteenth century, the Pennsylvania Germans recorded the birth of a child on a hand-colored fraktur. Daniel Witmer was born on January 10, 1812. The heart, birds, and trees are typical decorations. (Photo: Conestoga)

white margin below the picture. The artist's name is important even if you cannot tell if the picture is a print, a photograph, or a painting. If you find a signed work of art, it is a relatively simple task to determine the fame of the artist. The Internet is a good place to start. Go to a search engine like Google or Yahoo and type in the artist's name. Web sites have information on thousands of American artists. Libraries and museums can also help you search for information on a particular artist.

Etchings, engravings, woodcuts, and lithographs are printed on paper, but each is produced with a different method of printing and drawing. Many of these pictures depict the happenings of the day. The photograph has replaced the lithograph as a news medium, but the lithograph remains as an art form and as a collector's delight.

"Copyright 1890 by The Strobridge Litho Co., Cincinnati, New York & London" is printed in the lower right corner of this chromolithograph. The picture shows a sulky race. Chromolithography is a method of making colored lithographs invented in 1837.
(Photo: Cowan)

The first copyright laws published in England give clues to dating an English print. If the front of the print is labeled *Published According to Act of Parliament,* usually in the white margin, the picture is an English print made after 1735. Prints that are labeled *Published by Act of Parliament 1845* or *Published London by Mr. John Doe 1845* are even easier to date. Unless the picture is a very modern, twentieth-century photographic copy or a late reprint of an original work, labels on prints mean what they say. Prints made in the United States after 1802 were often labeled with the words *Entered according to act of Congress in the year ____.*

Early engravings and lithographs that were copyrighted tell their own story. In the United States, the first copyright laws were passed in May 1790. In April 1802 engravings were listed among the items eligible for a copyright under the new law. The district courts were given jurisdiction over all copyright applications in February 1819. The laws protecting artists and writers with copyrights were revised in 1831 and 1909. Most American lithographs were not marked with the year and copyright words until after 1848.

If you would like specific information on your copyrighted print, check the *Catalog of Copyright Entries*, which is available at larger libraries. Information is also available for a fee from the Copyright Office, Library of Congress, Washington, DC 20559.

CURRIER & IVES PRINTS

If your print is American, it could be a Currier & Ives lithograph. Nathaniel Currier began his career as a lithographer in 1828. He was working for his own firm in 1834, and made James Ives, an artist who was his bookkeeper, a partner in 1857. The first print marked *Currier & Ives* was made in 1857.

Currier & Ives made more prints than anyone else in America during the nineteenth century, and more of their prints have survived. The prints were always marked with the name of the firm, and they often included the company's address. If there is no name on the print, it is either a copy or the print has been trimmed. It is important that prints have their original margins. A trimmed print is of less value, so if you are tempted to trim a picture to fit an old frame, remember that you might be cutting off future dollar bills.

Scenes of everyday life made Currier & Ives prints the most popular nineteenth-century picture for the home. "Home from the Woods: The Successful Sportsmen" is a hand-colored Currier & Ives lithograph made in 1867. (Photo: Skinner)

It is possible to determine if your print is an original Currier & Ives print or if it is a copy. Measure the print. Most original Currier & Ives prints were made in four sizes: very small (7 by 9 inches); small (8.8 by 12.8 inches); medium (9 by 14 to 14 by 20 inches); and large (anything larger than 14 by 20 inches). Most reproductions were made in sizes differ-

HOME FROM THE WOODS.
THE SUCCESSFUL SPORTSMEN.

Dating Currier & Ives Prints

Marked Currier & Ives prints are easily dated. The restless firm moved from building to building in New York City, and it is possible to fix an almost exact date by checking the address. Workrooms were at either 2 Spruce Street or 33 Spruce Street. The retail store was at several addresses on Nassau Street and for a brief time in 1842 at 169 Broadway. Some pictures are labeled with an address but no name.

Name	Address	Date picture was printed
Currier & Stodart	137 Broadway	1834–1835
N. Currier's Lith.	1 Wall Street	1835–1836
N. Currier	148 Nassau Street	1836–1837
N. Currier	2 Spruce Street	1838–1856
N. Currier	152 Nassau Street	1838–1857
N. Currier	169 Broadway	1842
Charles Currier*	33 Spruce Street	1845–1846
Currier and C. Currier	33 Spruce Street	1847
Currier & Ives	2 Spruce Street	1857–1865
Currier & Ives	152 Nassau Street	1857–1872
Currier & Ives	33 Spruce Street	1866–1907
Currier & Ives	125 Nassau Street	1872–1874
Currier & Ives	123 Nassau Street	1874–1877
Currier & Ives	115 Nassau Street	1877–1894
Currier & Ives	108 Fulton Street	1894–1896

* Charles Currier was Nathaniel Currier's brother

ent from the originals. Some prints were made only in the large folio size, but they have been copied during the twentieth and twenty-first centuries in smaller sizes. If you examine a new copy of a print under a magnifying glass, you will see a series of small dots. If you look at an original print, you will see a series of short lines. The copies made by today's methods of printing print the black, white, and color at the same time. An original Currier & Ives print was printed black on white and then hand colored or partially printed in color and finished by hand. The inaccuracies of hand coloring show on the old prints.

There have been many copies of Currier & Ives prints. Chromolithographs were first made in 1858. *Chromos* had a sharper color than early lithographs. Currier & Ives always hand colored the lithographs and never used chromos. An insurance firm printed calendars with fine photographic reproductions of Currier & Ives prints from 1936 until the 1990s. These reproductions themselves have become collectible.

Black-and-white and colored Currier & Ives prints have a value. As a general rule, the countryside scenes and the political cartoons are of most interest. The still-life vases of flowers, portraits of children, and religious pictures are of less value. The known works of Currier & Ives are catalogued in many books, such as *Currier & Ives Prints: An Illustrated*

Check List by Frederick A. Conningham and *Currier & Ives: An Illustrated Value Guide* by Craig McClain.

OTHER TYPES OF PICTURES

Paper Pictures

Any old, odd picture made from paper in an unusual style is probably a worthwhile antique. Popular paper pictures include cutout pictures, pinprick pictures, quillwork, silhouettes, tinsel pictures, and woodblock prints.

Cutout Pictures

Elaborate and intricate cutout paper designs known as *scherenschnitte* were made from about 1840 to the early 1900s. This folk art was brought to the United States by German immigrants and is still popular in parts of Pennsylvania. Most cutout pieces were made as personal treasures by artistic women. A few exceptionally gifted artists made and sold the cutouts. The cut white paper was usually mounted on a dark paper and framed to be hung as a picture. The more elaborate the cutout, the better the picture.

Look carefully at this unusual paper picture. Cutout flowers, leaves, and dried moss have been assembled in a picture of an urn. It is inscribed Henriette Luuterbach, 1884.

Pinprick Pictures

A picture made with pinholes of various sizes is called a *pinprick picture*. These pictures were popular in England from about 1820 to 1840. The picture was made by pricking the paper with one of several sizes of pins. The holes could be made from either side of the paper. The more talented of the amateur artists who tried this technique applied watercolors over the pinpricks to develop textured color.

Quillwork

Opposite page: Quillwork was used to decorate boxes. The ends of the paper spirals have been colored to create the design on this tea box. The date 1800 is part of the quillwork.

Paper filigree work, or quillwork, was first made in the seventeenth century. Samuel Pepys's diary mentioned it. Quillwork was popular during the eighteenth century, and it was made as late as 1870. To make quillwork, small strips of paper were cut about one-eighth of an inch wide and rolled into tight spirals of different sizes. The rolled spirals were about the size of a pencil eraser, and they were bent into shape and glued on a background. The edges of the spiral rolls formed designs, which were painted to make the pattern more obvious. Some artists added shells, dried grass, or small pictures to the filigree pattern. French and English quillwork is still considered the finest, but quillwork was made in many other countries, including the United States and Canada.

Silhouettes

A silhouette is a cutout paper picture. The word *silhouette,* meaning "a simple outline picture," was added to the French dictionary in 1835. In eighteenth-century America, the word *shade* was used to describe this style of picture until the French word came into use. Silhouettes are still popular today.

Any silhouette made before 1900 is a collector's prize. Important American silhouettes were made by Charles Willson Peale and are marked *Peale Museum* or *Peale's Museum.* To make his hollow cut silhouettes, Peale cut out the shape of a head from a piece of white paper. He discarded the head-shaped piece of paper and placed the remaining outline on a backing of dark silk or paper. The finished silhouette was a black shape showing through a hole in the white foreground, not the familiar black shape pasted on a white background.

Silhouettes are still popular pictures. These early nineteenth-century American silhouettes, all hollow cut, suggest the hairdos and dress of the day.
(Photo: Cowan)

Another famous silhouette maker, Auguste Edouart, worked in the United States and abroad. In 1813 he went to England, where he spent several years making hair pictures and portraits. He cut his first silhouettes in 1825 and traveled from

Scotland to Ireland to the United States, where he worked in many cities. He signed his silhouettes *Aug Edouart*. There is a sad ending to this artist's story: Returning to France with duplicates of his silhouettes (about fifty thousand pictures), Edouart's ship was wrecked, and all of his work was lost at sea. Auguste Edouart was so upset he never worked again.

Other early signed American silhouettes were made by William Bache, William Henry Brown, Augustus Day, William Doyle, Charles Peale Polk, and William King.

Japanese woodblock prints have inspired many designs in other countries. This print by Toyokuni II (1777–1835) is part of a series of pictures of Japanese women.
(Photo: Degener)

Woodblock Prints

JAPANESE WOODBLOCK PRINTS

Japanese woodblock prints were produced in quantity during Japan's Edo Period (1600–1868). They are called *ukiyo-e*, which means "pictures of the floating world" of everyday existence. Typical subjects shown in the pictures were courtesans, geisha, Kabuki actors, historical events, warriors, and landscapes. The woodblock masters best known to collectors outside Japan are Hokusai (1760–1849) and Hiroshige (1797–1858), famous for landscapes; Kiyonobu (1664–1729) and Toyokuni (1769–1825), who specialized in theater prints; Harunobu (c.1725–1770), who developed multicolored prints; and Utamaro (1753–1806), known for his portraits of beautiful women.

The prints were the result of the cooperative effort of four men: the artist, who created the design; the engraver, who carved the woodblocks; the printer, who mixed the paints and registered the prints; and the publisher, who provided the money and materials, supervised the operation, and marketed the prints.

Japan was closed to the West until 1868. This changed after Commodore Perry sailed into Tokyo Bay in 1853 and the Meiji emperor was restored to power. Printmaking during the Meiji Era (1868–1912) began to break with the traditions of the past and turned to Western subjects and techniques. Prints made in Nagasaki and Yokohama featured Western men, women, and children; steamships and sailing vessels; and European clothing, furnishings, and leisure activities.

Prices for prints vary widely, depending on the artist, the color and clarity of the impression, and the print's overall condition. An edition was usually limited to about two hundred prints. Additional prints might have been made from the blocks, but first- or second-edition prints are most desirable.

ARTS AND CRAFTS WOODBLOCK PRINTS

Woodcuts and wood engravings appeared in Europe during the fifteenth century. This type of print was revived in the late nineteenth century, inspired by the popularity of the Japanese woodblock print favored by Arts and Crafts artists. The style became popular in England and later in the United States.

One of the most important American artists to be inspired by the Japanese woodblock print was Arthur Wesley Dow. In 1895 Dow exhibited his color woodblock prints at the Museum of Fine Arts in Boston, the first exhibit of its kind by an American artist.

Burned Wood Pictures (Pyrography)

The earliest burned wood pictures known to collectors were made about 1790, but they were not made in quantity. Pictures made with hot pokers were at the height of their popularity from about 1850 to 1895. To create this kind of landscape or portrait, artists used a red-hot poker as their only tool to burn pictures into basswood. Kits, patterns, burning tools, and designs could be purchased by amateurs. Some pieces were made and sold by companies. The Flemish Art Company and Thayer & Chandler were two of the best-known firms.

This pyrographic picture was burned on a board, then enhanced with paint. The 17-by-11-inch picture was made by a talented amateur and is unmarked.

Hair Pictures

Hairwork of all kinds was a popular form of art during the early eighteenth century and remained in style until about 1890. Flowers, fruit, portraits, and jewelry were woven from human hair. Some hairwork was homemade, but many items were made by professionals.

The mourning picture made from human hair was a Victorian custom. It was made in memory of a departed family member or friend, but the hair of the deceased was not always used. Pictures were also made with hair from still-living family members.

This cameo-like head of Captain John Paul Jones is made of wax. The eighteenth-century picture is mounted in its original tiger maple frame.

Wax Portraits

Wax pictures were molded or cast, then mounted on a darker background. The art of making portraits in wax was practiced during the eighteenth century in England and France and remained popular until about 1850 in America. Some portraits were signed. Many wax pictures were portraits of royalty or politicians. Others were copies of classical designs, like cupids or Grecian women. A few were pornographic.

Beware of wax portraits of U.S. presidents. Some clever fakes have been created by casting wax heads from plaster models. The models were made from bronze medals originally produced at the U.S. Mint.

Reverse Paintings on Glass

The art of glass painting is not lost or difficult, but it is currently out of vogue.

Reverse paintings on glass have been made since the fourteenth century. Several types of paintings were made by transferring or painting a design on the back of glass with oil paints. During the eighteenth century, Jean Glomi invented a method of framing prints against glass with black and gold bands that were painted as borders on the glass. *Églomisé* is the French term for a special type of reverse painting on glass that is backed with gold- or silver-leaf foil. It is doubtful, however, that Monsieur Glomi ever made the type of glass painting that has been named for him. Early eighteenth-century pictures were painted on glass that had an uneven surface. Nineteenth-century pictures were painted on heavy glass and resembled colored prints that were pasted onto the glass.

An old reverse painting on glass is almost always in its original frame. The painting is so delicate that it might be destroyed if the frame is removed.

The best reverse paintings on glass were made in England from 1770 to 1825. The English method of transfer-glass pictures was developed about 1700. The pictures were usually signed, and the person or scene was identified on the glass. Early reverse glass paintings are more detailed than Victorian paintings.

In the United States, reverse painting became the vogue during the eighteenth and nineteenth centuries, and it was a hobby for

The value of a reverse painting on glass is determined by the subject matter, the excellence of the painting, and the condition of the paint. If the subject matter is interesting, your glass painting is valuable. Peeling paint lowers the value and is very difficult to restore.

The colored flowers in this picture were reverse painted on glass. Then the glass was mounted over a crinkled piece of metal foil to make one type of tinsel picture. The 15-by-18-inch picture was made about 1840.

many women. In July 1857 *Godey's Lady's Book and Magazine* published an article that explained how to paint on glass. Most American reverse paintings were made by using a simple five-step transfer process. First a piece of glass was covered with turpentine, then a wet print was pressed facedown on the turpentine-covered glass. As the print dried, the paper was rolled off the glass and the outline of the picture remained on the glass, ready to be painted.

American glass paintings are often crude portraits of heroes or religious subjects. Portraits of George Washington were especially popular. Some glass paintings were done by Americans, while others were imported from China and Europe. New England painters preferred the still life. Artists often pasted metal foil to the inside of the glass to add glitter to the finished picture. Landscapes and sea battles were also painted. Many paintings were made for clock and mirror decorations.

Cabinet cards were the family pictures of the days before the small, easy-to-use camera. This framed cabinet card is a wedding portrait taken about 1880 in Minneapolis, Minnesota.

Tinsel Pictures

The tinsel picture was a popular art form during the late eighteenth and early nineteenth centuries. In America tinsel pictures were reverse paintings on glass that were mounted on crinkled metallic paper. The shiny paper showed through the painting and added interest to the background. Another type of tinsel picture is the English theatrical tinsel print. Theater ads printed in the 1820s were embellished with beads and bits of glitter or foil that were pasted on the print.

PHOTOGRAPHY

The nineteenth century saw the development of several new photographic processes that produced an image on a hard surface, either metal or glass.

One of the earliest types of photographs was the *daguerreotype*, a picture made on a copperplate coated with silver. It was developed by Louis-Jacques-Mandé Daguerre of France in 1839. Daguerreotypes were soon replaced by the cheaper ambrotype and then by the tintype. The *ambrotype* was a picture produced on glass that was coated with collodion, a thick, sticky liquid. This photography process was developed in the early 1850s and used until the mid-1860s. Ambrotypes were fragile, however, and were replaced in popularity by the tintype.

A *tintype* is a picture made on a thin piece of iron that is coated with black japan varnish. The tintype was developed by Hamilton L. Smith of Kenyon College in Gambier, Ohio, in 1856. He sold the patent to Peter Neff, who continued the work. A competitor, Victor Griswold, developed a japanned iron plate that he more accurately named a *ferrotype,* but the term *tintype* continued to be used to describe this type of picture.

Early tintypes and daguerreotypes are collected for the subject matter of the picture. Pictures of famous people are best. Collectors also like pictures of children with toys, people at work or holding tools, identifiable street scenes, Civil War soldiers and places, and pictures of ethnic groups—especially African-Americans, American Indians, or Asians living in the United States. Photos of unusual subjects, such as corpses posed as if they were asleep or men dressed as women, are very collectible. The cabinet card (1850–1920s) and the carte de visite (popular from 1859 to 1906) were photographic prints posted on standard-size card stock. Stereographic views made from two photographs mounted together were first made about 1850. ☙

If you collect old pictures made by any type of camera, always look for the unusual subject. Civil War pictures, early views of cities and work, and pictures of life in the West are among the best.

Remember—There are no photographs of George and Martha Washington. They died years before the first permanent photograph was made in 1822.

DAGUERREOTYPE CASES

The early daguerreotype case was made of wood and covered with a thin leather that often had embossed designs. A papier-mâché case in the shape of a book with velvet covering or inlaid pearl became popular in the 1850s. In 1854 Samuel Peck patented a composition case, known as a Union Case, which was made of shellac and sawdust that had been heated and pressed into a mold. The inside of the case was velvet-lined on one side, and the picture was on the other side. Cases were also made from gutta-percha, a plastic substance made from the resin of a Malaysian tree. The label of the daguerreotype casemaker can sometimes be found under the picture.

Chapter 20

Paper Antiques

COLLECTORS ARE COMPULSIVE PEOPLE. Almost every family has at least one relative who saves everything. Saving becomes ridiculous when it results in the accumulation of huge piles of old newspapers, magazines, boxes, cans, and other debris that is strewn throughout the house. Behavior of this sort is known as the Collyer Brothers Syndrome. The Collyer brothers collected and saved everything. When they died amid the debris in their New York City apartment, they were not found for days. Fortunately, saving mania is most often seen in milder forms, but if any of your relatives have lived in one house for more than twenty-five years, the attic will usually show evidence of collectivitis. Attics can, and do, store boxes and packages of unlabeled pictures, unwanted books, and assorted useful and useless junk for years.

It is every collector's dream to be turned loose in an attic that has been untouched for more than fifty years. China, glass, old furniture, jewelry, toys, and even household tools are usually sorted and saved; but many old newspapers, books, catalogs, and other paper materials are often thrown away as rubbish. But some paper *is* of value.

Opposite page: Color pictures were uncommon in the nineteenth century. Calling cards and greeting cards were mounted in this Victorian scrapbook. Labels, ads, and other ephemera were also saved.

It is virtually impossible to save everything, but there are some things worth keeping. Go back into your wonderful dream attic and sort the piles of debris. Study each pile carefully to see what you really have.

NEWSPAPERS

Old newspapers are not as valuable as most beginners believe. Some newspapers published in America from 1690 to 1860 are important, but most libraries today keep copies on microfilm, not the original, fragile paper. Do not destroy any newspaper printed before 1860 without contacting a local historical society or an antiquarian bookseller first. Newspapers printed after 1860 that describe important events or places are rare and desirable. The first issue (volume one, number one) of any newspaper is of value.

The first newspapers printed in Western states and territories appeared years after many Eastern newspapers were well-established. Sometimes a late nineteenth-century Western paper is of great importance. To find out if your old newspapers are worthy of a finer fate than the trash can, look up information in several sources. Your local library may have access to databases that list locations of old issues of newspapers. The *United States Newspaper Program National Union List* (1999) is available in large public and university libraries. Other libraries may own *American Newspapers, 1821–1936: A Union List of Files Available in the United States and Canada*, edited by Winifred Gregory (1967); and *History and Bibliography of American Newspapers, 1690–1820* by Clarence Brigham (1947). These publications list newspapers and the institutions that hold copies of them. Any newspaper that is not listed and even those listed as available in just a few locations may be rare and of value. Early papers may be desirable if a full year or a long

Beware. Many old-looking newspapers are reproductions like these. The 1861 New York Times *discusses the imminent Civil War, and the* Herald *describes the battle at Fort Sumter in Charleston, South Carolina.*

run of the paper is available. Local historical societies and libraries often search for this sort of reference material.

The content of a newspaper is often what makes it valuable to the collector. Interesting early advertisements, announcements of important historical events, drawings by such artists as Thomas Nast or Frederic Remington, or the first publication of a great literary work are always in demand.

Old Historic Newspapers

There are a few single issues of important old historic newspapers, but they have been reprinted so often that the chance of owning an original is slight. The Library of Congress Serial and Government Publications Division publishes information circulars that describe how to distinguish originals and copies of eighteen famous issues. The circulars are posted on the Internet.

The historic papers that are most often copied include the New York *Morning Post*, November 7, 1783, with Washington's farewell address to the Army; the Ulster County *Gazette,* January 4, 1800, which reports Washington's death; the *Daily Citizen*, Vicksburg, Mississippi, July 4, 1863, a newspaper printed on wallpaper during the Civil War when newsprint was unavailable; and the *New York Herald,* Saturday, April 15, 1865, which reported the death of President Lincoln.

Care of Old Newspapers

Wood-pulp paper is a mass of cellulose fibers. Lignin, a component that acts as a binder, makes paper like newsprint brittle, weak, and short-lived. To preserve the information in a newspaper article, photocopy it on acid-free paper. If you want to preserve the newspaper article itself, try a milk of magnesia and club soda bath. Dissolve a milk of magnesia tablet in a quart of club soda and chill the mixture. Let the paper soak in the fluid for an hour. Remove the paper and pat it dry between white paper towels. Then allow the paper to air dry. There are also commercial sprays and solutions, such as Wei T'o and Bookkeeper, that remove acid from newsprint. These can be found at any art supply store or Internet site that sells archival materials.

POSTERS

The art poster that was popular in the 1890s had evolved from the illustrated advertising poster. The development of lithography and high-speed presses in the first half of the nineteenth century made possible a boom in the production of advertising posters for everything from steamship voyages to patent medicines.

At first the posters had more text than pictures, but images and graphics became increasingly important. French lithographer Jules Chéret began working in the 1860s and is considered the father of the nineteenth-century art poster. His work, often advertising theatrical events, featured colorful illustrations with few words. Chéret influenced artists in Europe and America, especially Henri de Toulouse-Lautrec and Pierre Bonnard in France and art nouveau artists such as Aubrey Beardsley (English), Alphonse Mucha (Czech-French), Gustav Klimt (Austrian), and Will Bradley (American). The first exhibition of posters as art was shown in Paris in 1884.

Most nineteenth-century advertising posters were meant to be disposable, so they were not printed on high-quality paper, and they deteriorate easily. A professional conservator can repair and restore a poster and properly frame, mount, and mat it. Store or display a poster in a clean, pollution-free environment with humidity around 55 percent, at a constant temperature (cooler is better), and away from direct natural or artificial light.

OTHER PRINTED EPHEMERA

Judge Taft is pictured on this colorful, embossed cigar band from the late 1800s. Every good cigar had a label that identified the brand.

Unusual bits of printed paper—from labels to paper napkins—are known as *ephemera*. There isn't space enough to list all the old paper items that are interesting to collectors, but it is worth noting that there are large, well-documented museum collections of valentines, advertising cards, baseball cards, broadsides, railroad passes, circus posters, and other paper memorabilia. Don't throw away

any ephemera before checking if it is wanted by collectors or historians. Here are a few collectibles to watch for.

Cigar Boxes and Labels

Cigar bands and wooden cigar boxes with paper labels were made starting in the early nineteenth century, when cigars first became popular. The best wooden cigar boxes were made of cedar. The brand name was die-stamped onto the wooden top. Paper labels were used on the sides and inside the lid. The boxes and labels were collected even in Victorian times. The boxes were always useful for holding small items.

There were nearly twenty thousand different brands of American cigars by 1870, and labels were needed for each. Early cigar box labels were made using a stone lithography process. As many as twenty colors were used on a single label. The designs were often embossed and decorated with gold highlights. Old cigar box labels became popular collectibles in the late 1970s. A rare label can sell for hundreds of dollars.

Collecting cigar bands was a popular hobby around 1900, but it lost favor by the 1940s. Thousands of different cigar bands were produced from the 1890s until the 1920s. Glass ashtrays decorated with early twentieth-century cigar bands can still be found.

Melrose tobacco used this Egyptian-style design popular in the 1880s. The exotic woman and palm trees attested to the enticing aura of smoking.

Top: Citrus fruit growers in California and Florida used colorful crate labels in the 1890s. This label was used about 1900 for South Carolina-grown cantaloupes. It is a rare early example. (Photo: PaperStuff.com)

Bottom: Color was not often used on labels made in the 1870s. A black and white label is on this box of Tasteless Blazers, an improved type of matches patented in 1877.

Fruit Crate Art

Orange growers in California began using colored lithographed labels on their wooden crates during the 1880s, and soon growers of other fruits followed suit. Growers tried to outdo each other in the color and appeal of their individual labels, which were used on crates of oranges, lemons, apples, pears,

asparagus, lettuce, and other fruits and vegetables. Early labels were produced using the stone lithography process. From the 1880s until World War I, designers favored flowers, animals, birds, and scenic views.

Matchbox Labels and Matchbooks

Matchbox labels came into use about 1826 with the invention of the friction match. The first label on a matchbox was strictly utilitarian. The design was black and white and included directions on how to the use the new invention. In 1830 N. Jones & Company of England produced a crude, pale green matchbox label picturing an Englishman and a Highlander smoking, with two serpents breathing flames to add interest.

Early manufacturers discovered that the labels were good selling devices, and by 1880 people began collecting them. The best labels came from Italy, Belgium, Spain, and Australia. The oldest labels feature royalty, important people, and buildings. By the end of the nineteenth century, animals and birds were extremely popular.

The oldest known American printed matchbox label was produced by P. Truesdell of Warsaw, New York. The Truesdell matches were made from 1855 to 1857. Safety matches were invented in 1855, and many labels after that date have those words printed on them.

There are no official matchbox label catalogs, and prices depend mainly on the individual collector and personal tastes. If a label is worn, dirty, or torn, the price of the matchbox drops. Labels that were made to wrap around three sides of a box, no matter how old, are valueless if they have been cut apart. Beginners should not pay high prices for labels before they are familiar with what is available. Remember, forged labels do exist.

Book matches were patented by a U.S. attorney in 1892. The first matchbook issued by the Diamond Match Company was an advertisement for the Mendelssohn Opera Company. By 1896 book matches were made by the thousands. Book matches should be saved without the pad of matches or the staple.

Catalogs

Old store catalogs are important to historians and collectors, and they offer hours of fun to readers. Of special importance and value are old Sears, Roebuck or Montgomery Ward catalogs, or any catalog printed before 1900. Any catalog that includes a new invention, or a catalog published within the first few years of the invention has wanted information. A catalog listing tools, jewelry, silverware, porcelains, farm machinery, garden statuary, lamps, and many other everyday items is also of value. All unusual illustrated catalogs can be either saved or sold to others who need them for research. Reprints of old catalogs will also sell. Some collectors search for recent catalogs that offer reproductions of antiques so they can identify the confusing fakes.

Old catalogs are valuable sources of historic information. This Larkin Soap Company catalog of the 1890s pictures a clock, tea set, and lamp given free with cartons of soap.

SHEET MUSIC

The history of illustrated sheet music began in the fifteenth century, when music was often hand decorated with elaborate colored letters. Today's collectors want sheet music that was published after the 1820s and includes interesting graphics. Most lithographed vignettes and covers were printed on the East Coast. Many early published songs had been composed in England, but by the 1830s sheet music publications of American tunes with typically American illustrations were being produced.

There is a general rule to dating sheet music: the smaller the picture on the title page, the older the sheet music. By the 1870s, sheet music title pages included a full picture with the title in decorative type. Most title pages or covers were lithographed in black and white. A few color lithographs began to be used in the 1840s. The look of sheet music changed in the early 1900s, when designs began to include the song's title as part of the art. Photographs were often part of these covers. Before 1917 most sheet music was printed on pages measuring 13½ by 10½ inches. After the United States entered World War I, four sizes were made: regular (13½ by 10½ inches), 10 by 7 inches, 4 by 5 inches, and 12 by 9 inches. After 1920 most sheet music was published on sheets measuring 12 by 9 inches.

The value of sheet music is determined by its age, the popularity of the song or music, the rarity and condition of the sheet music, the fame of the artist, and the type of picture. Music with pictures of automobiles or political events often sells for higher prices than earlier, more artistic covers.

Date sheet music by the copyright date, which was required after 1871. Many pieces were copyrighted before that year as well. Keep in mind that sheet music often was printed long after the copyright year that was engraved on the original plates used for printing.

Chapter 21

Packaging and Advertising

MUSEUMS AS WELL AS ANTIQUES collectors are interested in commercial packaging, company advertising, and country store memorabilia. Many museums display eighteenth- and nineteenth-century commercial whiskey flasks and glass containers in their collections of early blown glass. Restaurants and stores want walls filled with ads and shelves of old bottles and boxes. Items that were found in the old general store or a supermarket, even though many of them are only forty years old, are an important part of our country's history. Shaving cream jars with Pratt transfer lids, lithographed tin boxes, and other commercial packages made before the late nineteenth century are desirable collectibles. Historical museums are using even more recent advertising, packaging, and store display pieces to complete room exhibits of the decorative arts of the nineteenth and twentieth centuries.

Look for advertising on cans, signs, trade cards, and even dishes for the kitchen. Canned condensed milk was set on the table to use as cream. This attractive porcelain can holder advertised the milk on the inside, where it would not show.

Top: Fish, especially salmon, was one of the first types of canned food. This tin can with an old-style embossed paper label held salmon. The label instructs the user to heat the salmon by putting the unopened can into boiling water. Bad idea!

Right: Early cans, like this Carolina Brand Tomatoes can, were sealed with a lead-soldered metal disk. To open it, just put a hot coal on the disk and melt the lead. Not a method considered safe today.

Tin Cans—To Help an Army Travel on Its Stomach

The first metal containers for food or tobacco were used in England about 1780. Snuff was sold in small lead drums marked with engraved paper labels. Large metal drums were used to store varnish by the early nineteenth century.

Cans, or canisters as they were first known, were important because they solved a problem: Napoleon's army had to eat. The problem of feeding a large, moving body of men was the key to victory in war. Realizing this, Napoleon offered a reward to the person who could develop a safe way to preserve tasty food for long periods of time. Nicolas-François Appert developed a method of canning in 1795, opened a factory to can meats, vegetables, and fruit in 1805, and in 1810 received the prize. His products were stored in glass jars. Breakage was a problem, so most manufactures soon switched to tin cans. Peter Durand patented an iron-coated tin can with a soldered cover in 1810. He canned food for the British army in 1813. Today food is preserved in tin- or plastic-coated steel cans.

The earliest cans were made by hand. Isaac and Nathan Winslow of Portland, Maine, sold handmade cans in 1842. The can had a small hole in the top and was sealed with a soldered disk. A workman could make about six cans an hour.

Cans were partially shaped by machine in 1847. By 1858 manufacturing was more mechanized, and a single workman could make 1,000 cans a day. By 1883 automation had speeded up production to about 2,500 cans per hour. These cans were made with a small hole in the top and a soldered closure.

The type of can we use today was first made in 1898. It has crimped ends and a soldered lock-seam, a side seam that can be felt on the body. Some earlier handmade cans are smooth at the joints. Cans with a baked varnish interior that appears golden in color were first made in 1903.

Lithography on Cans

Some containers had embossed or raised designs. A method of printing on metal cans was invented about 1850. Lithography was done directly on the tin about 1875, when the process was developed and patented by Robert Barclay and John Doyle Fry in England. The printing process was successful, and the elaborately designed cans were favored by many firms. Americans developed the process for lithographing cans in the 1870s, and lithographed cans with the dates 1878, 1879, and 1880 have been found. A few early lithographed American-made tin containers include the name of the company as part of the tin's design. The name is usually printed in very small letters near a seam or near the bottom of the can. One of the names often found on early tins is Somers Brothers, the first American firm to make containers with designs lithographed directly on the metal. Daniel, Joe, and Guy Somers were making tins by 1869. Somers Brothers went out of business in 1901.

Canned Goods

Thomas Huntley started packing biscuits (cookies) in tins in England about 1830, when his brother, a tinsmith, developed a watertight package for shipping biscuits. William Underwood of London, England, came to Boston in 1821 and sold pickles, sauces, and other foods in glass jars and tin cans. By 1835 he was offering canned tomatoes. He also canned deviled ham and milk. Americans Ezra Daggert and Thomas Kensett patented their containers in

Any lithographed can with a picture as part of the design is of more value to the collector than a lithographed can with only names. A well-known manufacturer's name also adds value.

Today some lithographed cans show crazing because the paint that was applied was thick and has shrunk slightly.

EARLY TIN CAN MANUFACTURERS

Companies that manufactured cans in the United States before 1900 include Ginna and Company (1870s) of New York City; S.A. Ilsley and Company (1865) of Brooklyn, New York; Somers Brothers (1869) of Brooklyn, New York; and Hasker and Marcus Manufacturing Company (1891) of Richmond, Virginia.

General stores sold bulk goods like cream of tartar from large containers. The label was lithographed directly on this tin, then the paper picture of a woman's head was pasted on as an added decoration.

VALUE

All tin containers are judged by the same criteria: rarity, condition, and maker. Extras that add value include a figural three-dimensional shape like a book or a royal carriage, or a can label picturing an animal, sports figure, Uncle Sam, woman (especially nude), car, train, or airplane.

1825. After a few years of manufacturing, Mr. Kensett moved to the Baltimore area, where he canned fruits, oysters, tomatoes, and other foodstuffs in his patented can. Gail Borden canned condensed milk and milk products in 1856.

The 1860s saw a surge in the canning industry in America. Van Camp started packing pork and beans in 1861. Burnham & Morrill, established in Portland, Maine, in 1867, canned vegetables, meat, and fish, including lobsters. Anderson and Campbell of Camden, New Jersey, began packing more than two hundred food items starting in 1869. (The firm became Joseph Campbell Preserve Company in 1892, and it was the forerunner of the Campbell Soup Company of today.) Libby McNeil started packing meat in 1872. Schepps coconut products were sold in cans during the 1890s. Many types of spices were also offered in tins.

Food was not the only product that was packaged in the new tin cans. In 1866 Dr. Israel Lyon used the first metal box for his tooth powder. Tobacco products such as snuff, pipe tobacco, cigars, and cigarettes were available in tins. Before safety matches were invented (1855), matches sometimes ignited in a pocket. Many burns were prevented after 1845, when matches were packed in tins.

Many tin collectors specialize. The most popular collectibles are beer, tobacco, tea, coffee, and oil cans. Also of interest are containers for oysters, face powder, food, condoms, and gunpowder.

Labels

In the early nineteenth century, cans were labeled with printed or engraved labels or with tin-soldered metal labels. The oldest known paper food-can label in America is a steel engraving of tomatoes by Rechbow and Larne of New York, dating from the mid-nineteenth century.

Any paper-labeled can that can be dated before 1900 is rare. Although paper can labels are easy to find, old cans with intact original paper labels are among the most difficult items to locate.

Especially desirable are can, box, and packet labels that mention the Shakers, who packed vegetables, flower seeds, jellies, and herbs. Can labels that feature scenes of the past, houses, or people in period dress are good. A label picturing a maid serving soup, a Victorian factory building, or a sports figure helps to date the package. It is also possible to date a can or box label from the name of the company or lithographer.

Large boxes and crates with unusual original labels can still be found. These were either wholesale-size containers or boxes made to hold retail-size packages of a product. Many wooden boxes had stenciled names, not labels. Collectors feel that the best boxes have paper labels on the sides and on the inside of the lid.

Labels can be dated from the design, the brand, or the company. The cut glass bowl containing peas was stylish about 1910. Ocean View is a brand that was packed in Wisconsin from 1907 to 1924.

Product Packages to Look For

Baking Powder Cans

In the middle of the nineteenth century, women had many new preparations to help them with their baking. Phosphate baking powder was first sold in the United States by the Rumford Chemical Works in 1859. Horsford self-rising bread preparation, a self-rising flour for pancakes, and Rumford yeast were also developed. Royal Baking Powder was first made in 1873. Baking powder was first marketed in glass, but after 1880 it was packaged in metal cans with paper labels. Baking powder tins were made with a completely removable lift-off lid that could be used to reseal the can. Other early baking powder tins include those used by Amazon (c.1900); Andrews & Company (c.1890); Arm & Hammer (c.1867); Calumet (c.1814); Charm (c.1900); Clabber Girl (1899); Cleveland's (c.1880); Climax (c.1890); Cowbrand (1876); Crescent (c.1900); Czar (c.1900); Davis & Davis (c.1900); De Land and Company (c.1890); Dr. Price's (c.1900); Gillet's (c.1900); Golf Label (c.1900); Grant's (c.1900); Hansfords (c.1890); Hecker's (c.1900); Horsford (c.1880); Lewis (c.1900); Pearl (c.1900); Pioneer (c.1900); Pure Gold (c.1880); Redhead's (c.1900); Royal (c.1867); and Snow Flake (c.1900). Fiber cans were used for a short time around 1900 and then off and on after 1934.

Spice cans were made of tin in the nineteenth century. This lithographed tin can for French's imported paprika is 3¼ inches high.

Spice Tins

All types of spices were put in tins soon after the Civil War. Large store bins held spices in bulk, and small tins held them in ounces. The earliest examples were japanned and stenciled. Later, lithographed designs and paper labels were used on the tins. Many spices were packaged for wholesale grocers and labeled with the company name. Early cans had full lift-off lids. The lift top with a half opening for a spoon measure first appeared in the 1930s. Spice cans were made for Eagle Spice Company (1870–1892); Emmett Spice Company (before 1896); Forbes Spice Company (1853–1880); John Hancock and Sons (1865–1904); Heeker Spice Company (1899–1919); Justice Spice Mills (1892–1895); Slades Spice (1888–1935); Steinwinder-Stoffregan Spices (1894–1934); Thompson and Taylor Spice (1883–1920); Watkins (c.1880–present); and Woolson Spice Company (1880–present).

Some of the major companies that sold spices were national brands, and their spices were marketed nationwide. McCormick and Company (founded in 1889) had many labels, including Bee Brand, Silver Medal, Clover Brand (1895), Banquet Brand (1902), Clover Blossom Brand (1905), and Green Seal (1909). Stickney and Poor's was established in 1815 and Durkee in 1857. These companies are all still operating.

Mustard was another well-packaged product. It was sold in tins and other containers starting in the 1860s. Westmoreland Glass made milk glass mustard holders for sale in stores. Pottery mustard containers are also known. Companies packaging mustard include Colburn's (c.1870–present); Colman's (c.1814–present); and Keen's (1742–present).

Biscuit Boxes

The first biscuit tins were made in England in the 1830s. Thomas Huntley, a baker, asked his brother Joseph, a tinsmith, to make some boxes to ship biscuits by stagecoach. The tin container kept the biscuits fresh. The brothers founded a firm that is still in operation. A method of transfer printing directly on tinplate was patented by London printer Benjamin George about 1860.

Huntley and Palmers biscuits were packaged in tins with paper labels, but by 1868 printed tins were made. The words *By Appointment*, which means the biscuits were used by the royals, appear on Huntley and Palmers' tins after 1885.

Biscuit manufacturers, especially in England, found tins that had attractive shapes helped sell the product. A. S. Henderson & Sons used this log cabin tin to hold cookies. It is 5¼ by 6 inches.

Elaborately shaped and decorated biscuit tins were being made in quantity by the early 1880s. The designs on the tins often reflected the styles of the times or special events. Tins were decorated with scenes of China, India, Arabia, and other exotic lands. The art nouveau influence is apparent in tins made during the late 1890s. In the early 1900s, tins shaped like a motor bus and a telephone—both issued in 1907—reflected new technologies of the times. Novelty tins shaped like games or toys were popular after 1918. The tins continued to be made after the 1930s, when simpler shapes were used. After World War II, the fancy tins almost completely disappeared because of their high cost.

English biscuit companies using the figural tins include John Buchanan and Brothers Confectioners; William Crawford and Sons, Ltd; W. Dunmore and Sons; Huntley and Palmers; W. R. Jacob and Company; MacKenzie and MacKenzie; McVitie and Price, Ltd.; Meredith and Drew, Ltd.; and Peek Frean and Company.

Coffee Cans

Coffee has been a popular drink since the late seventeenth century. At first green coffee beans were sold, and they had to be roasted and ground at home before making the beverage. By the nineteenth century, stores were roasting and grinding coffee. The first unground roasted beans and ground coffee were sold in paper bags, but soon they were available in tin containers. Large store

containers with colorful lithographed labels appeared in the 1870s. Lithographed tins or paper-labeled cans held a pound of coffee. Early cans were made in many sizes and shapes, but by the 1920s can manufacturers tried to standardize their packages. A rectangular or cylindrical package was used for standard one-, two-, and three-pound sizes. The vacuum-packed can was first used about 1900.

In 1906 the Pure Food and Drug Act was passed, and claims on packaging were required to be true. For example, medical claims for coffee were not permitted. Careful reading of a package's label will date the package as being produced before or after 1906.

All cans can be dated by the techniques used to design and produce the tin, the tin's shape, and the age of the company. Early nineteenth-century cans were stenciled or hand painted on japanned tin, which has an orange black background made of asphaltum. Later designs and labels were hand painted, decorated with applied decals, or lithographed on the colored tin.

Gunpowder Flasks

The gunpowder flask is probably the earliest tin container used in America that is still found by collectors. One of the earliest gunpowder cans has a paper label that reads *Kentucky Rifle Gunpowder Hazard Powder Co. founded 1843*. Early tins had paper or stenciled labels. Later tins were either printed with a lithographed design or had a paper label.

Gunpowder was sold in tin cans with small pouring spouts. Dupont used an Indian on its product. Look carefully at old tins. This is a reproduction.

Opposite page: The most common coffee can of the past is a cylinder that holds one pound. This cardboard Royal Blend container has an embossed tin lid. On the back of the can, the paper label pictures a large building and a horse-drawn carriage.

Talcum Powder Cans

The talcum powder sprinkle-top can is a specialized area of collecting. Mr. Mennen invented the sprinkle-top can in 1883. These cans can be dated by the picture of a baby on the side. The child looks more attractive on later labels.

Mr. Mennen, who invented the sprinkle-top for talcum powder, was said to be the baby shown on the can. The lithographed tin cans remained in use over the years, but the decorations were updated.

Right: Tea was sold in bulk or in small tin boxes. The box was lithographed or used a paper label like this one on a nineteenth-century, oriental-style Forest City tea container. The instructions for making tea said "use a stone or agate pot."

Opposite page: "Hand Made" was a well-known brand of tobacco. This lithographed flip-top tin, used about 1900, is 3½ by 4 inches. Variations of the hand logo were used.

Many other firms marketed talcum powder in a variety of sprinkle-top cans. A screw top was used about 1910. Sprinkle-top tins held many other types of products, such as tooth powder (especially Dr. Lyon's, a brand started in 1886).

Tea Caddies

Tea was a popular eighteenth-century drink. It was so valuable that it was stored in tea caddies that were locked. Tea caddies were made of porcelain, silver, or, for the less well-to-do, painted tin. Caddies had flat or domed tops, and commercial packages used in stores were designed in the same shape. Tea was sold loose from bins for years. Large store bins were known by the Civil War. The bin was labeled with the name of the type of tea, such as oolong, gunpowder (a Chinese green tea), or orange pekoe. Bins often had a cylinder that revolved so the storekeeper could show which tea was in stock. Small commercial tin containers for coffee and for tea were used by the end of the nineteenth century.

Tobacco Cans

Another specialized type of can that is much in demand is the tobacco can. Most of the tobacco cans collectors want were made to hold pipe tobacco. Other tins were made to hold chewing plugs, snuff, cigars, or cigarettes, and there were also containers to dispense or display tobacco in stores. Tobacco was sold in cloth or paper bags until about 1880, when tobacco tins were made. Often attractive scenes of interesting people were lithographed on the metal, and there are collectors who specialize in this sort of container. A few tins were roly-poly, shaped like fat men or women. Stoneware and glass jars were also used.

There are several ways to date a tobacco tin. Examine the method of decoration, the design elements, and the lettering. Check the name on the can, and then research the tobacco company or the manufacturing company that made the can at the library or on the Internet. Tax stamps can be of some help, but they are not always as useful as it might seem. The stamp will suggest the date the tin was sold, but the date of the sale could have been several years after the stamp was issued. There were tax stamps in use at least as early as 1864. These are not dated with a year, and they must be recognized by the design.

Package Design

Design is the key to dating almost any type of antique or collectible. Styles were copied years later, but an art deco piece designed in the 1920s could not date from an earlier period. Some knowledge of the history of packaging design helps identify packaged items and signs. Most packages were designed with a look that was familiar to consumers but not daring or odd. For example, the art nouveau style was popular in packaging in the early 1900s, about ten years after it had been prominent in the decorative arts.

It is best to first learn the differences among Victorian (1850–1900), art nouveau (1880s–1914), and art deco (1920s–1930s) designs in type styles and border designs to help you determine age. The pseudo-Egyptian (1870s–1890s) and the Japonisme (1860–1900) movements of the late nineteenth century also influenced package designs for short periods.

Pictures were used on packages throughout the nineteenth and twentieth centuries. Pictures of company buildings were popular by the 1880s. Medals and awards, usually from world's fairs, were used on many packages, and they can often help to date a tin. But remember these awards were used on packages for many years after the award was given. A picture of an attractive woman was first used on a tin at about the time of the Civil War. If a tin has a picture of a familiar comic figure, like the Yellow Kid, the image dates the tin to within a few years of the figure's popularity.

Trademarks—Icons of Advertising

Some trademarks that originated in the nineteenth century are still being used. Many have been updated to a more modern look. Collectors like these icons of advertising, and all are collectible. Some of the most famous are the Quaker Oats man (1876); Baker's Chocolate lady (1883); Coca-Cola logo (1886, registered in 1893); Aunt Jemima (1889); Mennen Talc baby (1892); Cream of Wheat man (1893); and Nabisco's boy in a yellow raincoat (1899).

In dating labels, look for wording that seems old-fashioned. At the turn of the twentieth century, a can label might say, *Carefully selected fruit prepared by experienced women*. Products had names like *washing fluid* or *telephone peas*. Some products included additives, like quinine, which would seem strange today.

During the nineteenth century, paper labels were produced in elaborate styles using various printing techniques. The raised, embossed labels of the mid-nineteenth century, often found on tobacco boxes, needle cases, and fabric bolts, lost favor by the twentieth century because of the high cost of producing them.

Bottles

Bottles are described in detail in Chapter 7. Remember that any bottle made before 1900 or any specially shaped bottle, like a pickle bottle or a figural liquor bottle, is a collector's treasure. Many bottles, including milk bottles, soda bottles, candy

Store Collectibles: "Firsts"

Printed matchbook label: *"Percussion Matches Manufactured by P. Truesdell, Warsaw, New York. Warranted New Yorker Print"* was printed on the first matchbook label, which was made from 1855 to 1857.

Cigarette cards: In 1885 Allen and Ginter of Richmond, Virginia, issued ten cigarettes in a box plus a picture card for five cents. These eventually inspired baseball cards.

Paper advertising fans: Paper fans were made in the eighteenth century. A Crystal Palace exhibition in New York in 1853 used advertising fans.

Paper napkins: The first paper napkins, which were plain tissue paper squares, were introduced at the Chicago World's Fair in 1893. The first printed paper napkin appeared in 1898.

U.S. advertising wall calendar: An 1863 calendar advertising medicine for John L. Hunnewell of Boston, Massachusetts, is the earliest.

Paper bags: Paper bags appeared in Europe in the seventeenth century and in the United States in the nineteenth century. In 1852 Frances Wolle of Bethlehem, Pennsylvania, invented a machine that made bags. By 1884 the Union Bag & Paper Company was making brown bags with flat bottoms and pleated sides. Advertising soon was printed on the bags.

containers, canning jars, and ink bottles from the nineteenth and twentieth centuries, should be saved. Protect the labels, because they add value even if they are damaged.

Store Furnishings

Anything that was used in a store before 1900—from coffee grinders to bill hooks and ledger books—is of historic interest to collectors today. Cabinets, candy containers, signs, and displays from the old stores are now valuable.

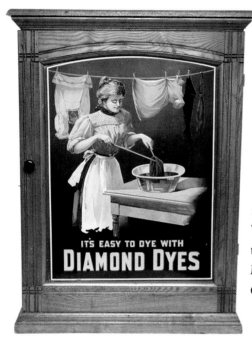

Dye was sold in small paper packets. The store kept the packets in dye cabinets that often had embossed and lithographed tin fronts. This Diamond Dye cabinet appropriately shows a woman dyeing clothes. This is one of ten different Diamond cabinet fronts.
(Photo: Randy Inman)

Cabinets

The store cabinet, which was used to store thread or dye, may have been refinished, repainted, and reworked, or had its hardware replaced, and then found a place in the living room in the 1960s. Today the collector prefers a cabinet that is in good original condition.

Old store spool cabinets had very narrow drawers, often with glass on the front. They were used as display pieces and containers for spools of thread from about 1880. Many had labels that read *Clark Company O.N.T.* (Our New Thread) or *J. and P. Coats Spool Cotton.* These two companies were competitors in the thread business from about 1830 until 1896, when they consolidated their interests and formed a single selling agent, the Spool Cotton Company. By then, a new style of thread cabinet was popular in stores. It was a tall, four-sided chest with glass panels on two sides, louvered doors on the other two sides, and a swivel base that allowed more spools of thread to be displayed.

A dye cabinet or a medicine cabinet was usually made with a lithographed tin panel on the door. Inside the cabinet were many small compartments that held the merchandise. Tin-front Diamond Dye cabinets, first made about 1890, are so popular they have been reproduced.

Other large cabinets were used in country stores. Deep bins for grains, coffee, collars, or sundries are popular with both the country store collector and those who want a country look in the family room. There are a surprising number of collectors, museums, and historic villages that have stores or store-like setups and display numerous cans, bottles, boxes, signs, tools, toys, and even working household goods.

Coffee Mills and Grinders

Until about 1860, coffee drinkers roasted and ground coffee beans at home. Grocery store owners began to equip their stores with coffee mills during the second half of the nineteenth century. The large Enterprise No. 1 Store Mill, which was patented in 1870, had one side wheel. The two-wheel model was made in 1873. The large floor-model store grinder or the large counter-model mills or grinders date from about the same time. The best store grinders have the original paint and all the original parts. Repainting lowers the value.

The first commercially ground coffee in America was sold in the 1860s. By 1873 roasted whole-bean coffee was packaged and marketed, and manufacturers developed small grinders for home use. At the end of the nineteenth century, some coffee mills were operated by electric motors. Coffee mills were listed in hardware catalogs by 1894, and there were advertisements for Royal and The Telephone Coffee mills. By 1912 the Lightning, Kin, Fast Grinder, Superior, Queen, Premier, and Swift's Family mills were being made. The coffee mill lost favor by the 1930s. Home-ground coffee came back into fashion in the 1980s, and coffee grinders became available again for home use.

About 1950 someone decided that a coffee grinder would make an unusual lamp. Thousands of reproductions of the early home coffee grinders were made. These reproductions are often found at flea markets and look older than they actually are.

Coffee was ground at the store in a large coffee grinder like this Enterprise No. 6. It dates from about 1873 and has the original red paint and decorative decals.
(Photo: Randy Inman)

Signs of the Times

Some old store signs were lithographed directly on tin and designed
to look like a picture with a frame. These signs are hard to find in
good condition. The Grape Nuts sign featuring a girl and her St.
Bernard is one of the best known examples. Any early sign that
includes a picture of an American flag, Uncle Sam, a black person,
or an unusual scene has added interest. Recognizable brand names
like Coca-Cola or Pepsi-Cola are also of greater value.

The Apothecary Shop and Drug Store

The apothecary shop was the place to buy medicine in the years
before the twentieth century. The shop's owner dispensed the medicine in bottles, cans, wooden boxes, and paper packets. Consumers
could buy medicine without a prescription from a doctor.

By the end of the nineteenth century, a soda fountain had been
added to the apothecary shop. It was the druggist who first served

Coca-Cola or Moxie. Elaborate soda fountains were made with marble and brass trim. The syrups for drinks were squirted from ceramic dispensers that were often made in imaginative shapes, perhaps like a lemon or an orange. These figural dispensers command high prices. A Hires root beer urn dispenser that pictures the Hires boy and the words *Drink Hires Rootbeer 5¢* sold in 1997 for a record $106,700. ☙

Carbonated drinks made from a mixture of flavored syrup and carbonated water were sold at the drugstore counter. This Hires syrup dispenser can be dated from the dress and bib on the Hires boy. It was used from 1891 to 1906. (Photo: Pettigrew)

Chapter 22

Kitchenware

KITCHEN UTENSILS OF ALL TYPES, from eggbeaters to bowls, are collected today. Handmade wooden and metal items, like ladles and choppers, were made in the early nineteenth century. Later, items like iron apple peelers and graniteware were mass produced. The late Victorian period was the era of the mechanical gadget, and tools like the cherry pitter, cabbage chopper, and eggbeater were popular. Most of the early kitchen tools were made of iron. Many iron utensils have a patent date molded into the handle. Look for the date, because it is the best clue to the age of the item.

Cooks have used rolling pins for making pastry for hundreds of years. In colonial America, they were most often made of sycamore, walnut, beech, fruitwood, or oak. Early rolling pins usually had handles or knobs at one or both ends, but some had no handles and were merely tapered at each end. Toward the end of the eighteenth century, glass rolling pins were made to be used as decorations, but they could also be used in the kitchen. Early glass rolling pins were solid, usually opaque white, but by 1790 some were hollow and could be filled with cold water or sand when they were used to roll pastry.

Opposite page: Food choppers were in general use by the 1890s. This amusing poster touted the uses of the Universal chopper patented in 1897. It could be screwed onto the kitchen counter, then used to chop meat, vegetables, fish, and more.

This heavy copper mold is tin lined to make it safe to use with acidic foods. It is 6½ by 5½ inches. It was probably used to mold blancmange, a thick, sweet milk pudding popular in England in the nineteenth century.

Early cans were opened with simple tools: a hammer and chisel. In 1858 Ezra J. Watson patented the first can opener, and in the 1860s a variety of utensils to stab and open cans were invented. Cans with thin tops that could be cut off with a knife and cans with caps that could be loosened by pulling a tin strip were developed in the 1870s.

The first rotary-crank eggbeater was invented by Ralph Collier of Baltimore in 1856. Dover Stamping Company of Dover, New Hampshire, manufactured the first mass-produced eggbeaters in the 1870s. The eggbeater was useful for mixing batters and sauces and for whipping cream as well as eggs. Eventually more than one thousand different patents were issued for various types of this practical kitchen tool.

Graniteware is an enameled tinware that has been used as cooking pots in the kitchen from the late nineteenth century to the present. Early graniteware was green or turquoise blue with white spatters. Later graniteware was gray, either a solid color or with white spatters. Reproductions are made in all colors.

Early iron kitchen tools are scarce and pricey. Griswold Manufacturing Company (founded in Erie, Pennsylvania, in 1865) and Wagner Manufacturing Company (founded in Sidney, Ohio, in 1881) were two important makers of cast-iron cookware and tools. By the early 1900s, they were producing cast aluminum ware as well. Both companies were acquired by General Housewares Corporation in the middle of the twentieth century. Other inventions for the kitchen were solutions to everyday problems in the nineteenth century: the wooden mouse trap with a mallet that hit the mouse on the head, the flytrap maze baited with honey, ice tongs made to lift fifty-pound blocks of ice. There are hundreds of other tools and utensils that are no longer needed and almost unrecognized today.

Any old kitchen tool or utensil that is in original condition and made before 1900 is of interest to the collector. If you plan to collect, try to specialize. A complete collection of apple peelers or eggbeaters showing the continuous improvements and changes is of great interest to historians and inventors.

Never, never repaint, refinish, or restore an old metal or wooden piece if it interests you because of its value as an antique. If you are going to use the item, refinishing or restoring might add to its beauty or usefulness, but it will detract from its worth to the serious collector. Rusty iron can be cleaned and the rust removed, but you should *never* repaint the piece.

Early graniteware in the United States was usually turquoise, green, or gray with white marbling, although many other colors were used in Europe. This large water kettle has a wooden bail handle.

Chapter 23

Tools

BEFORE THE TWENTIETH CENTURY, cabinetmakers, blacksmiths, tinsmiths, and other tradesmen made their own tools for particular jobs. These one-of-a-kind tools were patterned after tools the tradesmen had used or seen while learning their trade. Planes, saws, wrenches, hammers, slide rules, and other tools seen at flea markets today were used by blacksmiths, farmers, homesteaders, doctors, and people working in foundries, mills, dairies, buggy shops, and other businesses.

Woodworking

Woodworking tools have been used for centuries, and many of the tools used today are similar to old ones. The ancient Egyptians put models of tools into tombs, and these, together with many wall paintings, have left a good record of early woodworking. By the first part of the sixteenth century, houses were built by carpenters. Then cabinetmakers, who built furniture, and joiners, who did interior trim, began to specialize. The man known as a wood turner made rounded pieces that he turned on a lathe. Soon there were even more specialists. The chairmaker made a chair frame, then had it enhanced by a carver.

Opposite page: The purpose of many old tools is sometimes a mystery because manufacturing methods have changed. This pair of paddles with sharp needle points was used to card wool in the nineteenth century. After untangling, the strands of wool were spun into thread.

Furniture produced before the nineteenth century was made by hand, but a single workman did not construct an entire chair alone. Groups of workers were employed in a shop, and each had a special task. Each specialty required special tools. Most tools were hand-made by the craftsman. By the nineteenth century, craftsmen were assisted by machinery. Boards were no longer cut by a man using a pit saw; a machine did the job more efficiently.

Specialists worked in many crafts, not just building and furniture making. Wheelwrights made wheels and axles for wagons. Pattern makers made a wooden pattern for each metal part to be used in machines.

Early construction tools include axes, adzes, saws, planes, chisels, drills, turning tools, hammers, vises, wrenches, screwdrivers, and rules, among many others. It is difficult to date early tools, but some nineteenth- and twentieth-century tools were marked with the name of the company that made them.

Stanley—A Famous Name in Tools

New Britain, Connecticut, was an early center for ironwork. The shop belonging to William and Frederick Stanley was the first in the city to use steam power. In 1842 the brothers began to manufacture bolts and door hardware. They soon expanded, and by 1852 they were able to cast, forge, and manufacture metals, and make many types of hardware. Other members of the family started A. Stanley & Company to make boxwood and ivory rules. The successful company acquired two other firms and became the Stanley Rule & Level Company. Over the years, it acquired many other companies that made a variety of tools, enabling the firm to obtain valuable patents and expand its product line. By 1900 Stanley was the world's largest maker of planes. The company continued to grow, and today the Stanley Works makes many tools that are sold around the world. Stanley is the best-known name for tool collectors, and the name adds value.

Fire-Fighting Equipment

For collectors, fire-fighting equipment is in a field of its own, and there are many who will buy anything that relates to a fire department, including helmets, hose nozzles, belts, photographs, and fire-chief trumpets.

Fire marks were first used in the eighteenth century and could be found on many homes until the 1870s. These plaques were made of wood, lead, cast iron, or stamped tin and were placed on insured homes as an indication to firemen that the owner of the house had paid for special fire protection. Each insurance company had its own symbol. All firemen knew that if the house was marked, the insurance company paid a reward to the volunteer firemen. The fire mark went out of use when firemen's salaries began to be paid by the community, a practice that started in most communities soon after the Civil War. Many modern copies of fire marks have been made.

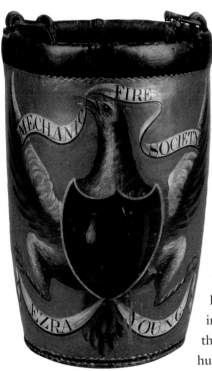

Leather fire buckets with the name of the firehouse, the city, or the city's insignia painted or stamped on them were used in America from the seventeenth century. Some were decorated with elaborate paintings of arms, eagles, figures, and insignias. The leather bucket was used in larger cities until the 1840s and in rural areas for many years after that. Old leather buckets sell for hundreds of dollars each.

This leather fire bucket is decorated with the words Mechanic Fire Society, Ezra Young, *and an eagle and shield with the symbols of a bootmaker. This bucket sold for over $54,000 in 2000.*
(Photo: Skinner)

APPENDIX

Nineteenth-Century Jewelry and Metalwork Designers and Manufacturers

This table lists the maker or factory, date, mark, and other information about jewelry designers of the nineteenth century. Parentheses enclose the birth and death dates of the artist. Other dates given are approximate working dates of the factory or artist. The names of workers or designers connected with jewelry factories are also in parentheses in the third column. One mark, if available, is used for each listing although the makers often used a variety of marks. Many pieces are unmarked or marked with the seller's or designer's, not the maker's, name.

Workshop or Artist and Location	Dates	Artists, Factories and Related Information	Mark
AUSTRIA			
Hoffmann, Josef Vienna	(1870–1956)	Jewelry, metalwork designer	
Moser, Koloman Vienna	(1868–1918)	Jewelry, glass, ceramics, metalwork	
BELGIUM			
Dubois, Fernard	(1861–1939)	Jewelry, silver, silver plate	
Van de Velde, Henri Clemens Brussels; Berlin, Germany	(1863–1957)	Jewelry, furniture, bronze, silver, architecture, porcelain, metalwork, ceramics	
Wolfers Frères Brussels	1812–1910	Jewelry. Phillipe Wolfers (1858–1929) worked with jewelry, metalwork, sculpture, ceramics. He joined the family's firm c.1880.	
CANADA			
Birks, Henry & Sons Montreal	1879–present	Silver, gold, jewelry. Founded by Henry Birks (1840–1928).	
FRANCE			
Aucoc, Maison Paris	1821–c.1900	Gold, silver, jewelry. Brothers Louis and André Aucoc and René Lalique (see below) worked at the factory.	A.A. or L.A.
Babst & Falize Paris	1880–1892	Jewelry, gold, silver. Partnership of Falize (see below) and Germain Bapst (1853–1921).	

Workshop or Artist and Location	Dates	Artists, Factories and Related Information	Mark
Boucheron, Maison Paris, London	1858–present	Jewelry. Founded by Frédéric Boucheron (1830–1902).	$\mathbb{B}$
Boutet de Monvel, Charles Paris	(1855–?)	Jewelry, enamel, engraver, painter	
Cardeilhac Paris	1802–1951	Silver (Vital-Antoine Cardeilhac, Ernest Cardeilhac [d.1904], Edward Cardeilhac)	Cardeilhac . Paris
Cartier Paris London New York, N.Y.	1847–present	Jewelry (Louis-François Cartier; his son, Alfred Cartier; Alfred's sons, Louis Cartier, Pierre Cartier, and Jacques Cartier)	Cartier
Chaumet et Cie Paris London	c.1780–present	Jewelry. Chaumet was successor to the firm of Etienne Nitot, founded c.1780. Joseph Chaumet (1854–1928) joined in 1874. (Jules Fossin [1808–1869])	
Christofle, L'Orfevrerie St. Denis	1839–present	Silver, silver plate (Charles Christofle, Henry Bouilhet, E. Reiber, J. M. Olbrich)	
Colonna, Edward Paris; New York, N.Y.	(1862–1948)	Jewelry. Born in Cologne, Germany; worked in New York (Tiffany's, Associated Artists, 1883–1884), Paris (S. Bing, H. Vever, 1898–1905)	COLONNA
de Ribaucort, Georges	(1887–1907)	Jewelry	
Epinay de Briort, Prosper	(1836–?)	Jewelry, sculpture	$\mathbf{B}$
Falize Paris	1838–1936	Founded by Alexis Falize (1811–1898); succeeded by his son, Lucien (1839–1897); succeeded by Lucien's sons, André, Jean and Pierre; continuing as Falize Frères	AXF
Feuillâtre, Eugene Paris	(1870–1916)	Silver, jewelry, enamel, sculpture (R. Lalique)	Feuillatre

Workshop or Artist and Location	Dates	Artists, Factories and Related Information	Mark
Fontana et Cie Paris	1840–1930s	Gold, jewelry (J. Fontana, A. Templier, C. Fontana, P. Fontana)	
Fontenay, Eugene Paris	(1823–1887) 1847–1882	Jewelry	
Fouquet Paris	c.1860–?	Jewelry Founded c.1860 by Alphonse Fouquet (1828–1911); joined by son, Georges Fouquet (1862–1957) in 1891. (Alphonse Mucha and Charles Desrosiers)	G. FOUQUET
Froment-Meurice Paris	1794–?	Gold, jewelry. Founded in 1794 by François Froment; taken over by his son François-Désiré Froment-Meurice (1802–1855) in 1825; taken over by François-Désiré's son Emile (1837–1913) in 1859. (Designer Jules Wièse [see below] worked at the firm before 1860.)	FROMENT MEURICE
Gaillard, Lucien Paris	(1861–1910)	Silver, jewelry Succeeded father, Ernest Gaillard, in his firm in 1892.	L Gaillard
Hirnè Paris	1880–1900	Jewelry (A. F. Thesmar)	Hirnè
La Maison Moderne Paris	c.1889	Jewelry (Meier-Graefe)	
LaCloche Frères Paris	1897–?	Jewelry, enamel. Founded by brothers Fernand LaCloche, Jules LaCloche, Leopold LaCloche, Jacques LaCloche.	
Lalique, René Paris	(1860–1945)	Jewelry, silver, glass	LALIQUE
Lim, Auguste	(1830–1895)	Jewelry, chains	
Mellerio, Maison Paris	c.1818–after 1914	Gold, jewelry	

Workshop or Artist and Location	Dates	Artists' Factories and Related Information	Mark
Obry, Hubert Paris	(1808–1853)	Jewelry, seals, signet rings	
Thesmar, André-Fernand Paris	(1843–1912)	Jewelry, enamel, metalwork	
Vever, Maison Metz, Paris	1821– at least 1981	Jewelry. Founded 1821 in Metz by Pierre Vever (1795–1853); joined by son Ernest Vever (1823–1884) in 1848 and by Ernest's sons Paul Vever (1851–1915) and Henri Vever (1854–1942); moved to Paris in 1871. (Eugene Grasset [1841–1917])	VEVER PARIS
Wagner, Karl Paris	(1799–1841)	Jewelry, silver. Born in Berlin; worked for the firm Mention & Wagner in Paris in 1830.	
Wièse, Jules Paris	1860–1880	Gold, jewelry. Founded by designer Jules Wièse (1818–1890).	

GERMANY

Workshop or Artist and Location	Dates	Artists' Factories and Related Information	Mark
Fahrner, Theodor Pforzheim	(1868–1928)	Silver, jewelry	
Gross, Karl Munich	(1869–?)	Jewelry, pewter	
Hueck, Eduard Lüdenscheid, Westphalia	1864–?	Metalwork, pewter (P. Behrens, J. Ohlbrich)	
Lettré, Emil Berlin	(1876–1954)	Jewelry, silver	
Olbrich, Josef Maria Darmstadt	(1867–1908)	Designer of pewter (Eduard Hueck), silver plate (C. Schroeder), silver (Christofle), jewelry (D. & M. Loewenthal, Theodor Fahrner)	
Sy & Wagner Berlin	Sy (1827–1881) Wagner (1826–?)	Gold, silver, silver plate, flatware and tableware (Emil Wagner, Francois Sy)	SY & WAGNER.
Von Cranach, Wilhelm Lucas Berlin	(1861–1918)	Gold, jewelry	

Workshop or Artist and Location	Dates	Artists, Factories and Related Information	Mark
GREAT BRITAIN			
Adie Brothers Birmingham	1879–?	Silver, silver plate (Percy Adie, Tony Adie)	
Antrobus, Philip, Ltd. London	1810–?	Jewelry	
Ashbee, Charles Robert London	(1863–1942)	Silver, jewelry, furniture. Founded Guild of Handicraft in 1888.	
Asprey & Company, Ltd. London	1781–present	Jewelry	
Attenborough, Richard London	c.1850–1862	Gold, silver, jewelry	
Benson, J. W. London	1874–present	Jewelry. Merged with Alfred Benson and Henry Webb, c.1897.	
Birmingham Guild of Handicraft Birmingham	1890–present	Metalwork, jewelry, silver (Arthur Dixon [founder], Montague Fordham, Claude Napier Clavering, E. & R. Gittins Co.)	
Brogden & Garland	1826–1835	Jewelry	
Brogden, John	1842–1885	Gold, jewelry (See Watherston & Brogden.)	
Bromsgrove Guild of Applied Art Bromsgrove	c.1890–1966	Jewelry, metal (Walter Gilbert, Arthur Gaskin, Georgina Gaskin)	B.G.A.A.
Burges, William	(1827–1881)	Jeweler, architect, designer	
Child & Child London	1880–1916	Jewelry, enamels	
Clavering, Claude Napier		Birmingham Guild of Handicraft	

Workshop or Artist and Location	Dates	Artists, Factories and Related Information	Mark
Collingwood and Company London	1817–present	Silver, jewelry. Founded by Joseph Kitching; Henry Collingwood apprenticed in 1830s and took over in 1855; joined by Henry's son Robert Nelson Collingwood.	C&C
Comyns, William & Sons London	1848–present	Silver	W.C
Connell & Co.	c.1890–1910	Silver (William Connell [d.1902]; George Connell)	C C
Cooper, John Paul Westerham	(1869–1933)	Silver, copper, jewelry (Artificer's Guild)	JPC
Courthope, Frederick	1880–1930s	Silver	F C
Cuzner, Bernard London	(1877–1956)	Jewelry, silver. Worked for Liberty & Co. c.1900.	B.C.
Dawson, Edith Robinson London	c.1900–?	Jewelry, enamel. Married to Nelson Dawson in 1893.	
Dawson, Nelson London	(1859–1942)	Jewelry, silver, metalwork, enamel. Married to Edith Robinson Dawson in 1893.	N·D
Dixon, Arthur Birmingham	(1856–1929)	Founded Birmingham Guild of Handicraft	G B H LD
Dixon, James & Sons Sheffield	1806–present	Silver, silver plate, Britannia metal (Christopher Dresser, 1879–1882)	J.W.D
Doria, Carlo	c.1860–1880	Gold, jewelry. Worked for Robert Phillips.	
Dresser, Christopher	(1834–1904)	Designed for many companies	Chr. Dresser
Elkington & Co. Birmingham	1830–present	Silver, silver plate, metalwork, enamel (Christopher Dresser, c.1885–1888)	E&CºLª
Emanuel, Harry London	1860–?	Gold, jewelry	HE

Workshop or Artist and Location	Dates	Artists, Factories and Related Information	Mark
Fisher, Alexander London	(1864–1936)	Silver, jewelry, enamel	AF
Garland & Watherston	1835–1841	Jewelry	
Garrard, R. and S. London	1802–1952	Silver, gold, jewelry (Robert Garrard, James Garrard, Sebastien Garrard)	
Gaskin, Arthur Joseph Birmingham	(1862–1928)	Metalwork, jewelry (Liberty & Co.)	G
Gaskin, Georgina	(1868–1934)	Silver, enamel, jewelry. Married Arthur Gaskin 1894; joint work began 1899.	G
Giuliano, Carlo London	(1831–1895)	Jewelry, gold	CG
Goldsmiths' & Silversmiths' Co. London	1890–1952	Silver, jewelry (William Gibson, Harold Stabler [1872–1945])	G.&S.Cº Lᴰ
Guild of Handicraft London	1888–1908	Silver, jewelry, furniture, leather, books (Charles Robert Ashbee [1863–1942])	GoHLᴰ
Hancocks & Co. London	1848–present	Jewelry	
Hardman, John & Co. Birmingham	1838–?	Ecclesiastical silver, jewelry. Founded by John Hardman (1811–1867). (A. W. N. Pugin)	J.H.&ᵒ
Harris, Kate	c.1890–1910	Silver (W. Hutton & Sons, Goldsmiths' & Silversmiths' Co.)	
Haseler, W. H. & Co. Birmingham	1870–1927	Silver, jewelry, Cymric silver, Tudric pewter (Liberty & Co.)	W·H·H
Heaton's Cloisonne Mosaics, Ltd. England, Switzerland, United States	1912–1940	Jewelry, stained glass, enamel Founded by Clement Heaton (1861–1940).	Jewelry not marked

Workshop or Artist and Location	Dates	Artists, Factories and Related Information	Mark
Hennell Limited London	1735–present	Jewelry. Became R.G Hennell & Sons in 1837; now Hennell, Frazer and Haws.	**RGH**
Horner, Charles Halifax	1885–present	Mass-produced enameled silver, jewelry	**C.H.**
Hukin & Heath Birmingham	1875–1953	Silver, silver plate (Christopher Dresser, c.1878–1890)	JWH JTH
Hunt & Roskell London	1844–1939	Silver, silver plate, jewelry Originally Storr & Mortimer (1823–1826), Storr, Mortimer & Hunt (1826–1838), Mortimer & Hunt (1839–1846), then Hunt & Roskell; acquired by A. Benson and H. Webb in 1897.	H&R L.TD
Hutton, William & Sons Birmingham	1800–1920s	Silver, silver plate, pewter, copper. Known as Hutton & Houghton, 1818–1820. (Kate Harris)	W & LD S
Jones, Albert Edward Birmingham	(1879–1954)	Silver, jewelry (Liberty & Co.)	A.E.J
Keswick School of Industrial Art Keswick	1884–1899	Jewelry, silver, copper (Harold Stabler 1898–1899)	K S I A
Knox, Archibald London	(1864–1933)	Jewelry (Liberty & Co.)	L⁷&C⁰
Liberty & Co. London	1875–present	Silver, pewter, furniture, ceramic, fabrics. Partnered with W. H. Haseler & Co.to produce Cymric line (1901–1926). (B. Cuzner [1877–1956], A. H. Jones, A. Gaskin [1862–1928], A. Knox [1864–1933])	L⁷&C⁰
Macdonald, Frances Glasgow, Scotland	(1874–1921)	Metalwork, jewelry	
Mackintosh, Charles Rennie Glasgow, Scotland	(1868–1928)	Furniture, architecture, silver, jewelry	

Workshop or Artist and Location	Dates	Artists, Factories and Related Information	Mark
Mackintosh, Margaret Macdonald Glasgow, Scotland	(1865–1933)	Metalwork, jewelry	MARGARET MACDONALD MACKINTOSH
MacNair, J. Herbert Scotland	(1868–1955)	Jewelry, enamel	J.HERBERT McNAIR
Marks, Gilbert Leigh Croydon, Surrey	1885–1902	Silver, metalwork, pewter, copper Founded by Gilbert Leigh Marks (1861–1905).	GM
Morris, May	(1862–1938)	Jewelry (Women's Guild of Arts)	
Morris, Talwyn Glasgow, Scotland	(1865–1911)	Metalwork, jewelry	
Mortimer & Hunt (See Hunt & Roskell.) London	1839–1846	Silver, silver plate, jewelry	JM & SH
Murrle, Bennet & Co. London	1884–1916	Jewelry	MBo
Newman, Mrs. Philip London	c.1870–1910	Jewelry (John Brogden [c.1870–1885])	Mrs. N
Phillips, Robert London	1851–c.1927	Jewelry. Founded by Robert Phillips (d.1881) (Carlo Giuliano [c.1860], Carlo Doria [c.1860–1880], Alfred Phillips)	
Pugin, Augustus Welby Northmore	(1812–1852)	Architecture, silver, jewelry, furniture (J. Hardman & Co.)	A.W.P.
Ramsden & Carr London	1898–1919	Jewelry, silver. Founded by Alwyn Carr (1872–1940) and Omar Ramsden (1873–1939).	OMAR RAMSDEN & ALWYN CARR MADE ME 1899
Rathbone, Richard Llewellyn Benson Liverpool, London	(1864–1939)	Copper, silver, jewelry	RATHBONE
Reynolds, William Bainbridge London	(1855–1935)	Silver	W.B.R

Workshop or Artist and Location	Dates	Artists, Factories and Related Information	Mark
Rundell, Bridge & Co. London	1788–1843	Gold, jewelry	
Simpson, Edgar London	c.1896–1910	Jewelry, silver, metalwork	
Stabler, Harold Keswick, London	(1872–1945)	Jewelry, metalwork, silver (Keswick School of Industrial Art, Goldsmiths' & Silversmiths' Co., Adie Bros.)	•HS•
Storr & Mortimer (See Hunt & Roskell.) London	1823–1826	Silver, silver plate, jewelry	
Storr, Mortimer & Hunt (See Hunt & Roskell.) London	1826–1838	Silver, silver plate, jewelry	
Watherston & Brogden	1842–1864	Jewelry (See Brogden, John.)	
Wilson, Henry J. London	(1864–1934)	Metalwork, jewelry (Art Workers' Guild)	HW

HOLLAND

Workshop or Artist and Location	Dates	Artists, Factories and Related Information	Mark
Amstelhoek Amsterdam	1894–?	Silver, metalwork, ceramics, furniture (J. Eisenloeffel, Christian van dar Hoef, W. Hoeker)	
Bonebakker & Sons	1767–present	Jewelry	
Eisenloeffel, Jan Amsterdam	(1876–1957)	Silver (Amstelhoek)	
Nienhaus, Lambert Amsterdam and The Hague	(1873–1960)	Silver, jewelry (W. Hoeker Silversmiths, c.1895)	

ITALY

Workshop or Artist and Location	Dates	Artists, Factories and Related Information	Mark
Bulgari Rome	1881–present	Jewelry (Sotirio Bulgari [1857–1932], Constantine Bulgari, Giorgio Bulgari)	BVLGARI

Workshop or Artist and Location	Dates	Artists, Factories and Related Information	Mark
Castellani, Alessandro Rome	(1824–1883)	Jewelry	
Castellani, Augusto Rome	(1829–1914)	Jewelry	
Castellani, Fortunato Pio Rome	(1793–1865)	Jewelry, gold, mosaic work (Fortunato Pio Castellani's son Alessandro and Augusto Castellani)	
Melillo, Giacinto	(1846–1915)	Gold, jewelry	
Saulini, Luigi	(1819–1883) 1836–1883	Jewelry, cameos	
Saulini, Tomasso	(1793–1864)	Jewelry, cameos	
RUSSIA			
Fabergé, House of Moscow, St. Petersburg	1842–1918	Goldsmiths, jewelers (Gustav Fabergé [1814–1881] and Peter Carl Fabergé [1846–1920])	ФАБЕРЖЕ
Hahn, Karl Karlovitch St. Petersburg	c.1896	Gold, jewelry, icons (A. Tillander)	К.ГАНЪ
Holström, August Wilhelm St. Petersburg	(1829–1903) 1857–1903	Gold, jewelry (Fabergé)	АН
Kollin, Eric St. Petersburg	(1836–1901) 1870–1886	Gold (Fabergé)	E.K.
Perkhin, Mikhail Evlampevich St. Petersburg	(1860–1903) 1886–1903	Gold (Fabergé, Imperial eggs from 1886 to 1903)	МЛ
Rückert, Feodor Moscow	c.1890s–1917	Gold, jewelry	Ф.Р.
Wigström, Henrik St. Petersburg	(1862–1923) 1903–1917	(Fabergé from 1886)	H.W

Workshop or Artist and Location	Dates	Artists, Factories and Related Information	Mark
SCANDINAVIA			
Andersen, David Oslo, Norway	1876–present	Silver, enamel (Carl Johansgate, G. Gaudernack [1892–1910])	D-A
Ängman, Jacob Sweden	1876–1942	Silver (Guldsmeds Aktiebolaget)	
Bindesbøll, Thorvald Denmark	(1846–1908)	Jewelry, architecture, furniture	
Bolin, W. A. Stockholm, Sweden	1791–?	Jewelry (Carl Edward Bolin, William James Bolin, Charles and Henrik Bolin, William Bolin, K.S. Bolin). Founded in St. Petersburg. Moved to Sweden in 1916.	BOLIN
Cohr, Carl M. Denmark	1863–present	Silver	
Hingelberg, Frantz Denmark	1897–present	Silver, jewelry	
Michelsen, Anton Copenhagen, Denmark	(1809–1877) 1841–present	Jewelry, silver	
Nielsen, Evald Denmark	(1879–1958)	Hand-hammered silver	
Rohde, Johan Denmark	(1856–1935)	Silver	
Tostrup, Jacob Oslo, Norway	1832–present	Metalwork, applied art	TORSTRUP
SPAIN			
Masriera, Luis	(1872–1958) Barcelona	Jewelry	
SWITZERLAND			
Bautte et Moynier Geneva	c.1840s	Jewelry, enamel, gold, watches	

Workshop or Artist and Location	Dates	Artists, Factories and Related Information	Mark
UNITED STATES			
Bailey, Banks & Biddle Philadelphia	1832–present	Jewelry	**BAILEY&CO.** **BAILEY BANKS & BIDDLE**
Black, Starr & Frost New York, N.Y.	1810–1929	Jewelry. Founded as Marquand & Co. in 1810; known as Ball, Tompkins & Black from 1839, Ball, Black & Co. from 1851, Black, Starr & Frost from 1876; merged with Gorham in 1929 to form Black, Starr, Frost-Gorham.	B S & F Black Starr Black, Starr & Frost Ltd
Blackinton, R. & Co. North Attleboro, Mass.	1862–present	Jewelry, silver. Founded by W. Ballou and R. Blackinton	Ⓡ ⬌Ⓑ⬌ Ⓒ
Caldwell, J. E. & Co. Philadelphia	1840–1919	Jewelry, silver	**J. E. C. & CO.**
Chicago Arts & Crafts Society	1897–c.1905	Metalworkers, designers, potters (Jessie Preston, James Winn [1866–c.1940])	Marked by individual artists
Dominick & Haff Newark, N.J.; New York, N.Y.	1872–1889	Silver, jewelry	**D. & H.**
Durgin, William B. Co. Concord, N.H. Providence, R.I.	1853–1935	Silver. Merged with Gorham in 1905. Moved to Providence in 1931.	
Foster, Theodore W. & Brother Co. Providence, R.I.	1873–1951	Jewelry, silver	**F. & B.**
Germer, George E. New York, N.Y.; Boston; Providence, R.I.	(1868–1936)	Jewelry, silver	
Glessner, Frances M. Chicago	(1848–1922)	Silver	
Gorham Corp. Providence, R.I.	c.1815–present	Silver, silver plate, bronze, metalwork, jewelry, copper, gold (Named Gorham Mfg. Co. in 1842.)	TRADE-MARK STERLING
Jaccard Jewelry Co. St. Louis	1829–present	Jewelry	MERMOD & JACCARD CO. TRIPLE

Workshop or Artist and Location	Dates	Artists, Factories and Related Information	Mark
Jarvie, Robert R. Chicago	c.1890–c.1920	Silver, metalwork, copper. Founded by Robert R. Jarvie (1865–1941).	Jarvie
Kerr, William B. & Co. Newark, N.J.	1855–1906	Silver, jewelry	
Kirk, Samuel Baltimore	1815–present	Silver	S.KIRK&SON
Koehler, Florence Chicago	(1861–1944)	Jewelry (Chicago Arts & Crafts Society)	
Marcus & Co. New York, N.Y.	1892–?	Jewelry, copper, silver (Herman Marcus and sons, George Elder & William E. Marcus)	MARCUS & CO. New York
Marcus, Herman New York, N.Y.	(1828–1899)	Jewelry (Tiffany, c.1850; Starr & Marcus, c.1864; Tiffany as co-partner, 1877; Marcus & Co., 1892–?)	MARCUS & CO. New York
Mauser Mfg. Co. New York, N.Y.	1890–1903	Silver	M
Reed & Barton Taunton, Mass.	1890–present	Silver, silver plate, jewelry	TRADE MARK R STERLING
Shiebler, George & Co. New York, N.Y.	c.1890	Silver	S
Shreve & Co. San Francisco	1852–present	Jewelry, silver. Founded by George C. Shreve (d.1893) and Samuel Shreve (d.1858).	S
Shreve, Crump & Low Boston	1796–present	Firm later known as Shreve, Crump & Low was founded by John MacFarlane in 1796. Benjamin Shreve joined the firm about 1854; Charles H. Crump joined the firm in 1869, when the name of the company became Shreve, Crump & Low.	SHREVE,CRUMP&LOW.
Spaulding & Co. Chicago	1888–present	Silver, silver plate, jewelry (Henry A. Spaulding)	S&C

Workshop or Artist and Location	Dates	Artists, Factories and Related Information	Mark
Stone, Arthur J. New Hampshire Detroit, Mich. Gardiner, Mass.	(1847–1938)	Silver (Stone Associates: Alfred Wickstrom, David Carlson, George Blanchard, Charles Brown, Arthur Hartwell, Herbert Taylor, George Erickson, Herman Glendenning, Edgar Caron, Earl Underwood)	
Tiffany & Co. New York, N.Y.	1834–present	Silver, metalwork (Charles Louis Tiffany, [1812–1902])	
Tiffany Studios New York, N.Y.	1879–1936	Metalwork, pottery, glass (Louis Comfort Tiffany [1848–1933])	
Unger Brothers Newark, N.J.	1878–1914	Silver, jewelry. Founded by Herman Unger and Eugene Unger	
Webster Co. North Attleboro, Mass.	1869–present	Silver (George K. Webster [d.1894])	
Whiting Mfg. Co. North Attleboro, Mass. Newark, N.J. Bridgeport, Conn. Providence, R.I.	1866–present	Silver, jewelry	
Whiting, Frank M. Co. North Attleboro, Mass.	1878–c.1960	Silver	
Winn, James H. Chicago, Ill. California	(1866–c.1940)	Jewelry (Chicago Arts & Crafts Society)	

BIBLIOGRAPHY

Information for *Kovels' American Antiques* came from many sources, especially books. We referred to many books written in the nineteenth and twentieth centuries, as well as important recent ones. This is a list of the books we think are most useful for readers who want to know more about a subject. Some can be found in bookstores. Others that are older and out of print are available in libraries or at antiquarian book sources.

GENERAL

Aslin, Elizabeth. *The Aesthetic Movement: Prelude to Art Nouveau.* New York: Frederick A. Praeger, 1969.

Clayton, Virginia Tuttle, Elizabeth Stillinger, and Erika Doss. *Drawing on America's Past: Folk Art, Modernism, and the Index of American Design.* Washington, DC: National Gallery of Art, 2002.

Green, Harvey. *The Light of the Home: An Intimate View of the Lives of Women in Victorian America.* New York: Pantheon Books, 1983.

Hornung, Clarence P. *Treasury of American Design.* 2 vols. New York: Harry N. Abrams, 1972.

Johnson, Diane Chalmers. *American Art Nouveau.* New York: Harry N. Abrams, 1979.

Kovel, Ralph, and Terry Kovel. *Kovels' Antiques & Collectibles Price List.* New York: Random House. Published annually.

Random House Collector's Encyclopedia: Victoriana to Art Deco. New York: Random House, 1974.

CHAPTER 1: POTTERY & PORCELAIN

Haggar, Reginald, and Elizabeth Adams. *Mason Porcelain & Ironstone, 1796–1853.* London: Faber and Faber, 1977.

Langham, Marion. *Belleek Irish Porcelain: An Illustrated Guide to over Two Thousand Pieces.* London: Quiller Press, 1993.

Savage, George, and Harold Newman. *An Illustrated Dictionary of Ceramics.* New York: Thames and Hudson, 1985.

CHAPTER 2: BRITISH POTTERY & PORCELAIN

Arman, David and Linda. *Historical Staffordshire: An Illustrated Check-List and First Supplement.* Danville, VA: Arman Enterprises, 1974, 1977.

Atterbury, Paul. *Moorcroft: A Guide to Moorcroft Pottery 1897–1993.* Somerset, England: Richard Dennis and Hugh Edwards, 1993.

Atterbury, Paul, and Maureen Batkin. *The Dictionary of Minton.* Woodbridge, Suffolk, England: Antique Collectors' Club, 1998.

Barnard, Julian. *Victorian Ceramic Tiles.* Boston: New York Graphic Society, 1972.

Bergesen, Victoria. *Encyclopaedia of British Art Pottery, 1870–1920.* London: Barrie & Jenkins, 1991.

Cushion, John, and Margaret Cushion. *A Collector's History of British Porcelain.* Wappingers Falls, NY: Antique Collectors' Club, 1992.

Eyles, Desmond. *Doulton Lambeth Wares.* London: Hutchinson, 1975.

_____. *Royal Doulton, 1815–1965: The Rise and Expansion of the Royal Doulton Potteries.* London: Hutchinson, 1965.

Godden, Geoffrey A. *British Porcelain: An Illustrated Guide.* New York: Clarkson N. Potter, 1974.

_____. *British Pottery: An Illustrated Guide.* New York: Harmony Books, 1975.

_____. *Godden's Guide to Ironstone: Stone & Granite Wares.* Woodbridge, Suffolk, England: Antique Collectors' Club, 1999.

_____. *An Illustrated Encyclopaedia of British Pottery and Porcelain.* 2nd ed. London: Barrie & Jenkins, 1980.

Harding, Adrian, and Nicholas Harding. *Victorian Staffordshire Figures, 1835–1875.* 2 vols. Atglen, PA: Schiffer, 1998.

Hawkins, Jennifer. *The Poole Potteries.* London: Barrie & Jenkins, 1980.

Mankowitz, Wolf. *Wedgwood.* New York: E.P. Dutton and Co., 1953.

Mankowitz, Wolf, and Reginald G. Haggar. *The Concise Encyclopedia of English Pottery and Porcelain*. New York: Hawthorn, 1957.

Neale, Gillian. *Miller's Collecting Blue & White Pottery*. London: Octopus Publishing Group, 2004.

Pugh, P.D. Gordon. *Staffordshire Portrait Figures and Allied Subjects of the Victorian Era*. Woodbridge, Suffolk, England: Antique Collectors' Club, 1980.

Reilly, Robin, and George Savage. *The Dictionary of Wedgwood*. Woodbridge, Suffolk, England: Antique Collectors' Club, 1980.

Sandon, John. *The Dictionary of Worcester Porcelain, 1751–1851*. Wappingers Falls, NY: Antique Collectors' Club, 1993.

Thomas, E. Lloyd. *Victorian Art Pottery*. London: Guildart, 1974.

Towner, Donald. *The Leeds Pottery*. New York: Taplinger, 1965.

Whiter, Leonard. *Spode*. London: Barrie & Jenkins, 1989.

Williams, Petra. *Flow Blue China and Mulberry Ware: Similarity and Value Guide*. Jeffersontown, KY: Fountain House, 1981.

CHAPTER 3: EUROPEAN POTTERY AND PORCELAIN

Bondhus, Sandra V. *Quimper Pottery: A French Folk Art Faïence*. Bondhus, 1981.

Csenkey, Eva, and Agota Steinert. *Hungarian Ceramics from the Zsolnay Manufactory, 1853–2001*. New Haven, CT: Yale University Press, 2002.

Gaston, Mary Frank. *Collector's Encyclopedia of R.S. Prussia*. 4 vols. Paducah, KY: Collector Books, 1982–1995.

Jacobson, Gertrude Tatnall. *Haviland China: A Pattern Identification Guide*. 2 vols. Iola, WI: Wallace-Homestead/Krause, 1979.

Kirsner, Gary. *Mettlach Book*. Coral Springs, FL: Glentiques, 1987.

Meadows, Adela. *Quimper Pottery: A Guide to Origins, Styles, and Values*. Atglen, PA: Schiffer, 1998.

Neuwirth, Waltraud. *Wiener Porzellan: Original Kopie Verfälschung Fälschung. (Vienna Porcelain: Originals, Reproductions, Fakes and Forgeries.)* Vienna, Austria: Neuwirth, 1979.

Winstone, H.V.F. *Royal Copenhagen*. London: Stacey International, 1984.

Röntgen, Robert E. *The Book of Meissen*. Atglen, PA: Schiffer, 1984.

CHAPTER 4: AMERICAN PORCELAIN AND POTTERY

Evans, Paul. *Art Pottery of the United States.* New York: Feingold & Lewis Publishing Corp., 1987.

Frelinghuysen, Alice Cooney. *American Porcelain, 1770–1920.* New York: Harry N. Abrams, 1989.

Kamm, Dorothy. *American Painted Porcelain.* Dubuque, IA: Antique Trader Books, 1999.

Karlson, Norman. *American Art Tile, 1876–1941.* New York: Rizzoli, 1998.

Kovel, Ralph, and Terry Kovel. *Kovels' American Art Pottery.* New York: Crown, 1993.

Rago, David. *American Art Pottery.* New York: Knickerbocker, 1997.

CHAPTER 5: ASIAN POTTERY & PORCELAIN

Beurdeley, Michael. *Chinese Trade Porcelain.* Rutland, VT: Charles E. Tuttle, 1962.

Karp, Herbert, and Gardiner Pond. *Sumida . . . According to Us.* Atlanta: KarPond, 2001.

Schiffer, Nancy. *Japanese Porcelain, 1800–1950.* Expanded 2nd edition. Atglen, PA: Schiffer, 1999.

POTTERY & PORCELAIN—MARKS

Godden, Geoffrey A. *New Handbook of British Pottery & Porcelain Marks.* North Pomfret, VT: Barrie & Jenkins, 2000.

Hartmann, Carolus. *Glasmarken Lexikon 1600–1945 (Glass Marks Encyclopedia 1600–1945).* Stuttgart, Germany: Arnoldsche, 1997.

Kovel, Ralph, and Terry Kovel. *Kovels' Dictionary of Marks: Pottery and Porcelain, 1650 to 1850.* New York: Crown, 1995.

_____. *Kovels' New Dictionary of Marks: Pottery & Porcelain, 1850 to the Present.* New York: Crown, 1986.

Kowalsky, Arnold A., and Dorothy E. Kowalsky. *Encyclopedia of Marks on American, English, and European Earthenware, Ironstone, and Stoneware, 1780–1980.* Atglen, PA: Schiffer, 1999.

Lehner, Lois. *Lehner's Encyclopedia of U.S. Marks on Pottery, Porcelain & Clay.* Paducah, KY: Collector Books, 1988.

Les Porcelaines Françaises (French Porcelain). Paris: Tardy, 1950.

Les Poteries Françaises (French Potttery). 3 vols. Paris: Tardy, 1949.

Michael, Ronald L., ed. *The East Liverpool, Ohio, Pottery District: Identification of Manufacturers and Marks.* Washington, DC: Society for Historical Archaeology, 1982.

Röntgen, Robert E. *Marks on German, Bohemian and Austrian Porcelain, 1710 to the Present.* Atglen, PA: Schiffer, 1997.

Zühlsdorff, Dieter. *Keramik-Marken Lexikon: Porzellan und Keramik Report, 1885–1935. (Dictionary of Porcelain and Ceramic Marks, 1885–1935)* Stuttgart, Germany: Arnoldsche, 1994.

CHAPTER 6: GLASS

Barlow, Raymond E., and Joan E. Kaiser. *The Glass Industry in Sandwich.* 4 vols. Windham, NH: Barlow-Kaiser Publishing Company, 1983–1999.

Billings, Sean, and Johanna S. Billings. *Peachblow Glass: Collector's Identification & Price Guide.* Iola, WI: Krause, 2000.

Blount, Berniece, and Henry Blount. *French Cameo Glass.* Des Moines, IA: Blount, 1968

Bredehoft, Neila, and Tom Bredehoff. *Hobbs, Brockunier & Co., Glass: Identification and Value Guide.* Paducah, KY: Collector Books, 1997.

Casper, Geraldine J. *Glass Paperweights of the Bergstrom-Mahler Museum.* Richmond, VA: U.S. Historical Society Press, 1989.

Casper, Geraldine J. *Glass Paperweights in the Art Institute of Chicago.* Chicago: The Art Institute of Chicago, 1991.

Grover, Ray, and Lee Grover. *English Cameo Glass.* New York: Crown, 1980.

Lee, Ruth Webb. *Early American Pressed Glass.* Pittsford, NY: Lee, 1933.

McCain, Mollie Helen. *A Field Guide to Pattern Glass.* Paducah, KY: Collector Books, 2000.

McKearin, George S., and Helen McKearin. *American Glass.* New York: Crown, 1948.

Pearson, J. Michael. *Encyclopedia of American Cut and Engraved Glass, 1880–1917.* 3 vols. Miami Beach, FL: Pearson, 1975–1978.

Reilly, Darryl, and Bill Jenks. *Early American Pattern Glass: Collector's Identification & Price Guide.* 2nd ed. Iola, WI: Krause, 2002.

Revi, Albert Christian. *American Art Nouveau Glass.* Camden, NJ: Thomas Nelson & Sons, 1968.

Selman, Lawrence. *The Art of the Paperweight.* Santa Cruz, CA: Paperweight Press, 1988.

Wilson, Kenneth M., *American Glass, 1760–1930: The Toledo Museum of Art*. 2 vols. New York: Hudson Hills Press, 1994.

Unitt, Doris, and Peter Unitt. *American and Canadian Goblets*. Arthur, Ontario, Canada: For the Love of Glass Publishing Inc., 1971.

_____. *American and Canadian Goblets*. Vol. 2. Arthur, Ontario, Canada: For the Love of Glass Publishing Inc., 1975.

CHAPTER 7: BOTTLES

Caniff, Tom, ed. *The Guide to Collecting Fruit Jars, Fruit Jar Annual*. Chicago: Jerome J. McCann. Published annually.

Covill, William E., Jr. *Ink Bottles and Inkwells*. Taunton, MA: William S. Sullwold, 1971.

Leybourne, Douglas M., Jr. *The Collector's Guide to Old Fruit Jars*. North Muskegon, MI: Altarfire Publishing, 2001.

McKearin, Helen, and Kenneth M. Wilson. *American Bottles & Flasks and Their Ancestry*. New York: Crown, 1979.

Ring, Carlyn, and W.C. Ham. *Bitters Bottles*. Downieville, CA: W.C. Ham, 1998.

_____. *Bitters Bottles Supplement*. Downieville, CA: W.C. Ham, 2004.

Toulouse, Julian Harrison. *Bottle Makers and Their Marks*. Nashville, TN: Thomas Nelson, 1971.

CHAPTERS 8 AND 9: FURNITURE

Bishop, Robert. *Centuries and Styles of the American Chair, 1640–1970*. New York: E.P. Dutton, 1972.

Boyce, Charles. *Dictionary of Furniture*. 2nd ed. New York: Facts on File, 2001.

Evans, Nancy Goyne. *American Windsor Chairs*. New York: Hudson Hills Press, 1996.

Fairbanks, Jonathan L., and Elizabeth Bidwell Bates. *American Furniture, 1620 to the Present*. New York: Richard Marek, 1981.

Forman, Benno M. *American Seating Furniture, 1630–1730: An Interpretive Catalogue*. New York: W.W. Norton, 1988.

Hanks, David A. *Innovative Furniture in America, From 1800 to the Present*. New York: Horizon, 1981.

Hepplewhite, A. and Co. *The Cabinet-Maker and Upholsterer's Guide*. Magnolia, MA: Peter Smith Pub, 1994.

Kenney, John Tarrant. *The Hitchcock Chair*. New York: Clarkson N. Potter, 1971.

Kylloe, Ralph. *Rustic Traditions*. Layton, UT: Gibbs Smith, 1993.

Miller, Judith, and Martin Miller, eds. *Antiques Directory: Furniture*. Boston: G.K. Hall & Co., 1985.

Montgomery, Charles F. *American Furniture: The Federal Period*. New York: Viking, 1966.

Richards, Nancy E., and Nancy Goyne Evans. *New England Furniture at Winterthur: Queen Anne and Chippendale Period*. Winterthur, DE: Winterthur Museum, distributed by University Press of New England, 1997.

Rieman, Timothy D., and Jean M. Burks. *The Complete Book of Shaker Furniture*. New York: Harry N. Abrams, 1993.

Sack, Albert. *The New Fine Points of Furniture*. New York: Crown, 1993.

Santore, Charles. *The Windsor Style in America: The Definitive Pictorial Study of the History and Regional Characteristics of the Most Popular Furniture Form of Eighteenth-Century America, 1730–1840*. Philadelphia: Running Press, 1992.

Saunders, Richard. *Wicker Furniture: A Guide to Restoring & Collecting*. New York: Crown, 1990.

Sheraton, Thomas. *The Cabinet-Maker and Upholsterer's Drawing-Book*. New York: Dover Publications, 1972.

Van Der Werff, and Jackie Rees. *Miller's Garden Antiques: How to Source & Identify*. London: Octopus Publishing Group, 2003.

CHAPTER 10: LIGHTING DEVICES

Barlow, Raymond E., and Joan E. Kaiser. *The Glass Industry in Sandwich*. Vol. 2. Windham, NH: Barlow-Kaiser Publishing Company, 1989.

De Falco, Robert, et al. *Handel Lamps: Painted Shades and Glassware*. Staten Island, NY: H & D Press, 1986.

Feldstein, William Jr., and Alastair Duncan. *The Lamps of Tiffany Studios*. New York: Harry N. Abrams, 1983.

Malakoff, Edward, and Sheila Malakoff. *Pairpoint Lamps*. Atglen, PA: Schiffer, 1990.

Russell, Loris S. *A Heritage of Light: Lamps and Lighting in the Early Canadian Home*. Toronto: University of Toronto Press, 1968.

Thuro, Catherine M.V. *Oil Lamps: The Kerosene Era in North America*. Radnor, PA: Wallace-Homestead Book Co., 1992.

_____. *Oil Lamps II: Glass Kerosene Lamps*. Paducah, KY: Collector Books, 1983.

_____. *Oil Lamps 3: Victorian Kerosene Lighting, 1860–1900*. Toronto: Collector Books & Thorncliffe House; distributed by Collector Books, Paducah, KY, 2001.

CHAPTER 11: CLOCKS AND TIMEPIECES

Baillie, G.H. *Watchmakers & Clockmakers of the World*. Vol. 1. London: N.A.G. Press, 1976.

Baillie, G.H., et al. *Britten's Old Clocks and Watches and Their Makers*. New York: Bonanza Books, 1956.

Bruton, Eric. *The History of Clocks and Watches*. New York: Crescent Books, 1989.

De Carle, Donald. *Watch & Clock Encyclopedia*. London: N.A.G. Press, 1978.

Loomes, Brian. *Watchmakers & Clockmakers of the World*. Vol. 2. London: N.A.G. Press, 1976.

Palmer, Brooks. *Book of American Clocks*. New York: Macmillan, 1950.

_____. *Treasury of American Clocks*. New York: Macmillan, 1967.

CHAPTER 12: SILVER

Culme, John. *Directory of Gold & Silversmiths, Jewellers & Allied Traders, 1838–1914 (from the London Assay Office Registers)*. 2 vols. Wappingers Falls, NY: Antique Collectors' Club, 1987.

Fales, Martha Gandy. *Early American Silver for the Cautious Collector*. New York: Funk & Wagnalls, 1970.

Kovel, Ralph, and Terry Kovel. *Kovels' American Silver Marks, 1650 to the Present*. New York: Crown, 1989.

Newman, Harold. *An Illustrated Dictionary of Silverware*. London: Thames & Hudson, 1987.

Pickford, Ian, ed. *Jackson's Silver & Gold Marks of England, Scotland & Ireland*. 3rd ed. Wappingers Falls, NY: Antique Collectors' Club, 1989.

Rainwater, Dorothy T., and H. Ivan Rainwater. *American Silverplate* Atglen, PA: Schiffer, 1988.

Rainwater, Dorothy T., Martin Fuller, and Colette Fuller. *Encyclopedia of American Silver Manufacturers*. 5th ed. Atglen, PA: Schiffer, 2004.

Wyler, Seymour B. *Book of Old Silver*. New York: Crown, 1937.

_____. *Book of Sheffield Plate*. New York: Crown, 1949.

CHAPTER 13: PEWTER

Cotterell, Howard Herschel. *Old Pewter: Its Makers and Marks.* Rutland, VT: Charles E. Tuttle, 1973.

Kauffman, Henry J. *The American Pewterer: His Techniques & His Products.* Nashville, TN: Thomas Nelson, 1970.

Laughlin, Ledlie Irwin. *Pewter in America: Its Makers and Their Marks.* 3 vols. Barre, MA: Barre Publishers, 1969–1971.

Montgomery, Charles F. *History of American Pewter.* New York: E.P. Dutton, 1978.

CHAPTER 14: TINWARE AND TOLEWARE

Coffin, Margaret. *The History & Folklore of American Country Tinware 1700–1900.* Camden, NJ: Thomas Nelson & Sons, 1968.

Gould, Mary Earle. *Antique Tin & Tole Ware: Its History and Romance.* Rutland, VT: Charles E. Tuttle, 1958.

Lea, Zilla Rider. *The Ornamented Tray: Two Centuries of Ornamented Trays (1720–1920).* Rutland, VT: Charles E. Tuttle, 1971.

CHAPTER 15: MUSIC MAKERS

Michel, Norman Elwood. *Michel's Piano Atlas.* Rivera, CA: Michel, 1953.

Pierce Piano Atlas. 11th ed. Albuquerque, NM: Larry E. Ashley, 2003.

CHAPTER 16: TEXTILES

Anderson, Clarita S. *American Coverlets and Their Weavers: Coverlets from the Collection of Foster and Muriel McCarl.* Williamsburg, VA: Colonial Williamsburg Foundation, 2002.

Brackman, Barbara. *Clues in Calico: A Guide to Identifying and Dating Antique Quilts.* McLean, VA: EPM Publications, 1989.

Burnham, Harold B., and Dorothy K. Burnham. *"Keep Me Warm One Night," Early Handweaving in Eastern Canada.* Toronto: University of Toronto Press, 1972.

Checklist of American Coverlet Weavers. Williamsburg, VA: Colonial Williamsburg Foundation, Abby Aldrich Rockefeller Folk Art Center, 1978.

Collins, Herbert Ridgeway. *Threads of History: Americana Recorded on Cloth, 1775 to the Present.* Washington, DC: Smithsonian Institution, 1979.

Kiracofe, Roderick. *The American Quilt.* New York: Clarkson Potter, 1993.

Mackrell, Alice. *Shawls, Stoles and Scarves.* London: B.T. Batsford, 1986.

Orlofsky, Patsy, and Myron Orlofsky. *Quilts in America*. New York: Abbeville Press, 1992.

Rehmel, Judy. *The Quilt I.D. Book*. New York: Prentice Hall, 1986.

CHAPTER 17: JEWELRY

Bennett, David, and Daniela Mascetti. *Understanding Jewellery*. Wappingers Falls, NY: Antique Collectors' Club, 1989.

Newman, Harold. *An Illustrated Dictionary of Jewelry*. New York: Thames and Hudson, 1987.

Poynder, Michael. *The Price Guide to Jewellery, 3000 B.C.–1950 A.D.* Wappingers Falls, NY: Antique Collectors' Club, 1976.

Rainwater, Dorothy T. *American Jewelry Manufacturers*. Atglen, PA: Schiffer, 1988.

Romero, Christie. *Warman's Jewelry Identification and Price Guide*. Iola, WI: Krause, 2002.

CHAPTER 18: TOYS, GAMES, DOLLS, AND HOLIDAY ANTIQUES

Cieslik, Jürgen, and Marianne Cieslik. *German Doll Encyclopedia 1800–1939*. Cumberland, MD: Hobby House Press, 1985.

Coleman, Dorothy S., Elizabeth A. Coleman, and Evelyn J. Coleman. *Collector's Encyclopedia of Dolls*. 2 vols. New York: Crown, 1968, 1986.

Fondin, Remise, and Jean Fondin. *The Golden Age of Toys*. Boston: New York Graphic Society, 1967.

Fraser, Antonia. *A History of Toys*. New York: Delacorte Press, 1966.

Greenberg, Bruce. *Greenberg's Guide to Lionel Trains*. 8 vols. Waukesha, WI: Kalmbach, 1985–1994.

Kurtz, Henry I., and Burtt R. Ehrlich. *The Art of the Toy Soldier*. New York: Abbeville Press, 1987.

Love, Brian. *Great Board Games*. London: Michael Joseph and Ebury Press, 1979.

———. *Play the Game*. London: Michael Joseph and Ebury Press, 1978.

Penny Toys from Heaven: The Legendary Tin Penny Toy Collection of the Late Jane Anderson. Annapolis, MD: Theriault's Gold Horse Publishing, 2004.

Pressland, David. *The Art of the Tin Toy*. New York: Crown, 1976.

White, Gwen. *Toys, Dolls, Automata: Marks & Labels*. London: B.T. Batsford, 1975.

CHAPER 19: PRINTS, PICTURES, AND PHOTOGRAPHS

Bénézit, E. *Dictionnaire des Peintres, Sculpteurs, Dessinateurs et Graveurs (Dictionary of Painters, Sculptors, Designers and Engravers)*. 10 vols. Paris: Librairie Gründ, 1976.

Carrick, Alice Van Leer. *A History of American Silhouettes: A Collector's Guide—1790–1840*. Rutland, VT: Charles E. Tuttle, 1968.

Conningham, Frederic A. *Currier & Ives: An Illustrated Check List*. New York: Crown Publishers, 1983.

Fielding, Mantle. *Mantle Fielding's Dictionary of American Painters, Sculptors & Engravers*. Poughkeepsie, NY: Apollo, 1986.

Hughes, Therle. *Prints for the Collector: British Prints from 1500 to 1900*. New York: Praeger, 1971.

Mallett, Daniel Trowbridge. *Mallett's Index of Artists: International–Biographical*. New York: Peter Smith, 1948.

McClain, Craig. *Currier & Ives: An Illustrated Value Guide*. Lombard, IL: Wallace-Homestead, 1987.

Who Was Who in American Art 1564–1975. 3 vols. Madison, CT: Sound View Press, 1999.

CHAPTER 20: PAPER ANTIQUES

Brigham, Clarence S. *History and Bibliography of American Newspapers, 1690–1820*. Worcester, MA: American Antiquarian Society, 1947.

Gregory, Winifred. *American Newspapers, 1821–1936: A Union List of Files Available in the United States and Canada*. New York: Kraus Reprint Corp., 1967.

Rickards, Maurice. *The Encyclopedia of Ephemera*. New York: Routledge, 2000.

United States Newspaper Program National Union List. Dublin, OH: OCLC, 1999.

CHAPTER 21: PACKAGING AND ADVERTISING

Davis, Alec. *Package & Print: The Development of Container and Label Design*. New York: Clarkson N. Potter, 1968.

Johnson, Laurence A. *Over the Counter and on the Shelf: Country Storekeeping in America, 1620–1920*. Rutland, VT: Charles E. Tuttle, 1961.

Kovel, Ralph, and Terry Kovel. *The Label Made Me Buy It: From Aunt Jemima to Zonkers—The Best-Dressed Boxes, Bottles, and Cans from the Past*. New York: Crown, 1998.

CHAPTER 22: KITCHENWARE

Franklin, Linda Campbell. *300 Years of Kitchen Collectibles.* 5th ed. Iola, WI: Krause, 2003.

CHAPTER 23: TOOLS

Diderot, Denis. *A Diderot Pictorial Encyclopedia of Trades and Industry.* 2 vols. New York: Dover, 1959.

Pascal, Dominique. *Collectible Hand Tools.* Paris: Flammarion, 2004.

Salaman, R.A. *Dictionary of Woodworking Tools, c.1700–1970.* Mendham, NJ: Astragal Press, 1997.

Sellens, Alvin. *Dictionary of American Hand Tools.* Atglen, PA: Schiffer, 2002.

Photo Credits

333 Auction
333 N. Main Street
Lambertville, NJ 08530

American Bottle Auctions
1507 21st Street, Suite 203
Sacramento, CA 95814

Antiquarian Traders
9031 West Olympic Boulevard
Beverly Hills, CA 90211

Antiquorum Auctioneers
609 Fifth Avenue, Suite 503
New York, NY 10017

Auction Team Breker
P. O. Box 50 11 19
D-50971 Köln, Germany

Bertoia Auctions
2141 DeMarco Drive
Vineland, NJ 08360

Brunk Auctions
P. O. Box 2135
Asheville, NC 28802

Canada Council for the Arts
Instrument Bank
350 Albert Street, P. O. Box 1047
Ottawa, Ontario K1P 5V8 Canada

Charlton Hall Galleries, Inc.
912 Gervais Street
Columbia, SC 29201

Cincinnati Art Galleries
225 East 6th Street
Cincinnati, OH 45202

Conestoga Auction Company
768 Graystone Road
Manheim, PA 17454

Copake Auction
Box H, 266 Route 7A
Copake, NY 12516

Cottone Auctions
15 Genesee Street
Mt. Morris, NY 14510

Cowan Auctions
673 Wilmer Avenue
Terrace Park, OH 45226

Craftsman Auctions
333 N. Main Street
Lambertville, NJ 08530

Dargate Auction Galleries
214 North Lexington
Pittsburgh, PA 15208

David Rago Auctions
333 N. Main Street
Lambertville, NJ 08530

DeFina Auctions
1591 State Route 45
South Austinburg, OH 44010

Degener Japanese Fine Prints
40637 Meerbusch, Germany

Doyle New York
175 East 87th Street
New York, NY 10128

Duomo Antiques
P. O. Box 200
Aquetong Road
Carversville, PA 18913

Fontaine's Auction Gallery
1485 West Housatonic Street
Pittsfield, MA 01201

Gene Harris Antique Auction
Center, Inc.
P. O. Box 476
203 South 18th Avenue
Marshalltown, IA 50158

Glass Works Auctions
P. O. Box 180
East Greenville, PA 18041

Green Valley Auctions
Rt. 2, Box 434-A
Mt. Crawford, VA 22841

Hesse
350 & 385 Main Street
Otego, NY 13825

Isham-Terry House
The Antiquarian and Landmarks
Society
255 Main Street
Hartford, CT 06106

Jackson's Auctioneers &
Appraisers
2229 Lincoln Street
Cedar Falls, IA 50613

James D. Julia, Inc.
Rt. 201, Skowhegan Road
Fairfield, ME 04937

John McInnis Auctioneers
76 Main Street
Amesbury, MA 01913

Joy Luke Auction Gallery
300 East Grove Street
Bloomington, IL 61701

Leslie Hindman Auctioneers
and Appraisers
122 North Aberdeen Street
Chicago, IL 60607

L. H. Selman Ltd.
123 Locust Street
Santa Cruz, CA 95060

Live Free or Die Antique Tools
Auctions
P. O. Box 281
Bath, NY 14810

M. S. Rau Antiques
630 Royal Street
New Orleans, LA 70130

Neal Auction Company
4038 Magazine Street
New Orleans, Louisiana 70115

New Orleans Auction Galleries
801 Magazine Street
New Orleans, LA 70130

Noel Barrett Antiques
Carversville Road
Carversville, PA 18923

Norman C. Heckler & Company
79 Bradford Corner Road
Woodstock Valley, CT 06282

Pacific Glass Auctions
1507 21st Street, Suite 203
Sacramento, CA 95814

PaperStuff.Com
P. O. Box 9938
Seattle, WA 98109

Pettigrew Auction Company
1645 South Tejon Street
Colorado Springs, CO 80906

Phillips, de Pury & Company
450 West 15th Street
New York, NY 10011

Pook & Pook, Inc.
P. O. Box 268
Downingtown, PA 19335

Randy Inman Auctions
P. O. Box 726
Waterville, ME 04903

Richard & Eileen Dubrow
920 166th Street
Whitestone, NY 11357

Robert C. Eldred Co., Inc.
1483 Route 6A
East Dennis, MA 02641

Skinner, Inc.
357 Main Street
Bolton, MA   01740

Smith & Jones
12 Clark Lane
Sudbury, MA 01776

Sotheby's Auctions
1334 York Avenue at 72nd Street
New York, NY 10021

Swann Galleries, Inc.
104 East 25th Street
New York, NY 10010

Syracuse China Archives
Libbey Inc.
2900 Court Street
Syracuse, NY 13208

Theriault's
P. O. Box 151
Annapolis, MD 21404

Treadway Gallery, Inc.
2029 Madison Road
Cincinnati, OH 45208

Treadway Toomey
John Toomey Gallery
818 North Boulevard
Oak Park, IL 60301

Van Dyke's Restorers
P. O. Box 278
39771 S.D. Highway 34
Woonsocket, SD 57385

Village Doll & Toy
P. O. Box 70
Adamstown, PA 19501

Waddington's
111 Bathurst Street
Toronto, Ontario M5V 2R5
Canada

Web Wilson's Online Auctions
P. O. Box 506
Portsmouth, RI 02871

Weschler's
909 E Street, NW
Washington, DC 20004

William H. Bunch Auctions
One Hillman Drive
Chadds Ford, PA 19317

Woody Auction
P. O. Box 618
Douglass, KS 67039

Index

Candlewood, 171
Candy containers, 114, 288
Canes, glass, 97
Caneware, 33
Cans, tin, 316–317, *324–325*
Canton ware, 73, *73*
Cardeilhac, *342*
Carder, Frederick, 108
Carnelian, 256
Carpenter, Francis W., 273
Carpets, 242, 243
Carte de visite, 305
Carter & Co., 29, *38*
Carter, Jesse, 29
Carter, Stabler and Adams, 29
Cartier, *342*
Cartlidge, Charles, 60
Carver, Governor John, 129
Castellani, *351*
Cast-iron cookware, 334
Castor sets, 208–209, *209*
Cat's-eye, 261
Caughley Pottery Works, 74
Cauliflower ware, 33
Celluloid, 265
Centennial Exhibition, U.S., 26, 62, 129, 157, 168
Ceramic Art Company, 9, *9*, 60, *60*
Ceramic Art Pottery, 9
Challinor, Taylor & Company, 91, 92
Chamberlain and Company, *36*
Chamberlain, Robert, 36
Chandeliers, 177, *177*
Chandler, John Greene, 178
Charles G. Tuthill & Company, *96*
Chaumet et Cie, *342*
Chautauqua furniture, 153
Chelsea grape, sprig, and this-tle, 14, 18, 19
Chelsea Keramic Art Works, 26, 63, *63*, *67*

Chéret, Jules, 310
Chesapeake Pottery, 13, *67*
Chicago Arts & Crafts Society, *353*
Child & Child, *345*
Chinese export porcelain, 13, 71–73
Chippendale, Thomas, 132, 151
Christmas, 287–290; cards, 290; decorations, 288–289; electric lights, 288–289; ornaments, *287*, 287–288, 290; plates, 8, 46, 47, 290; trees, 287; spoons, 290
Christofle, L'Orfevrerie, *342*
Chromolithographs, 296; Strobridge, *294*
Chrysanthemum sprig, 92
Cigar boxes and bands, 311
Cincinnati Art Pottery Company, *67*
Clark Company O.N.T., 328
Clavering, Claude, *345*
Clocks, 182–191; acorn, 187; alarm, 188; animated, 188; banjo, 184, 186, *186*; blink-ing-eye, 190; bobbing-doll, 190; calendar, 188, 189; cases, 187; coil works, 183; cuckoo, 189; dials, 184; electric, 189; face numbers, 184; girandole case, 186; grandfather, 184, mantel, 186–187; novelty, 190, *190*; octagon drop, 186; regula-tors, 189; schoolhouse, 186; shelf, 186; skeleton, 190; specialty, 188; spring driven, 187; tall case, 184, *184–185*, 188; tambour, 188; wag-on-the-wall, 190; wall, 184, 186; walnut, 187; water, 190
Clothing, 245

Coalbrookdale Iron Foundry, 149
Coalport, 19
Coca-Cola, 331
Cocheco Manufacturing Company, 287
Coffee cans, 20, 321–323
Coffee grinders, 329, *329*
Coffeepots, 206, 218, *223*
Cohr, Carl M., *352*
Coiffe, Delinieres & Company, 51
Collier, Ralph, 334
Collingwood and Company, *346*
Colonna, Edward, *342*
Commondale Pottery, *39*
Comyns, William & Sons, *346*
Connell & Co., *346*
Consolidated Lamp and Glass Co., 181
Cooper, John Paul, *346*
Copeland & Garrett, 29, 30, *40*
Copeland, 26
Copyright laws, U.S., 294–295
Coral, 102, 256–257; carved, *257*
Coralene, 106, *106*
Cotton cloth, factory-made, 235
Courthope, Frederick, *346*
Coverlets, *235*, 235–238; marks, 237; overshot, 236; Jacquard, 236, *237*
Cox, Paul, 64
Crackle glass, 106
Crackleware, 63
Crandall, Benjamin Potter, 276
Crane, Walter, *39*
Creamers, *82*; shapes, 206
Crewelwork, 240
Crosby, Nichols and Company, 278
Crown Milano, *106*, 107, *107*
Currier & Ives, *295*, 295–297

Cut glass, 84, 93–96
Cuzner, Bernard, *346*
D. F Haynes and Son, *68*
Daggert, Ezra, 317
Daguerre, Louis-Jacques-
Mandé, 305
Daguerreotypes, 304; cases,
305
Dallas Pottery, *67*
Dalpayrat, Pierre-Adrien, *57*
Dalzell, Gilmore and Leighton,
86, 107
Dammouse, Albert, *51*
Danforth, Joseph, *216*
Daum Frères, 105
Daum Nancy, 105, *105*
Davis, William, 36
Dawson, Edith Robinson, *346*
Dawson, Nelson, *346*
Day, Augustus, 300
De Morgan, William, *39*
De Ribaucort, Georges, *342*
Deck, Theodore, *57*
Dedham Pottery, 63, *63*
Deerfield Society, 240
Delaherche, Auguste, *57*
Delft, 10, 12, 25
Della Robbia Pottery, *39*
Diamond Dyes, 328
Diamond Match Company,
313
Diamonds, 257
Diapering, on ceramics, 79
Dickens Ware, 66
Dionne Quintuplets, 286
Dip-molding, 82, 113
Dixon, Arthur, *346*
Dixon, James & Sons, 218, *346*
Doat, Taxile, 45, *57*
Dolls, 282–287, advertising,
286; Barbie, 286; bébé,
284–285; bisque, 284; char-
acter, 285; Chatty Cathy,
286; china head, 282–284;
cloth, 286; dollmakers, 285;

French, *282*; Frozen Charley
and Charlotte, 286; hair-
styles, *282*; kewpie, 286;
marks, *284*; Raggedy Ann,
286; Santa Claus 286; walk-
ing, *282–283*; wax, 285
Dominick & Haff, *353*
Doorknobs, *168*
Doria, Carlo, *346*
Doulton & Co., 27, *27*, 28,
39, 41
Dover Stamping Company, 334
Dow, Arthur Wesley, 301
Doyle, William, 300
Drake, Edwin L., 176
Dresden, 53
Dresser, Christopher, *39*, *346*
Dubois, Fernard, *341*
Duche, Andrew, 59
Dumaine, Guillaume, 51
Dummer, Jeremiah, 193
Durand art glass, 105
Durand, Peter, 316
Durgin, William B., Co., *353*
Dutch delft, *10–11*
E. Woods and Sons, 41
Eastlake, Charles Lock, 142
Edgerton Art Clay Works, *67*
Edgerton Pottery, *67*
Edison, Thomas Alva, 227
Edouart, Auguste, 298, 300
Edward Miller & Company,
181
Edwin Bennett Pottery, 13, *67*
Eggbeaters, 334, *334*
Églomisé, 302
Egyptian Revival, 128–129,
188
Eisenloeffel, Jan, *350*
Electroplated nickel nilver, 197,
199
Electroplated white metal, 197,
199
Electroplating, 108
Elizabethan Revival, 140

Elkington & Co., *346*
Eloury, François, 51
Elton's Sunflower Pottery, *39*
Emanuel, Harry, *346*
Embroidery, 231
Emeralds, 256
End-of-day glass, 92
English patents, 4
English registry marks, *1–4*
Enoch Wood and Sons, 30
Eocean, 66
Epergnes, 209
Ephemera, 310
Epinay de Briort, Prosper, *342*
Erickson, Ruth, *64*
Excelsior Glass Company, 88
F. & R. Pratt, 23, 24
Fabergé, House of, *351*
Fahrner, Theodor, *344*
Faience Manufacturing
Company, 13, *58–59*, *67*
Faience, 10, 12, 25
Fairings, 20, *20*
Falize, *342*
Famille Rose porcelain, 73–74
Fans, 248
Faries Manufacturing Co., 181
Favrile, 104
Federzeichnung, 108
Fenton Glass Company, 88
Fenton, Christopher Webber,
62
Ferrotype, 305
Feuillâtre, Eugene, *342*
Filigree work, paper, 298
Filigree, 97, 264
Findlay Onyx, 107, *107*
Fire marks, 339
Fire-fighting equipment, 339
Fire-polishing, 85
Fish plates, 20–21
Fisher, Alexander, *347*
Fiske Foundry, 149
Flame stitch, 240
Flashing, 88